Social Work Skills Demonstrated
Beginning Direct Practice

Text-Workbook, CD-ROM, and Website

Second Edition

Linda K. Cummins
Barry University

Judith A. Sevel
Illinois State University

Laura E. Pedrick
University of Wisconsin – Milwaukee

PEARSON

Boston   New York   San Francisco
Mexico City   Montreal   Toronto   London   Madrid   Munich   Paris
Hong Kong   Singapore   Tokyo   Cape Town   Sydney

ISBN 0-205-40610-6

Printed in the United States of America

10 9 8 7 6 5 4 3 2   09 08 07 06 05

DEDICATION

We would like to thank our students and colleagues for their valued guidance and input in bringing this project to fruition. The Excel Communication staff did a wonderful job helping us to revise and greatly enhance the CD-ROM and develop a comprehensive website. Thank you to Patricia Quinlin, our editor at Allyn and Bacon. And finally, thank you to our families for their love, understanding, support, and patience throughout this two-year process.

Linda Cummins, Judith Sevel and Laura Pedrick
(Collaborators, friends and sisters forever!!)

TABLE OF CONTENTS

Chapter		Page
1	An Introduction to Social Work and the Helping Process	1
	Defining Social Work	1
	The Helping Process	3
	Social Worker Roles	11
2	Values and Ethics in Social Work	17
	Social Work Mission	18
	Social Work Values	18
	Self-Determination	19
	Empowerment	21
	Inherent Worth and Dignity	22
	Confidentiality	24
	Social Work Ethics	25
	Ethical Dilemmas	28
	Conclusion	31
3	Social Work Practice and Theory	33
	Systems Theory	34
	Ecological Perspective	37
	Life Model of Social Work Practice	40
	Person-in-Environment (PIE) Assessment and Classification System	40
	Strengths Perspective	42
	Empowerment-Based Practice Model	45

Chapter		Page
4	The Cultural Context of Practice: Using Interviewing Skills Effectively	49
	Self-Awareness	53
	Evolving Self-Awareness	54
	Cross-Cultural Knowledge	58
	Cross Cultural Skills	65
	Conclusion	67
5	The Engagement Process	71
	The Professional Relationship	71
	Getting Down the Basics: Know Yourself	83
	Confidentiality	85
	Preparing for the First Meeting	87
	The First Face-to-Face Meeting with the Client	89
	Home Visits	90
	Signs of Successful Client Engagement	96
	Conclusion	98
6	Social Work Skills	101
	Interviewing Skills	101
	Lead-in Responses	101
	Paraphrasing	102
	Reflection of Feeling	104
	Open-Ended Questions	106
	Closed-Ended Questions	110
	Clarification	111
	Summarization	112
	Information Giving	114
	Confrontation	117
	Interpretation	122
	Attending Behaviors	124

Chapter			Page

6   Social Work Skills

     Integrating Social Work Skills and Attending

        Behaviors   129

     Conclusion   131

7   Pitfalls   135

     Detecting Mistakes   135

     The Pitfalls   136

       Advice Giving   136

       Inappropriate Use of Humor   139

       Interrupting the Client and Abrupt

         Transitions   141

       Inappropriate and Irrelevant Questions   142

       Judgmental Response   146

       Inappropriate Social Worker Self-Disclosure   148

       Premature Confrontation   151

       Overwhelming the Client with Too Much or

         Irrelevant Information   153

       Premature Problem Solving   155

       Offering False Assurance/Minimizing the

         Problem   156

     Learning from Mistakes   160

     Conclusion   162

   Workbook   165

     Social Work Skills   165

       Paraphrasing   165

       Reflection of Feeling   171

       Open-Ended Questions   178

       Closed-Ended Questions   184

       Clarification   190

       Summarization   195

       Information Giving   206

       Confrontation   213

       Interpretation   218

     Pitfalls   223

     Putting it all Together   239

PREFACE

It has been more than four years since we first started discussing the possibility of a second edition of *Social Work Skills Demonstrated: Beginning Direct Practice.* We have encountered many false starts, and faced unexpected obstacles, but we believe that these bumps in the road actually served us in providing the necessary time to bring to fruition all of the changes that evolved in this second edition. Many of the changes would not have surfaced if we had pursued this work in the usual 12 month production pattern. Cesar Madrigal was not able to continue as a co-author on this edition, but his original idea of creating a skills workbook and CD-ROM remains at the core of this three part learning system. We remain grateful to Cesar for pushing us down this road where most of us were not anxious to go. Now we are hooked on technology and social work education. We were fortunate to have Laura Pedrick join the writing team as the third co-author on the second edition. Laura served as the multimedia editor on the first edition, so was well prepared to step into the role of co-author on this project. The extra time we have taken to complete this book, CD-ROM, and website, provided us with time to meld as a writing team, and we all agree we that we have never worked with a more collaborative, generous and supportive group. We now characterize ourselves as 'sisters.'

The student manual and CD-ROM in the first edition has now evolved into a three-part multimedia learning system that includes an expanded text with workbook, fully revised and technologically updated CD-ROM, and a resource website for instructors and students. The text and workbook has been expanded by more than 100 pages. The additions we have made will complement any primary text for an introduction to social work practice. Each chapter has been revised with a special emphasis on integrating cultural content across chapters and adding more culturally relevant case studies. In all, three new chapters have been added to the text and workbook. Chapter 4 in this new edition, *Cultural Context of Practice: Using Interviewing Skills Effectively,* replaces Chapter 5 (*Cultural Diversity*) in the first edition. This new chapter provides students with insights and exercises on how to become a culturally competent social work practitioner. Chapter 3, *Social Work Practice and Theory,* adds a much-needed discussion of the use of theory in social work practice, and provides a theoretical lens through which students can view the application of skills and techniques; and Chapter 5, *The Engagement Process,* provides students with a glimpse of the multidimensional nature of practice, even at the entry level, and the preparations necessary before meeting the client for the first time. This chapter also helps students to understand how to use skills and attending behaviors to enhance client engagement, and provides a discussion of home visits and the special considerations that go with meeting clients on their own turf. The exercises in the workbook at the back of the text have been updated and enhanced by integrating more culturally relevant examples into the case studies. Also added are exercise designed for practice partners or small groups.

We are particularly excited about the changes to the CD-ROM in this second edition. Realizing the degree to which college students today are digital natives and learn best in an interactive environment, nearly all of the text that appeared on the first edition of the CD-ROM has been removed, and replaced with an online instructor. Co-author Judith Sevel makes her video début as Professor Sevel, who expertly guides students through the application of skills and attending behaviors, and the identification of common pitfalls in social work practice. Concepts maps have been added as well, to visually and systematically provide students with a framework for approaching each skill and attending behavior. The framework includes 1) definition of skill; 2) how it helps in relationship building; 3) appropriate use of the skill with three video clip examples; and, 5) inappropriate use of the skill. Video examples are provided with each skill and attending behavior as in the first edition, but we have added an audio analysis of each skill as it is played out in the video vignettes. A new addition to the pitfalls portion of the CD-ROM is the use of video clips that demonstrate pitfalls. Each video clip is followed with a work screen where students are asked to reflect on the pitfall they have just viewed, provide feedback on how they think the client may have emotionally reacted to the pitfall, and how the social worker might have avoided the pitfall in the first place. Students are provided with an electronic notebook where they can answer the reflective questions, save their work to a disk and email it to the instructor, or simply print off their responses and hand them in at the next class period.

A major addition to this second edition CD-ROM is a new and fourth case study that features a grandmother (Mrs. Anderson) with Multiple Sclerosis, raising her multicultural granddaughter (Maria) while trying to provide support to her daughter (Crystal) who has lost custody of her daughter due to involvement in domestic violence and drugs. Caught in the conflict between granddaughter and daughter, Mrs. Anderson is assisted by her social worker, who helps her assume the role of primary caregiver and establish appropriate boundaries with her daughter and granddaughter. At the same time the social worker guides Maria through the tumultuous changes in her young life and helps her begin to see what is possible for her, in spite of the difficulties she faces. This fourth case study is set in the home environment and social worker/client interviews take place in Mrs. Anderson's home, and in a park setting with Maria. To enhance the *person-in-environment* perspective across all case studies, cases analyses using concept maps that graphically present the multiple forces influencing clients' lives are provided to help students understand the complexity and context of clients' lives. The case analyses are accompanied by a voice narrative, and can be found at the beginning of each case study. Individual session analyses are also available on the companion website.

As in the first edition of the CD-ROM, students still have the opportunity to interact with the virtual clients, now under the 'try it' menu. Students receive feedback on their responses and after choosing the correct response, can see it enacted on the CD-ROM by the virtual social worker. The comprehensive video quiz remains a central feature on the CD-ROM where students can assess the extent to which they have mastered the skills of practice.

Finally, a third component has been added to this multimedia learning system: a resource website for instructors and students. This new website goes beyond the traditional 'instructor's manual' format usually seen on companion website for texts. While it does include all those wonderful items in the traditional online 'instructor' manual' we have also provided instructors and students with a multitude of resources relevant to practice. Many practice tools are included on the website, such as online treatment plans, case notes, and contracts that students can apply to the virtual clients on the CD-ROM. Instructors are provided with a completed set of treatment plans for each client. Multiple URLs are provided to assist the instructor in web-based teaching in the classroom or they can be used to support the student in web-base research related to practice. Instructors are provided with an exhaustive list of creative ways to use the interactive CD-ROM and website in the classroom along with classroom exercises for maximizing the multimedia learning system. Students and instructors can provide electronic feedback to the authors on how well the text, workbook, CD-ROM, and website are working for them, and suggestions for the third edition.

We are grateful to all of you who have been consistent users of the first edition of *Social Work Skills Demonstrated: Beginning Direct Practice* and who were generous enough to share your experiences using it with us. Your feedback was instrumental in moving us forward in this second edition. We hope to continue this working partnership with social work educators and students in the future. We sincerely hope that this second edition of *Social Work Skills Demonstrated: Beginning Direct Practice* will bring to life the art of social work practice for beginning social work students.

In service to social work education, we are very truly yours.

Linda K. Cummins, PhD
Judith A. Sevel, M.S.W., L.C.S.W, A.C.S.W.
Laura Pedrick, M.A.

About the Authors

Linda Cummins is an Associate Professior in the School of Social Work at Barry University in Miami Shores, Florida. Linda has an extensive practice career in nursing before completing her MSW and PhD in social work at the Ohio State University. She has been a social work educator for 15 years in the areas of groups, community organizing, rural social work, policy, political advocacy, and research. She has served as Curriculum Chair in the Policy and Research Sequences at Illinois State University. She has co-authored books on practice and policy. Linda has worked with various homeless populations, including homeless youth in Chicago, polyaddicted, severely mentally ill homeless in Indianapolis, the rural homeless in Ohio, and Appalachian homeless women in Southern Ohio. Active in promoting the use of technology in social work education and practice, Linda served as the Chair of the Technology Committee at the Indiana University School of Social Work while on faculty there, and has worked as an independent consultant on technology based learning. She is currently working on co-authoring a policy practice book with a companion virtual practice environment.

Judith Sevel is graduate of the University of Pittsburgh (BASW) and Howard University (MSW), and has been a social work practitioner and educator since 1986. She has practiced in the fields of mental health, domestic violence, family and children services, incarcerated juveniles, and people with developmental disabilities. Currently she is Director of Field Education for the BSW and MSW programs at Illinois State University (ISU) in Normal, IL, where she also teaches courses in interviewing and assessment. Judith is also the chair of the Field Sequence Committee and serves on the

Practice Sequence Committee at ISU. Judith has been a disaster mental health services volunteer for the American Red Cross since 2001.

Laura Pedrick is the assistant to the provost at the University of Wisconsin-Milwaukee. She holds an M.A. in Journalism and Mass Communication from the University of Minnesota. Laura has worked on a variety of technology projects throughout her career. She served as project manager for UWM's campus portal and has helped develop numerous university websites. Her contributions to this project have centered on ensuring that the CD-ROM is highly usable, incorporating current research on interactive instructional design. As a freelance editor, she has worked on many social work projects, including the first edition of *Social Work Skills Demonstrated*. She is also a Ph.D. student at UW-Madison, with research interests in how adolescents use the Web in decision making. Laura is currently working with Linda Cummins on co-authoring a policy practice book with a companion virtual practice environment.

Suggestions for Using the CD-ROM and website (www.ablongman.com/cummins2e) to Enhance Skills Learning

The *Social Work Skills Demonstrated: Beginning Direct Practice* CD-ROM and website have many applications for skill learning in the classroom, lab, and homework settings. Below is a list of suggestions on how the product might enhance your teaching of the Methods I curriculum. This is by no means an exhaustive list, and we encourage you to be creative and to use the product in ways that fit your teaching style.

- The CD-ROM and website are useful tools for beginning Social Work Methods instructors in preparing for class. It provides them with a wealth of material for structuring student learning inside and outside the classroom;

- Use the video clips to initially demonstrate the skills in the classroom;

- After viewing the video clips, have student try to identify the exact portion of the interview exchange where the skill use occurred. Play the voice analysis afterwards to confirm or correct the student's assessment.

- Use the video clips to demonstrate a skill and then have students role-play the skill using their own problem focus;

- Use the T*ry It* video clips, or the cross-session case studies in class, asking students to identify the skills in use as the videotape progresses. Using the pause button on the video bar, the instructor can stop the video intermittently while waiting for students to identify the skill that was most recently viewed in the interviewing session;

- By using the cross-session case studies, the instructor can help students identify the appropriate time frame within which to use specific skills, and thus enhance the development of the social worker-client relationship;

- Instructors can structure a round-robin class exercise around selected video clips. For example, after viewing a short clip that ends with a client statement, the instructor can ask students to give a variety of skill responses to the client in turn. You may ask the first student to give a reflection of feeling response, the second student to give a paraphrase response, and the third, a clarification response.

- Longer video clips can be used to support the discussion of the relationships among skills, and how they build on each other in the developing social worker-client relationship;

- The *Try It* skills and the comprehensive *quiz* features can be used in the classroom for test preparation, as well as for preparing students in doing their own videotapes for class assignments;

- The vignettes can be used as a standard against which to critique students' skill level of expertise when rating student videotapes;

- The case analysis with each case study can provide students with a theoretical lens of the *person-in-environment* perspective to help student understand the complexities and contexts of clients lives.

- The skills concept maps and guided narrative can be used to reinforce skills, definitions, and appropriate and inappropriate usage of each skill. The guided narrative of the online professor can be used to support in class lectures, and to integrate other social work concepts (values, theory, problem solving, cultural issues, etc.) into the helping relationship;

- The video clips can be used to demonstrate and support lectures on creating professional boundaries, and rules of self-disclosure;

- The instructor can select a variety of video clips to be shown in the classroom or lab setting that demonstrate the different levels of empathy;

- With the audio off, attention to nonverbal communications from the client as well as the social worker could be addressed and discussed in the classroom;

- Use the scripts of the CD-ROM videos located on the website to have students reenact the scenes and practice the skills. Have them practice the complexities of interviewing by including skills, attending behaviors, and empathy in the reenactment.

- Students may use the CD-ROM for self-tutoring in the social work lab or at home;

- The pitfall videos can be viewed and can support a classroom discussion lead by the instructor on the nature of the pitfall, why it was considered a pitfall, and how the social worker might recover the pitfall in the interview process;

- The guided questions following the pitfall videos and the electronic notebook can be used as homework assignments or lab assignments to help students build empathy for the clients and also to learn recovery techniques in the interview process;

- The practice tools and web links provide students with wonderful opportunities to apply practice skills to the virtual clients on the CD or clients they may come in contact with in the field or in a volunteer setting; such as building treatment plans, writing a contract, or writing case notes.

- Use the exercises on the website for homework assignments or in class assignments;

- The CD-ROM is helpful in training teaching assistants for Social Work Methods. It provides a quick method of reviewing the skills;

- Teaching assistants can use the CD-ROM to tutor individual students experiencing difficulty in learning specific skills or attending behaviors;

- The CD-ROM has application in training nonprofessional or paraprofessional social service personnel in appropriate interviewing techniques; in preparing non-BSW masters students for the MSW curriculum; and, in teaching interviewing techniques for a wide range of undergraduates enrolled in other helping professional schools or majors such as nursing, school counseling, teaching, sociology, psychology, medicine, speech pathology, etc.

An Introduction to Social Work and the Helping Process

DEFINING SOCIAL WORK

Social work is the art and science of helping others. The field has a long tradition of helping the disadvantaged and disenfranchised, and in influencing social policy to meet the dynamic continuum of human needs. Social workers are represented in an array of professional settings and positions; the clinical social worker, case-manager, school social worker, community educator, agency administrator, program planner and the legislator are just a few career choices available to social workers. To be a professional social worker, one must have graduated from an accredited school of social work with a minimum of a bachelor's degree or BSW. BSW social workers can work under supervision to perform tasks that assist in evaluating client psychological needs or providing services that help people meet their physical, emotional and psychological needs. For example, common positions for BSW-prepared social workers include intake worker at a substance abuse center, group home counselor, case manager for the chronically mentally ill, and caseworker for foster care, adoption, and child protective services at child welfare agencies. Jobs in management, supervision and clinical social work require a master's degree in Social Work (MSW). In most states, social workers must pass a state licensing exam in order to practice and call themselves social workers. Beyond the MSW level, the National Association of Social Workers (NASW) provides credentialing for specialization in social work practice. With additional credentials beyond the MSW, social work practitioners gain access to increased autonomy in their practice. For example, an MSW can become a member of the Academy of Certified Social Workers (ACSW), a Diplomate in Clinical Social Work (DCSW), or a Qualified Clinical Social Worker (QCSW) by completing the necessary requirements in supervision and continuing education (see http://naswdc.org/credentials/default.asp).

Regardless of your level of social work preparation, the profession is bound by common values and ethics that are grounded in client self-determination, respect for the individual, and helping individuals reach their potential by helping them function within the context of their environment. Whether it is a homeless person looking for shelter, a married couple addressing their differences, or an HIV/AIDS patient needing government assistance, social workers fulfill a variety of functions that meet the needs of individuals, families, organizations, communities and society at large.

The National Association of Social Workers has put forward this defining statement:

> "The primary mission of the social work profession is to enhance human well-being and help meet the basic human needs of all people, with particular attention to the needs and empowerment of people who are vulnerable, oppressed, and living in poverty. A historic and defining feature of social work is the profession's focus on individual well-being in a social context and the well-being of society. Fundamental to social work is attention to the environmental forces that create, contribute to, and address problems in living" (NASW, 1999, p.1).

Social workers bring the mission of the profession to life through the art of social work practice that requires the professional application of social work values, principles, knowledge, skills, and techniques to individuals, families, groups, organizations and communities. For example, social workers help people obtain a wide variety of tangible services such as counseling, housing, employment and training, child care, health service, and so on. Social workers help communities or groups provide or improve social and health services, assess community needs, run community agencies, and advocate for those in need through legislative processes. The practice of social work requires knowledge of human development and behavior; social, economic and political systems; and, diverse cultural norms. Social workers must understand the interaction of all these factors and the impact of these interactions on client groups. Social workers are highly trained professionals who care about people, who see what's possible in people, and who want to make a difference. There are over a half million professional social workers in the United States who are working to make a difference in the lives of people, in communities, and in the world (NASW, 2005).

Fundamental social work principles are based on the assumption that people aspire to reach their full potential. The aim of social work is to create enriched environments that support individuals' optimal personal development, allowing them to hone their innate abilities within their social setting. When people are confronted with problems in life, their levels of coping and ability to adapt to current circumstances can change their perceptions of reality. How individuals interpret reality is influenced by the levels of stress they experience in any given situation. For example, consider Elisa in the case study provided in Box 1.1

Box 1.1 Case Study: Elisa

Elisa is a 30-year-old Latina. She and her two sons moved from Mexico to New York City two years ago. She and her children are now living with her sister and her three children in a small apartment. Last week, Elisa's 14-year-old son Antonio was arrested for drug possession. This incident with Antonio has caused her to question whether she wants to remain in New York. In addition to Antonio's involvement with the legal system, Elisa has just been laid off from her position as a housekeeper. She anticipates going back to work, but in the meantime has been receiving a very small unemployment check. She is now feeling extremely hopeless and overwhelmed and is unable to figure out what she wants to do next. She has made a comment to the court services social worker that she has thought about running away and never coming back.

Points for reflection: When considering the level of strength and perseverance Elisa had to amass when she moved her family to the United States (leaving behind her community, country and her family, learning a new language, navigating in a completely unknown environment, getting a job, enrolling her children in school), the current "small" series of life events do not appear to be insurmountable from a social worker's perspective. However, to effectively engage Elisa, the social worker must be able to understand how Elisa is experiencing these events. From Elisa's perspective, what do you believe makes the current situation seem overwhelming to the point of wanting to run away?

THE HELPING PROCESS

Through direct practice, the social worker helps the client distinguish between healthy and unhealthy behaviors and ways of being. This can be a complex process, since many client problems and behaviors are long term, and have developed through the individual's interactions with multiple subsystems. For example, Trevor is a 12-year-old boy with attention deficient hyperactivity disorder. He presents with behavior problems at home and in school, demonstrating impaired academic performance, social isolation, and low self-esteem. At the individual level, there are biological influences that affect Trevor's behavior problems that may need to be treated with medication. At home and at school his behavior problems over time have caused him to be isolated from peers. In addition, Trevor has been labeled as a "difficult child and student." His behavior problems at school have interfered with his learning process and consequently he is lagging behind his peers academically. All of these problems collectively, over time, have led Trevor to conclude that he is in some way inadequate and contribute to his low self-esteem. The sorting out of the multiple influences in his life and deciding on appropriate interventions requires a significant amount of knowledge and skill on the part of the social worker.

Multiple interventions are often required to sufficiently alleviate the presenting and interconnected problems of clients. Social workers use the helping process, a problem-solving process, to guide them in structuring a plan of action aimed at improving the quality of life of clients. For the helping process to be successful, the social worker must establish a partnership with the client that is grounded in mutual respect and trust. Together, the client and social worker mutually identify goals to be attained. The social worker facilitates the helping process through the application of social work theory, skills, and techniques. The social worker guides the client through the following five stages of the problem-solving or helping process.

The first stage of the helping process is *engagement and assessment*. During this stage the social worker makes initial contact with the client and begins to establish the framework for the helping relationship. One of the primary tasks for the social worker in the helping relationship is to develop rapport and trust in order for the social worker to then gather information from the client and other important people in the client's life (for more information on engagement, see Chapter 5). Be aware that when the social worker wishes to talk with other people in the client's life (known as collateral contacts) the social worker must first request and receive written consent from the client. Most social service agencies use standardized consent and release of information forms (for an example of a common consent and release of information form, visit the website for this book at http://www.ablongman.com/cummins2e). During the information gathering process it is critical that the social worker not only identify and clarify the client's problem(s) but also the client's strengths. Client strengths will become central to helping the client resolve their problems and gain control over their life (Germain & Gitterman, 1995). During the engagement and assessment phase, the social worker and client are involved in forming a partnership for future work together. This work may include:

> Identifying client challenges;
> Inventorying client's resources and strengths;
> Encouraging the client to identify and name feelings;
> Envisioning broad goals together as a working team;
> Defining directions for action;
> Clarifying respective roles within the helping relationship; and,
> Identifying any cultural concerns that either party might have (Johnson & Yanca, 2001; Miley, O'Melia, & DuBois, 2001; Timberlake, Farber, & Sabatino, 2002; and Sheafor & Horejsi, 2003).

When the social worker has gathered sufficient information from the client about the current situation and concerns, the social worker then sorts through the information and analyzes the interacting dynamics of the actors and elements in the client's life that have contributed to the presenting problem(s). The social worker also takes stock of the resources and strengths the client possesses that can be used in resolving their problems. These strengths and resources are not limited to the client alone, but should be assessed of anyone in the client's environment (family, friends, community, and organizations) that may be available and willing to contribute to the client's recovery process and well-being. Finally, the social worker and client prioritize the challenges and obstacles facing the client. Assessment is a discovery process that is ongoing throughout the helping relationship (Haynes & Holmes, 1994; Johnson & Yanca, 2001; Miley et al., 2001; Timberlake et al., 2002; and Sheafor & Horejsi, 2003).

Through assessment and analysis, the social worker and client together mutually agree upon the problems to be addressed, and move into the next phase helping process, the *planning* stage. During the planning stage, the social worker and client:

> ➢ Set goals;
> ➢ Frame solutions to the client's challenges within cultural contexts;
> ➢ Explore strategies for successfully meeting client challenges; and
> ➢ Develop a plan of action that moves the client forward.

Setting goals provides focus and direction to the helping process (Hepworth, Rooney, & Larsen, 2003), helps in identifying obstacles that need to be overcome by the client (Haynes & Holmes, 1994), and establishes a clearer vision of life's possibilities for the client. Together, the social worker and client develop specific strategies for attaining the mutually determined goals of the helping relationship. During this stage the social worker and client develop a detailed treatment plan and contract defining the long-term and short-term goals and the specific tasks to be completed within a designated time period. The social worker-client contract can be written or verbal. The treatment plan and contract function to provide a means of accountability, for monitoring client progress, and determining when termination of the helping relationship is appropriate (Hepworth et al., 2003). For examples of treatment plans and contracts that reflect client goals and plans of action, visit the website for this book at http://www.ablongman.com/cummins2e and study the plans and contracts for the virtual clients (Mike, Anthony, Anna, Mrs. Anderson, and Maria) that you have met on the accompanying CD-ROM.

After the social worker and client have agreed on a plan of action, fulfilling the contract agreement occurs during the *intervention or implementation* stage. Successful implementation requires a goal-oriented interaction between the social worker and client. Both parties are accountable for completing specific tasks agreed to within the contract. Tasks may be directed toward the client's individual issues or may be related to other resource systems within the client's environment (Hepworth et al., 2003). Essential to successful implementation of the action plan is the development and mobilization of resources. This may include:

> ➢ Tapping into client resources and strengths identified in the assessment phase;
> ➢ Activating resources identified and committed by the client's family or friends;
> ➢ Creating alliances with community agencies who may possess important resources for the client; and,
> ➢ Using existing and future alliances to expand opportunities for the client (Johnson & Yanca, 2001; Miley et al, 2001; Timberlake et al., 2002; and Sheafor & Horejsi, 2003).

Together the social worker and client carry out the mutually agreed upon plan of action. In this process, the client and social worker take on specific roles. Roles are defined as the particular obligations and expectations that both have accepted as an outcome of the social worker-client contract (Zastrow & Kirst-Ashman, 2003). (For a more complete discussion of social work roles, see the 'social worker roles' section later in this chapter). For example, a client presenting with the problem of unemployment due to a work-related injury requires the social worker to be a broker of services. Expectations of this role may include the social worker seeking out training programs for reemployment, workers' compensation benefits, and transportation and childcare for the client if needed. Additionally, the social worker would take on the role of counselor and would provide emotional support as the client works through his or her issues of loss related to injury and job displacement. In the role of an advocate, the social worker might assist the client in campaigning for better safety measures being put in place at the work site in order to protect other workers from possible future injuries. Client roles would include following up on employment leads, completing necessary paper work for workers' compensation benefits, seeking out child care from friends and relatives, and exploring education and training opportunities. Successful implementation occurs in the context of a social worker-client relationship that is imbued with trust, a belief that change is possible, and a commitment to fulfilling the role expectations as defined by the action plan and contract (Hepworth et al., 2003).

After the plan of action has been put into place by the social worker and the client, the next phase of the helping process is *evaluation*. During this phase, the social worker assesses client successes and barriers to change and the extent to which the goals set by the client and social worker at the outset of the helping relationship have actually been attained. Ultimately, evaluation ask the question: How effective has the intervention been in resolving the client's presenting problem (Sheafor & Horejsi, 2003)? Does the problem still exist, or has it been mitigated or completely resolved? In order to answer these evaluation questions the social worker may assess some of the following factors that were identified as contributing to the client's presenting problem(s):

> Change in client specific attitudes, beliefs, and behaviors;
> Change in the ability and manner in which the client interacts with various members of their environment and success in completing transactions in various settings (home, school, work, community, etc.);
> Essential changes to the client's environment (for example, extracting oneself from an unhealthy relationship);
> Changes in the client roles within their family and peer structures, workplace, and community; and,
> Changes that have occurred outside of the client as a result of the intervention (for example, more autonomy in the workplace; greater respect from others in the client's environment; improved school performance by client's child as a result of better parent/teacher relationships) (Johnson & Yanca, 2001; Miley et al., 2001; Timberlake et al., 2002; and Sheafor & Horejsi, 2003).

Like assessment, evaluation is an ongoing process that occurs throughout the helping relationship to give direction to intervention strategies. When one intervention does not appear to be effective, the social worker and client may agree on an alternative approach.

This process may continue until the presenting problems and subsequent issues are resolved.

It is through the evaluation process that the social worker and client come to a conclusion about the effectiveness of the helping relationship. Based on this conclusion, the social worker and client may mutually decide if the therapeutic relationship should continue, be renegotiated, or be terminated. If the goals set forth at the beginning of the helping process remain relevant to the client's progress, the relationship will most likely continue. If the client's circumstances have changed and the goals are no longer relevant, the contract may be renegotiated, and new goals set and a new action plan developed. If the goals have been attained and the presenting problem resolved, the relationships will most likely be terminated.

Termination, the final stage of the helping relationship, is the process of mutually determining when and how the helping relationship will end. Optimally, termination is a planned process that begins at the outset of the helping relationship, and occurs when the client has reached treatment goals. In reality, the helping relationship may also be terminated because as a professional social worker, you determine that the client can be better served by another agency or worker, and you refer the client to that agency; or because the client disengages (or never fully engaged in the relationship) from the helping process. One of the cornerstones of social work is client self-determination and empowerment. The client and social worker come to a decision about termination by examining the client's willingness and ability to make healthy life decisions for himself or herself and follow through and act on those decisions. If the client is unable or unwilling to engage in the helping process (this can occur for many reasons, such as being an involuntary treatment situation [i.e., court-ordered counseling], a poor fit between the worker and client, or the client is not ready to address underlying issues that keeps them stuck in dysfunctional patterns or relationships, etc.), then the helping relationship is terminated. A client who is beginning to disengage from the relationship may signal this by:

> ➢ Showing up late for appointments;
> ➢ Canceling appointments or simply not show up;
> ➢ Neglecting or "forgetting" to carry out planned activities;
> ➢ Being inattentive at meetings;
> ➢ Becoming non-talkative and passive at appointments; or
> ➢ Displaying hostility and anger toward the worker.

When the client is giving signs of disengagement, the social worker should clarify with the client the intent to withdraw and validate the client's right to withdraw, if he or she so chooses. In this clarifying process, the social worker may come to realize that the client has attained a level of success that he or she is satisfied with even though it may fall short of the goals set at the outset of the helping process. This is a good time to help refocus the client on the original goal(s) as a means of motivating the client to continue in the helping relationship. If the client sees the level of success as sufficient, then the social worker is obliged to end the relationship, but leave the door open for the client to return in the future.

In the termination process, it is important to discuss with the client the possible consequences if the client prematurely terminates the relationship. For example, a resistant client may have been seeing the social worker because he was mandated by a parent and given the ultimatum of being thrown out of the house if he did not comply. In this situation, these consequences will need to be reviewed with the client so that he or she understands the possible outcomes of the decision to end the relationship. Recall the involuntary client Mike on the CD-ROM. Mike was mandated to alcohol treatment by his employer with the threat of losing his job. When Mike left the treatment center to have a drink with a fellow client, he risked being expelled from the program and losing his job. Karen, his social worker used this impending loss effectively in reengaging Mike in the alcohol treatment program. Pointing out and discussing the possible consequences of terminating the client-social worker relationship is also a part of information giving (a skill presented on the CD-ROM and in Chapter 6). That way, when the client does make a decision about prematurely terminating the relationship, he or she is well informed and is making a choice based on facts and a likely outcome. It is helpful to come to some agreement for mutual resolution of issues, and to review any client progress that has occurred thus far. Finally, the social worker should invite the client back for future work when the client feels ready and motivated to work on issues (Miley et al., 2001).

For those clients involved in meeting treatment goals, the social worker should periodically monitor and review the client's progress in moving toward established goals identified in the social worker-client contract. During these review periods, evaluation data are critical to making objective assessments about the client's progress. In the review process the social worker considers the client's:

> Ability to problem solve independently;
> Willingness to access available resources when problems arise in the future; and,
> Commitment to maintaining the progress made throughout the helping process.

As the social worker and client engage in problem solving throughout the helping relationship, they are, in fact, preparing for termination. The helping relationship provides the client with the steps for problem solving, and a repertoire of skills for successfully navigating life's problems beyond the helping relationship. As the social worker approaches successful termination with a client, it is important to frame termination for the client in three ways and respond to them appropriately. First, recognize that termination can be understood as a loss for the client. Often it is helpful to incorporate some ending ritual into your work with the client that recognizes the loss and provides the client the space to express their grief. This also provides the social worker with the opportunity to process, with the client, feelings of loss. Second, termination can be viewed as a period of new beginnings for the client. This moves the client beyond the grief of loss and into embracing their future armed with the new skills they have acquired during the helping process. Finally, social workers can use termination as an opportunity to affirm and integrate client gains throughout your work together (Johnson & Yanca, 2001; Miley et al., 2001; Timberlake et al., 2002; and Sheafor & Horsejsi, 2003).

The helping process is a fluid and dynamic sequence of social worker-client interactions directed toward problem resolution and growth. The stages of the helping process are not discrete, but build on one another as the helping relationship evolves. Neither are they strictly linear, as the social worker assesses the client situation, evaluates the client's progress and introduces new interventions, the helping relationship unfolds. Box 1.2 demonstrates the dynamic and complex nature of the helping relationship.

Box 1.2 Case Study: Sarah

You are a social worker at a not-for-profit social service agency that provides support services and training to help young single mothers achieve self-sufficiency. Sarah, a 17-year-old single pregnant female was referred to your agency by her school counselor. At intake the social worker tries to put Sarah at ease by providing her with a comfortable chair to sit in, asking about her general well being and letting Sarah guide the pace of the interview. Using these techniques, the social worker reaches out to *engage* Sarah in the helping process and to build a rapport that communicates care and concern. In such an atmosphere, Sarah is able to begin to tell the story of what has led her to seek services on this day. By taking the time to make Sarah feel comfortable and cared for, the social worker has learned that Sarah's *presenting problem* is that of impending homelessness. She is four months pregnant and has been kicked out of her parent's home. When Sarah informed her boyfriend of two years, Joseph, about her pregnancy, he broke up with her, saying he had plans for college and could not take on raising a family at this point in his life. Sarah is confused and depressed and uncertain about how to handle her situation. During the *assessment* process, you discover that Sarah is without family support, has dropped out of school, isolated herself from her peers, and has no money and no place to live. For the past week, Sarah has been spending the night at various classmates' homes, sometimes without the knowledge of their parents. She has worn out her welcome with her friends' families and last night she slept under a bridge about a mile from her parents' home. Although fearful, confused, and uncertain, prior to her current crisis, Sarah presented herself as a responsible student and daughter. Consequently, she is motivated to establish some stability in her life and is seeking help in improving her situation. Together you and Sarah identify problem areas that need to be addressed and accentuate her strengths in constructing a *plan of action* and *contract*.

Box 1.2 Case Study: Sarah, *continued*

The following treatment goals were mutually agreed upon:

1. Gain access to prenatal care;
2. Apply for Medicaid and TANF;
3. Explore temporary housing and apply for subsidized housing benefits;
4. Enroll in single teen parent support group;
5. Engage in ongoing individual counseling for dealing with issues of family disruption, self-esteem, and depression;
6. Enroll in GED classes;
7. Sign up for vocational training for job placement;
8. Begin parenting and family planning classes; and
9. Pursue child support payments.

Together you and Sarah prioritized the treatment goals and placed them within a specific time frame. During the *implementation stage,* Sarah was able to find temporary housing with a family friend until the birth of her child. Meanwhile, as her social worker, you linked her to a local public health clinic where she received prenatal care, and referred her to the public aid office where she applied for and received Medicaid and TANF benefits. Sarah attended her GED classes twice a week and planned on completing her diploma by the time her child is born. In addition, you referred her to the local housing authority where Sarah applied for subsidized housing. At the time she was facing a waiting list of six months. Sarah continued her weekly counseling session and was able to consider mending her broken relationships with her parents. Sarah enrolled in an early childhood development training program in preparation for employment after the birth of her child. Classes will begin when she completes her GED program. After six months of working with Sarah as her primary social worker, you *evaluate*d her progress and assessed the extent to which she had been able to attain her treatment goals. Over the five-month period, Sarah made the following progress on her treatment goals:

1. Consistently kept her prenatal care appointments, followed her physicians instructions, and gave birth to a full-term, healthy son;
2. Received Medicaid and TANF benefits and maintained her eligibility;
3. Moved into a one-bedroom public housing unit in a safe neighborhood;
4. Attended only two sessions of her single-teen parent support group;
5. Attended 90 percent of her weekly counseling sessions and was feeling more focused and less depressed;
6. Reestablished communication with her family;
7. Completed her GED;

Box 1.2 Case Study: Sarah, *continued*

8. Was scheduled to begin child care development classes in six weeks;
9. Had information on the local family planning clinic;
10. Received in-home parenting instruction from a home interventionist working with new mothers; and
11. Spoke to a Legal Aid attorney about pursuing child support.

Together, you and Sarah conclude that she has acquired a sufficient level of empowerment and determine that it is time to *terminate* the helping relationship. You and Sarah have created an environmental structure that will support and nurture her and her son, and as her social worker, you leave the door open for future contact.

SOCIAL WORKER ROLES

When effectively navigating the helping process, social workers take on a variety of roles that facilitate client change. Role is defined as expected professional behaviors and functions accepted by the social work profession, and frequently employed in social work practice (Zastrow & Kirst-Ashman, 2003). Over the course of a career, a social worker may fulfill several or all of the social worker roles and over time will develop competency in most of the roles. Several factors influence which roles a social worker will fulfill, such as the goals of the agency where one is employed; the latitude of the social worker's responsibilities in a given work setting; the needs of the client; and one's level of practice (see Box 1.4). The social worker's roles may be restricted to one level of practice, or may encompass all three levels (micro, mezzo, and macro). Roles will shift when the responsibilities of the social worker move across levels of practice (see Box 1.4). For example, as the social worker in the scenario presented in Box 1.2 you were required to practice at the micro and mezzo levels in order to serve the best interests of Sarah, your client. At the micro level, the social worker took on the roles of *enabler* and *counselor*. At the mezzo level the social worker acted as a *broker* where she connected Sarah to community resources (prenatal care, single parent support group; GED classes, vocational training, parenting classes, Medicaid and TANF benefits, housing assistance, and family planning). The social worker also served in the role of *mediator* (mezzo) in resolving the conflict between Sarah and her parents. If there had been no parenting classes available in Sarah's community, the social worker could have taken of the role of *planner* (macro), and developed a parenting class for Sarah and other expectant teen mothers in the community. For definitions of common social worker roles, see Box 1.3.

Box 1.3 Social Worker Roles

Activist: The social worker initiates and sustains change through social action. For example, in response to rising teen crime rates, the social worker may pull together a coalition of concerned citizens to push for change in the police department, schools, religious community and local agencies to address the growing gang problem in the community.

Advocate: The social worker champions the rights of others through empowerment or direct intervention. The social worker may advocate for a client, group, organization, or community.

Agency Administrator: The social worker is an agency director or assistant director and has responsibility for the functioning of an agency.

Broker: The social worker provides linkages between the client and other agencies or sources of needed resources. For a client recently diagnosed as HIV-positive, for example, the social worker investigates various medical and supportive services and assesses them in light of the client's insurance coverage and available financial resources.

Case Manager: The social worker creates and coordinates a network of formal and informal resources for the purpose of optimizing the functioning of clients with multiple needs. For example, as a case manager with a treatment program for severely mentally ill, polyaddicted drug addicts who are homeless, you will link clients with public supports and treatment services, and pull together formal and informal supports such as self-help groups, family members and friends for the purpose of keeping the clients mental illness well managed, limiting drug use relapses, stabilizing housing, providing job training and employment skills, and emotional supports to draw on during difficult periods.

Clinician/Counselor: The social worker helps improve client functioning through a variety of clinical intervention approaches and by providing ongoing support. The social worker may help the client gain insights into feelings, change unhealthy behaviors and acquires problem solving skills.

Coordinator: The social worker helps a variety of systems to work together at fulfilling goals. For example, the social worker may coordinate community efforts to develop a drug awareness program by working with the police department, local schools, public health department, and parents.

Box 1.3 Social Worker Roles, *continued*

Educator /Teacher: The social worker instructs or imparts knowledge to others at the individual, group, organizational, or community level. For example, the social worker may teach a client job search skills; teach a group of expectant mothers prenatal classes; train agency personnel on new intervention methods; or provide community education on transracial adoption. New knowledge can be empowering to clients, groups, organizations, and communities.

Enabler: Empowers clients in finding solutions to the challenges they face. The social worker offers support and encouragement to clients so that they can more easily accomplish tasks and solve problems. For example, the social work may help a mental health patient adjusts to day treatment.

Facilitator: The social worker leads a group, such as a rape survivors' recovery group, a community group investigating gang crime, or a professional peer group implementing organizational change.

Mediator: The social worker takes a neutral stance between two systems in order to help resolve conflict and to help establish a better communication flow. For example, divorce mediation, or business mediation between quarreling business partners.

Planner: The social worker may work in an agency as a program planner creating new services for clients; or in the community as a community planner enhancing social services and resources for the community.

Outreach Worker: The social worker works within the clients' environments to identify individuals with unmet needs and to engage them into the helping process and social service system. For example, as an outreach worker for the local homeless shelter, you may work with a team of workers who cruise or walk the neighborhoods looking for homeless individuals, engage them in conversation to assess their needs and link them to needed services.

Researcher/program evaluator: The social worker evaluates program effectiveness by gathering data, analyzing it, and interpreting the findings. For example, the social worker may be asked to assess how well the local health clinic is meeting the needs of uninsured community members.

Source: Sheafor & Horejsi, 2003; Zastrow & Kirst-Ashman, 2003; Boyle, Hull, Mather, Smith & Farley, 2006

Social workers can take on many roles at every level of practice. On any given day the social worker may find herself in the role of advocate, educator, clinician, facilitator, mediator, and broker. Often the social worker may find herself taking on the same role on many different levels of practice. For example, as a micro practitioner, you may find yourself advocating on behalf of an individual client (case advocate), a group of similar clients with the same problem (class advocate) or for agencies or organizations trying to address the unmet need of this group of clients (organizational advocate), or for community as a whole (community advocate) when it is discovered that the problem goes beyond your clients and agency to encompass the majority of similar people across the community. For example, as a case advocate, the social worker with a client who recently became disabled and was subsequently fired from his job, (though still able to do the work) may advocate for the client by pursuing legal recourse on his behalf. A class advocate advocating for low income disabled clients living in substandard housing may file a complaint with the local housing authority in an effort to improve the quality of housing for this group. On an organizational level, the social worker may advocate for more resources to meet the training and housing needs of disabled clients using the agency. As a community advocate, the social worker may lobby with other social workers for a more equitable application of the Americans with Disabilities Act to improve the plight of disabled people everywhere.

Given the complexity of the social service system, and the unpredictability of the human experience, social workers often have ethical and moral obligations to serve in multiple roles across all levels of practice if client needs are to be sufficiently met. The multidimensional nature of social work makes it unlikely that a direct practice social worker could restrict the social worker roles to one or two roles, or limit his or her practice to only one level. All social worker roles serve to move us in the direction of social justice by improving quality of life and structuring supportive environments at the family, community, organizational, and institutional levels. Box 1.4 provides a summary of common social worker roles across three levels of practice.

Box 1.4 Social Work Roles and Levels of Practice

Level of Practice	Role
Micro	Case advocate; case manager; client educator; clinician/counselor; enabler; group facilitator; outreach worker
Mezzo	Agency administrator; agency staff trainer; broker; class advocate; mediator; organizational facilitator; program planner; researcher/program evaluator
Macro	Activist; broker; community advocate; community educator; community facilitator; community planner; coordinator

Regardless of the roles you fill as a direct practice social worker, you will need interviewing skills to master the roles and meet the needs of your clients. Experienced social workers realize that interviewing is a skill that must be sharpened continually, and that it has an important place in direct practice at the micro, mezzo, and macro levels. Each new client has a story to tell, whether the client is an individual, family, community, or organization. The social worker must elicit and understand that story in order to be an effective helper. The skills that are explained in the following chapters cannot be learned in a single semester. Think of them instead as a career's work—and this CD-ROM, text, workbook, and accompanying website are your first steps toward mastery.

REFERENCES

Boyle, S., Hull,G., Mather, J.H., Smith, L.L., & Farley, O.W. (2006). *Direct practice in social work.* Boston: Allyn & Bacon.

Germaine, C. & Gitterman, A. (1996). *The life model of social work practice: Advances in theory and practice.* (2nd ed.), New York: Columbia University Press.

Hepworth, D., Rooney, R., & Larsen, J. (2003). *Direct social work practice: Theory and skills.* (6th ed.), Pacific Grove CA: Brooks/Cole.

Johnson, L.D. & Yanca, S.J. (2001). *Social work practice: A generalist approach.* (7th ed.) Boston, MA: Allyn & Bacon.

Miley, K.K., O'Melia, M. & DuBois, B. (2001). *Generalist social work practice: An empowering approach.* Boston, MA: Allyn & Bacon.

National Association of Social Workers (1999). *Code of Ethics.* Retrieved Feb. 18, 2005 from http://www.naswdc.org/pubs/code/code.asp.

National Association of Social Workers (2005). *Practice.* Retrieved Feb. 18, 2005 from http://www.naswdc.org/practice/default.asp.

National Association of Social Workers (2005). *NASW Credentials & Specialty Certifications.* Retrieved March 20, 2005 from http://www.naswdc.org/credentials/default.asp.

Sheafor, B.W. & Horejsi, C.R. (2003) *Techniques and guidelines for social work practice*, (6th ed.) Boston, MA: Allyn & Bacon.

Timberlake, E.M., Farber, M.Z., & Sabatino, C.A. (2002). *The general method of social work practice: McMahon's generalist perspective* (4th ed.) Boston, MA: Allyn & Bacon.

Zastrow, C. & Kirst-Ashman, K. (2003). *Understanding human behavior in the social environment.* (6th ed.), Florence, KY: Wadsworth.

CHAPTER TWO

Values and Ethics in Social Work

Social work is a practice-oriented profession grounded in the core values of self-determination, empowerment, confidentiality, and a belief in the inherent worth and dignity of all human beings. As practitioners, social workers are involved in the lives of people facing difficult and trying problems and circumstances. The actions of social workers can have a direct impact on the quality of life of their clients. When working with troubled individuals, we can just as easily add to the hardships of clients' lives, if our professional actions are not grounded in the values and practice theory of the profession, and guided by the mission of social work. It is therefore essential that social workers be self- aware about the possible outcomes of their interactions with clients.

Social work values are idealistic and can be difficult to sustain in our human condition. To be a social worker requires that you aspire to the values and mission of the profession, that you strive to derive your actions from them in your professional life, and that you recommit to them everyday. Social work values guide the profession toward the fulfillment of its mission of social justice, whose goal is that all members of society have equal access to resources sufficient for a healthy and supportive environment. It is important that individual social workers understand the nature of social work values and incorporate them into their daily practice with clients.

As we discussed in Chapter 1, social work practice can take many forms. At the micro level, social workers work with clients as individuals, in families, or in groups, in public, not-for-profit, or private agencies. At the mezzo level of practice, social workers may find themselves involved in program and policy development or research evaluation within community agencies or private corporations. On the macro level, social workers may be involved with community organizing and development, or working in the political arena as a state or federal employee, elected official, policy analyst, or lobbyist. Regardless of the setting of your social work practice, consideration must be given to how we personify the values of the profession. Social work values are exhibited in how we relate to clients, how service delivery systems are structured, and how, as social workers, we serve as a political voice for disadvantaged and marginalized people in society.

In most introductory skills courses, and in the accompanying CD-ROM, the focus of practice is on the individual client. Keep in mind however, that social work values infuse every level of practice, whether at the individual level or at the level of policymaking.

SOCIAL WORK MISSION

Ultimately, the purpose of social work is to advance the quality of life for all people through the enhancement of mutually beneficial interactions between individuals and society (Minahan, 1981). Social work stands for the social welfare of all people and is committed to social justice through social change at the individual, family, community, agency, and structural levels. As such, social work has historically been and continues to be in alliance with those members of society who live under difficult or oppressive conditions that keep them disadvantaged and marginalized. The profession of social work envisions a more decent and humane society (Ehrenreich, 1985).

Unique to social work as a helping profession is the *person in environment perspective*, which is based on the idea that one can not understand the problems of individuals without understanding the context in which they occur. The context, or environment, encompasses the individual's perceptions of self, family roles and conditions, community supports, agency functioning in meeting the individual's needs, and the interactions between the individual and societal institutions such as economic, political, educational, religious, family, and social welfare systems. Social work, then, has a dual focus, enhancing individuals' functioning in society by empowering them to achieve life goals, and pursuing social changes that are likely to provide a supportive environment for all members of society (Reamer, 1997a). Supportive environments give individuals access to opportunities and resources within all the institutions in society, without regard for attributes such as age, race, gender, religious or political affiliation, or sexual orientation. In doing so, disadvantaged individuals and groups have equal access to mainstream institutions that provide education, employment, wages, housing, nutrition, social supports, and health care. Equal access to these basic resources can alleviate distress and suffering for many people.

Opportunities to contribute to society are essential to one's well-being. Ultimately, human beings are created for the purpose of expressing the innate talents that we possess. Without opportunities for self-expression, human beings become withdrawn, fearful, and weighted down by a sense of having little worth. The social work profession supports the notion that people should be treated humanely and that transactions between individuals and the environment should enhance one's dignity, feelings of self-worth, and full self-expression (Haynes & Holmes, 1994). The mission of social work rests on professional values that ennoble men and women, and call forth their greatest being (Ehrenreich, 1985).

SOCIAL WORK VALUES

Social work values support the mission of social work and guide the profession in creating a humane vision of the world. The social work vision calls for individuals, regardless of their beliefs, practices, or backgrounds, to be treated with dignity, given equal access to societal institutions, opportunities and resources, and supported in contributing their unique talents to their families, communities, and country. At a fundamental level, social work values are congruent with and supportive of the values and beliefs reflected in the Declaration of Independence—that all are created equal and endowed with certain inalienable rights such as life, liberty, and the pursuit of happiness (Haynes & Holmes, 1994). And much like the visionaries who crafted the Declaration of Independence, social workers belong to a profession of action and passion in advocating for the downtrodden; they stand for social justice and human decency (Ehrenreich, 1985). However, for the passion of the profession's values to come alive, they must be put into action; that is, incorporated into one's way of being. Helen Harris Perlman (1976) captured this concept best when she wrote, "A value has small worth except as it is moved, or is moveable, from believing into doing, from verbal affirmation into action" (p.381). Social work practitioners, then, must relate to clients in a way that preserves or enhances their dignity and self-worth. They must structure services in a manner that gives equal access to resources, and support policies that reflect the belief in a just society and the belief that change is possible in individuals, communities, and organizations (Haynes & Holmes, 1994; Reamer, 1995). Only when we have moved social work values from the abstract ideal into empowering action in our professional lives can we claim them as our own (Reamer, 1995). Social work practice is the application of social work values to helping relationships with clients, groups, communities, organizations, and other professionals (Zastrow, 2003), in the context of evidence based social work theories, models and interventions.

Self-Determination

Self-determination is the act of giving clients the freedom to make choices in their lives and to move toward established goals in a manner that they see as most fitting for them, so long as clients' choices don't infringe on the rights of others (Zastrow, 2003). As social workers, we may not agree with our clients' choices, but supporting self-determination requires that we respect our clients in their life choices, whether or not we agree with them. Our job as social workers is not to tell clients what to do or what not to do, but rather to explore options with the client and the possible outcomes of life choices (Haynes & Holmes, 1994). In addition, a social worker can restrict a client's right to self-determination if the client's actions or potential actions could be harmful; or pose a serious danger to self or others. (Boyle, Hull, Mather, Smith & Farley, 2006). Often, we may experience conflicts between our personal or professional value base and that of clients (see Box 2.1).

Box 2.1 Self-Determination and Personal Value Conflicts

You are a drug and alcohol counselor employed at an outpatient treatment center. Tina is a new client of yours who was referred by her employer for alcohol treatment after having repeated "hangover" mornings at work. Recently she appeared at work fully intoxicated. Tina is an architect at a local firm, married, and the mother of two daughters, ages 12 and 14 years. During your third session with Tina, she mentions that she is having an affair. By the sixth session, you learn that Tina has had a series of affairs throughout her 16-year marriage, and that it is a common practice of Tina's to introduce her daughters to her lovers. Tina does not seem troubled by her extramarital affairs, and does not ask you for any help in this area of her life.

You are also married with children, but adhere to the middle-class traditional family values of monogamy, and honest and open communications in your marital relationship. You find Tina's behavior quite disturbing.

Points for reflection:
1. Are the value conflicts inherent in your relationship with Tina personal or professional?
2. How relevant are Tina's extramarital affairs to her alcohol problem and recovery program?
3. As a social worker committed to client self-determination, how would you proceed in your professional relationship with Tina?

Source: Reamer, 1995.

Since it is the client's quality of life social work is dedicated to enhancing, as social workers we must first and foremost allow the client's values to dominate their own lives. This is much easier said than done when we are confronted with client values and behaviors that contradict our own. We often struggle with the desire to impose our values on our clients in practice situations. All people are strongly attached to their personal value system. It is the base from which all our opinions and behaviors emanate. As social workers, we must give up the notion that our personal value system is the model that our clients should follow. We may prefer our personal value system to that of our clients, but it may not be a better value system, only different. For clients to be self-determining, it is essential that they be permitted to live within their own value system. Self-determination enhances clients' abilities to help themselves and fosters self-reliance and self-sufficiency. As we offer clients the opportunity to take on the power of decision-making in their lives, we also invite them to accept the responsibility that goes with the outcomes of those decisions. When we support clients through self-determination, we help create an avenue for clients' expressions of their inherent worth and dignity (Zastrow, 2003). Clients often know what is best for them, what is realistic and possible. Our job is to help them sort through their options, identify barriers, and develop problem solving strategies to "get the job done".

Empowerment

Empowerment lays the groundwork for informed self-determination. Although social workers provide opportunities for empowerment, only clients can empower themselves (the desire to change must originate within the client for it to be genuine). Through the decision making processes, and under the skillful guidance of the social worker, clients are able to move themselves toward their life goals. Social workers assist in this process by providing information, assisting the client in building support systems, and exploring possible outcomes of various life choices. Social workers guide clients to a position where they can make informed choices about their lives. On the surface, empowerment sounds like a fairly simple, yet ideal process. In reality, creating empowering options for clients whose behaviors violate our personal sense of what is right and wrong can be challenging at best. Knowledge is a fundamental ingredient of empowerment. As social workers, we impart new information and knowledge to clients, teach problem solving skills, and allow the power of their own decisions to dominate clients' lives. In the end, we hope, clients learn to seek out knowledge, problem solve, and advocate for themselves, and reap all the benefits and responsibilities that come with such self actions. When clients are able and willing to take theses steps, they have empowered themselves.

Box 2.2 Creating Empowering Options

As a case manager at the local Housing Authority office, you are responsible for helping low-income families gain access to safe, affordable, and when eligible, subsidized housing. Judy is a 30-year-old single mother of two who has been on welfare assistance for three years. For two years, Judy and her family drifted in and out of homelessness when her unstable housing arrangements fell apart. You have been working with Judy in finding her housing for 18 months. After being on the waiting list for public housing for a full year, you were able to help Judy secure a two-bedroom apartment in a public housing unit designated for young families that is located in a safe neighborhood. Judy and her family have been in their new apartment for six months, and for the first time in their young lives, her children are experiencing what it means to have a stable home. This afternoon, you received a call from the local police informing you that Judy has been arrested for drug trafficking in her apartment. The Housing Authority's policy forbids the use or selling of drugs in public housing units, and requires that residents who violate this rule be evicted immediately.

Points for reflection:
1. As a case manager with the local Housing Authority, what empowering options can you create for your client, Judy?
2. Do you see any value conflicts between the agency's drug policy and social work values? If so, what are they?
3. When you go to the jail to visit Judy, what will you say to her?
4. How would you feel about this case if Judy's children were not involved?

Inherent Worth and Dignity

A core value of the social work profession is respect for every human being's innate greatness. Social workers are trained to regard clients as having worth and to treat them with dignity, regardless of their outward behaviors. It is our job as social workers to provide the supportive environment for the client to fully express that innate greatness. In doing so, we create a process of affirmation that over time generates a growing sense of self-worth in the client.

To put into action the value of inherent worth and dignity, the social worker must be able to view people as unique individuals, and not impose preconceived notions, or stereotypes, on people possessing certain characteristic (see Box 2.3). This is the process of individualization (Zastrow, 2003), of knowing people for themselves, instead of "knowing" people through the distortions of our own biases.

Box 2.3 Stereotyping versus Individualization

Consider your initial impressions and assumptions about the following types of clients whom you may encounter in your practice. Write them down and then identify what is true for everyone with a particular characteristic; identify your beliefs that are based on stereotypes you've learned in your experiences and socialization.

1. A single African American welfare mother;
2. A homeless teenage prostitute of Mexican descent alone on the streets;
3. A 24-year-old white male recently diagnosed with AIDS;
4. A 52-year-old female executive working for a large corporation;
5. A 75-year-old male diagnosed with dementia.

The only indisputable things we can say about the potential clients described above are that you would be working with a poor African American mother, a Mexican teenager who has no home, and a young white male infected with AIDS, a very successful career woman and an elderly person. What other assumptions did you make about your potential clients? Consider where your impressions came from and the types of values reflected in your assumptions. Through honest self-reflection, we can begin to let go of our stereotypes, and move toward individualization and the possibility of knowing our clients as unique human beings.

Respecting people for their inherent worth and dignity also requires social workers to be willing and able to separate an individual's behaviors from who they are inherently as human beings. When our clients adhere to values, lifestyles, and behavior patterns that are similar to our own, relating to our clients with unconditional regard is easy to do. However, when a client's behaviors are at odds with our personal value system, engaging the client with unconditional regard can be very difficult (see Box 2.4).

Box 2.4 Separating Client Behaviors from the Client

Consider your reactions to the following clients. How difficult would it be for you to view these clients with respect? Identify the values and emotions that limit your ability to relate to these clients with unconditional regard.

1. A 35-year-old father who has sexually abused his six-year-old daughter;
2. A 15-year-old girl who shot and killed her mother while she slept;
3. A 45-year-old man arrested for selling drugs to grade-school children;
4. A 30-year-old single mother who left her three-year-old daughter locked in her room for a weekend while she went away with her boyfriend.

Zastrow (2003) offers two guidelines for working with clients whose behaviors appall and disgust us. First, accept that the individual and their behaviors can be separated. In doing so, you create an opening for treating clients with respect and viewing them as capable of change. By separating the behavior from the person, you can give yourself permission to despise the behavior without disrespecting the person. Second, recognize that with some clients, it will be difficult if not impossible for you to get past the heinousness of their behavior and treat them with the respect that is needed in order to establish a helping relationship. When this occurs, and it happens for almost all social workers at some point in their practice careers, it may be in the best interest of the client to transfer the case to another social worker. If you cannot conceive of the client as having inherent worth and dignity, a helping relationship cannot be created. Talk to your supervisor or a trusted colleague about your feelings. Then, assess your own values to determine what might be getting in your way (see self awareness in Chapter 4). We don't always have the option of transferring a case. Consider putting a plan in place with your supervisor for working through your biases. Begin with the question: "What buttons does this client push with me?"

All people are inherently great; it's just that some have forgotten. When we forget who we are innately, we become disconnected from ourselves, and express who we are *not,* through destructive behaviors. When we can stand in the possibility of our client's greatness, we have transcended our own biases and made an empathic connection with them. Only then can we effectively enter into our client's world and their lived experiences (Haynes & Holmes, 1994). The role of the social worker is to help individuals remember who they are, innately, and support them in expressing their greatness. Often this is unfamiliar territory, and clients will need considerable support, encouragement, and affirmation to engage in ways of being that have, to this point in their lives, been foreign to them. To stay in this process with the client requires us to acknowledge and draw upon our own innate gifts, and to have compassion for our clients when they fail, and for ourselves when we fail to stay in our commitment to our client's ability to change and create a better life. Social work practice requires an ongoing recommitment to the mission of our profession, the values that support it, and our clients' inherent worth and dignity.

Confidentiality

Confidentiality refers to the safeguarding of the information that passes between the social worker and the client. This aspect of the social worker–client relationship facilitates the evolution of a trusting relationship that is essential for client change. Trusting that what transpires during the interview session will remain private, clients can begin to express their concerns and aspirations within a safe environment. Once that occurs, the social worker can obtain the necessary information to create empowering options with clients and support them in their life choices. For more discussion on confidentiality in practice, see Chapter 5 on engagement.

State laws, the NASW code of ethics, and certain agency policies impose limitations on confidentiality within the social worker–client relationship. The NASW code of ethics and some state laws require that social workers report to the appropriate authorities clients' intentions to harm another individual or themselves. All states require that social workers report known or suspected cases of child abuse or neglect. Social service agencies that use a team treatment approach may require that all team members have access to pertinent information about the client. It is the ethical responsibility of the social worker to inform clients of the limits of confidentiality at the outset of the helping relationship (Gothard, 1997; NASW, 1997; Polowy & Gorenberg, 1997). However, even when we are knowledgeable about the legal and ethical limits of confidentiality, in the real practice world it is often difficult to identify when we have reached these limits within the helping relationship. Box 2.5 provides an example of this dilemma.

Box 2.5 A Confidentiality Issue

You are a caseworker at a Family Service Center where you have worked for one month since receiving your BSW. Richard is a 48-year-old construction worker whom you have been seeing weekly since your first week at the agency. Richard came to your agency seeking assistance after unexpectedly losing his job following a back injury that left him permanently limited in his abilities to lift or carry more than 20 pounds, or to climb or do twisting motions. Richard is a devoted husband and father and is feeling that he has let his family down because he has not been able to provide for them financially in recent months. With your help, Richard has been able to enter an eight-week reemployment-training program where he is being trained as a tax preparer for a local firm. He has done well in his classes, but has become depressed and frustrated in the past two weeks as his family's financial situation has worsened. Today, you notice that Richard seems more agitated and restless. When you asked him what is on his mind, he explains that the previous night he had been out at the local tavern having a few beers and on the way home was stopped for speeding and was given a DUI when he failed to pass the Breathalyzer test. The ordeal resulted in Richard being held in jail overnight, causing him to miss his tax preparer's class the following morning. He is feeling unjustly persecuted by the police, and fears that he will not be permitted to complete the class. As Richard is telling you of the events of the previous evening, he becomes enraged at the unfortunate hand that fate has dealt him and blurts out, "I feel like walking into the police station and shooting those bastards!"

Points for reflection:
1. How will you handle the issue of confidentiality in your relationship with Richard?
2. How do you determine whether Richard is serious about his threat or just venting his anger?
3. What actions would you take?
4. How would you address this with Richard, given confidentiality and issues of trust?
5. What safety issues do you need to consider for yourself, for Richard and the staff in your agency?

SOCIAL WORK ETHICS

Social work ethics provide social work practitioners with a set of guidelines for practice. These guidelines are established by the National Association of Social Workers (NASW), the major professional social work organization, and reflect the values of the profession. Social work ethics translate the abstract values of the profession into action statements and give social workers concrete guidelines for ethical ways of being in the practice setting. The first code of ethics was adopted in 1960, and was later revised in 1979 and again in 1996 to reflect the changing emphasis and direction of social work practice and changing social and political times (Haynes & Holmes, 1994; Reamer, 1997b). Box 2.6 summarizes the six ethical principles of the NASW Code of Ethics.

Box 2.6 Ethical Principles of the Social Work Profession

1. Social workers' primary goal is to help people in need and to address social problems;
2. Social workers challenge social injustice;
3. Social workers respect the inherent dignity and worth of the person;
4. Social workers recognize the central importance of human relationships;
5. Social workers behave in a trustworthy manner;
6. Social workers practice within their areas of competence and develop and enhance their professional expertise.

Source: NASW, 1997

The 1996 revisions to the Code of Ethics provide guidance on how to deal with issues in contemporary social work practice. Between 1979 and 1996, the social, economic and political contexts of society had changed in significant ways. Those changes directly impacted social work practice and called for a revision of the code. Some of the major societal changes affecting practice in this time period were:

> ➤ A shift to a more conservative philosophy of social welfare toward 'personal responsibility' that was reflected in a limited government role in the lives of people; conservative tax policies; reduction in human services federal budget from 28%-15%; fundamental changes in the welfare system and immigration laws, and tighter eligibility standards of accessing publicly funded social welfare benefits;
> ➤ Evidence of community disintegration emerging in social problems such as homelessness, domestic violence; poverty; substance abuse; job instability; unemployment; multiple jobs; and increased family stress;
> ➤ Population shift with growing numbers of people of color and the elderly;
> ➤ New health and information technologies and major changes in health policy favoring managed care; and,
> ➤ The development of a culture of consumerism reflected in "me first" attitudes; and "for protiftism" in the human services (Brill, 2001).

All of these changes called into question the ethics and commitment to public services by the public at large, the government, and professionals in the human services. Social workers are facing more complex issues in practice and are expected to work effectively and efficiently with fewer resources. The changes in the social, economic and political landscape of America have created a context of social work practice that has more ethical challenges. In response to these societal changes, the 1996 NASW revised code covered more areas of practice, and provided more specificity in professional behaviors. In all, the code now consists of 156 practice standards. Some of the new standards expand on old practice issues but in a new context; still others address practice issues for the first time (Brill, 2001; Reamer, 1998). Box 2.7 summarizes the areas included in the 1996 NASW Code of Ethics that are either new additions or a significant expansion of old standards.

Box 2.7 Summary of Practice Standards

1. Clearly states the limits to confidentiality;
2. Acknowledges the use and implications of technology in practice;
3. Gives special attention to dual and multiple relationships with clients and avoiding conflict of interests;
4. Expands standards of practice in regards to informed consent;
5. Considers issues of sexual relationships with or sexual harassment of clients, students, supervisees, and research subjects;
6. Addresses issues of ethical termination of clients;
7. Delineates expected behavior with colleagues;
8. Expands standards regarding administrators;
9. Speaks to general concerns about research, supervisory relationships, and faculty/student relationships;
10. Stresses the importance of cultural and ethnic diversity issues throughout the code;
11. Reasserts the focus of the profession; and
12. Clearly discusses the social worker's responsibility to call into question agency policies and procedures that reflect poor practice standards or that are discriminatory in any way.

Source: Brill, 1998.

It has been nearly ten years since the Code of Ethics was revised, and the country and the world has seen many changes that present new practice dilemmas for social workers. For example, today we are embroiled in a global war on terrorism. As social workers, we are confronted with clients returning from a type of war never before fought, to a country very politically polarized. As always, social work practitioners must focus on the client. As social workers are confronted with trying to effectively treat soldiers returning from war or deal with the personal and family adjustment to being deployed, one ethical response of profession has been to sponsor workshops on effective interventions with soldiers leaving for and returning from the war. These types of responses generate discussions within the profession on the obligations of social work to help soldiers and their families cope with issues surrounding deployment, war, and reentry, irrespective of the profession's political position on the war. Through these value-centered processes, our actions as a profession and the evolution of our code of ethics remain rooted in the values that have sustained the profession for over 100 years. As social workers, we commend the profession for responding to the changes of the times, and to living up to our values and mission by ethically responding to new client and social problems.

Charles Levy (1976) notes that social work ethics serve three functions for the profession: "It guides professional conduct, it is a set of principles that social workers can apply in the performance of the social work function, and it is a set of criteria by which social work practice can be evaluated" (p.108). By understanding the established ethics of social work practice, social workers can make the difficult moral and value-laden decisions that are an inescapable part of working with people from diverse walks of life. Social workers who find themselves within practice settings that may not adhere to the values of the social work profession have a supportive and clear set of guidelines. Box 2.8 outlines the areas of social workers' ethical responsibilities that are addressed in the NASW Code of Ethics. For a full reading of the NASW Code of Ethics, visit the NASW web site at www.naswdc.org, or go the website accompanying this book at http://www.ablongman.com/cummins2e to access the link.

Box 2.8 Social Workers' Ethical Responsibilities

1. Social workers have ethical responsibilities to clients;
2. Social workers have ethical responsibilities to colleagues;
3. Social workers have ethical responsibilities in the practice setting;
4. Social workers have ethical responsibilities as professionals;
5. Social workers have ethical responsibilities to the social work profession;
6. Social workers have ethical responsibilities to the broader society.

Source: NASW, 1997

Ethical Dilemmas

The social work profession is sanctioned by society through the passage of public laws, and through the appropriation of public funds to fulfill the mandates of public law. Social work therefore has an obligation to society to provide services, counseling, and interventions for those in need. In this sense, the public at large shows support for the values and mission of social work. Public laws and regulations also direct social work practice in so far as social workers are mandated by law to provide certain services and to structure those services in predetermined ways. Often the values inherent in the public laws directing social work practice are in conflict with the values inherent in social work practice. At times, this may put the social work practitioner in an ethical dilemma when trying to satisfy the demands of two competing value systems (see Box 2.9).

Box 2.9 Conflicting Values: Social Work and Social Policy

Let's return to the case of Sarah, presented in Chapter 1. Recall that you are a social worker at a not-for-profit social service agency that provides support services and training to help young single mothers achieve self-sufficiency. Over the past two years, you have seen Sarah intermittently. She has become one of your favorite clients, in part, because of her perseverance and her willingness to follow through on her commitments. Sarah is now 19 years old; her son, Seth, is two. Since you began working with Sarah, she has attended parenting classes and proven herself to be a loving and skilled mother. She has also completed her GED. With the help of housing assistance, she has been able to secure a two-bedroom apartment after being on the waiting list for six months. Eight months ago, Sarah got her first real job as an assistant teacher in a daycare center, working 20 hours per week. Sarah likes her job very much, and she excels at her work. The job only pays $7.25 per hour and provides no health care or paid time-off benefits. However, as an employee of the daycare center, Sarah receives free daycare for her son Seth. With her TANF (Temporary Aid to Needy Families) income, food stamps, Medicaid, subsidized housing, part-time job, and free daycare, Sarah has managed to create a stable life for her son.

In the state where you practice, clients can only receive TANF benefits for two years. As you review Sarah's case file, you see that her welfare benefits will expire in one month. Sarah needs the welfare check to meet basic survival needs for herself and her son. If she budgets carefully, her welfare check and work income together just cover her rent, secondhand clothing for Seth, bus fare to work, the phone bill, and essential items like toothpaste and soap that are not covered by food stamps. Without her welfare check, Sarah is likely to find herself in the same situation she was in two years earlier, homeless with her young son.

***Points for reflection*:**
1. What social work value does the state TANF policy contradict?
2. As a social worker, how do you comply with state law without violating social work values?
3. What options can you present to Sarah that will be empowering to her and her son?

As discussed earlier, changes in the complexity of society and social problems have created new ethical challenges to the contemporary social worker. Consider for example that cuts in human services funding have resulted in fewer salaried social workers and thus higher case loads for those social workers who have retained their jobs. How do you as a social worker provide adequate levels of care to 200 child welfare cases on your workload? The move toward contract/fee-for-service positions among social workers shifts the focus of the work from an internal altruistic motivation to one that is money driven. How will this affect the quality of service delivery? In the privatization of human services, service delivery has become competitive and funding driven rather than need driven, raising the question of who is getting served and who is not. Another ethical challenge is the increase in unionization among social workers....does this violate professional code? The use of technologies that computerize client records and allow for sharing of client information across agencies raises questions about our ability to insure client confidentiality (Brill, 2001). Consider the following three cases in box 2.10. Identify the ethical dilemma present in each case and then discuss how you would respond if you were the social worker in each case.

Box 2.10 Ethical Dilemmas: Case Examples

Case #1. A social worker employed in a county social services department as an eligibility worker has learned that local welfare reforms direct that she report any new children born to current welfare recipients. She fears that the new reporting requirement could prevent children born into welfare families from receiving income supports later in their lives. The worker is aware of the requirement that social workers should comply with the law. However, she is convinced that reporting newborns might preclude future essential services. The social worker also believes that the new regulations will create a new class of citizens (children born to welfare mothers) that might be discriminated against in various ways. She feels caught between complying with the law and ignoring the law to prevent what she views as likely injustice.

   A. What is/are the ethical dilemma(s) facing the social worker?
   B. Are these legitimate concerns? Why or why not?
   C. As the social worker in this county agency, how would you respond in this situation? What are your possible courses of action?

Case #2. A clinical social worker in a remote community trains paraprofessionals to do mental health counseling with members of their Asian, Pacific Islander, and Central American communities. She believes that well-trained paraprofessionals familiar with community members' cultures and languages could broaden mental health services by bringing cultural depth in service to those communities. Months after those she trained began providing services, the state department that licenses her agency adopted new policies prohibiting unlicensed social workers from providing mental health counseling services. A regional department representative reports that he is considering filing a complaint against the social worker for facilitating the unauthorized practice of social work.

   A. What do you see as the ethical dilemma here for the social worker? For the state department representative?
   B. Which action would provide the best services to the clients? Why do you think so?
   C. As the social worker at the agency, what would you do to protect your paraprofessionals and the services they provide to your clients?
   D. As a state department representative (which may well be social worker too), on what ethical grounds can you feel justified in enforcing the law?
   E. Is there a win/win solution to this dilemma? What do you think it might be?

Box 2.10 Ethical Dilemmas: Case Examples, *continued*

Case #3. When a nonprofit hospital downsized, all social work positions were eliminated. The social workers were transferred to an affiliated home health care agency. The hospital then offered to contract with the home health social workers for the same work they had done previously for the hospital. At times, the social workers who do both hospital and home based work experience conflicts of interest when faced with the need to refer hospital patients to home-based services. The social workers understand that they should not exclusively refer to the hospital's home health care agency and that self-determination requires that patients have information about a range of available, appropriate services. But, from the patient's perspective they also see that it would often be more desirable to be able to continue to work with the social worker who had been assigned during the hospitalization period. The hospital's risk management officer has argued, however, that when patients chose their home health care agency the same social worker should not continue to work with the patient because of the appearance of conflict of interest—that is, the social worker would receive compensation for services because of a referral he or she made.

A. If a patient chooses to continue with her hospital social worker as her home health social worker, is there really a conflict of interest for the social worker? If so, what do you believe the conflict to be?

B. What underlying social work values may be jeopardized in the above working arrangement?

C. Are there any standards of practice being violated in this working arrangement as set forth by the NASW code of ethics? Which one(s)?

Case studies reprinted with permission from NASW, 1998.

CONCLUSION

Social work as a profession is dedicated to social justice and the empowerment of all people through the creation of a just society where men and women are given equal access to resources and opportunities. These ideals often attract people to the profession who are committed to helping people. Putting social work values into practice is an ongoing challenge, especially in today's complex world. Ethical dilemmas are common to social work practice and social workers need to be familiar with the profession's code of ethics to guide them through the challenges of practice with people facing multiple problems in a rapidly changing world. Staying focused on creating a society where all people enjoy a safe and supportive environment helps us through the difficult cases. Witnessing our clients' successes as they reconnect with their own innate worth and create stable and fulfilling lives is the priceless reward that social workers reap in direct social work practice.

REFERENCES

Boyle, S., Hull,G., Mather, J.H., Smith, L.L., & Farley, O.W. (2006). *Direct practice in social work*. Boston: Allyn & Bacon.

Brill, C. K. (1998). Looking at the Social Work Profession through the eye of the NASW Code of Ethics. *Research on Social Work Practice, 11*(2), 223-234.

Ehrenreich, J. H. (1985). *The altruistic imagination*. Ithaca, NY: Cornell University Press.

Gothard, S. (1997). Legal issues: Confidentiality and privileged communication. In National Association of Social Workers *Encyclopedia of social work* (19th ed.). Washington, DC: NASW Press.

Haynes, K.S & Holmes, K.A. (1994). *Invitation to social work*. New York: Longman.

Levy, C. (1976). *Social work ethics*. New York: Human Sciences Press.

Minahan, A. (1981). Purpose and objectives of social work revisited. *Social Work, 26*(1), 5-6.

National Association of Social Workers (1997). *Encyclopedia of social work* (19th ed.). Washington, DC: NASW Press.

National Association of Social Workers (1998). *Current controversies in social work ethics: Case examples*. Washington DC: NASW Press.

Perlman H. H. (1976). Believing and doing: Values in social work education. *Social Casework, 7*(6), 381-390.

Polowy, C. I. and Gorenberg, C. (1997). Legal issues: Recent developments in confidentiality and privilege. In National Association of Social Workers *Encyclopedia of social work* (19th ed.). Washington, DC: NASW Press.

Reamer, F.G. (1995). *Social work values and ethics*. New York: Columbia University Press.

Reamer, F.G. (1997a). Ethics and values. In National Association of Social Work's *Encyclopedia of social work* (19th ed.). Washington, DC: NASW Press.

Reamer, F.G. (1997b). Ethical standards in social work: The *NASW Code of Ethics*. In National Association of Social Work's *Encyclopedia of social work* (19th ed.). Washington, DC: NASW Press.

Reamer, F.G. (1998). Ethical standards in social work: A critical review of the NASW Code of Ethics. In National Association of Social Work's *Encyclopedia of social work* (19th ed.). Washington, DC: NASW Press.

Zastrow, C. (2003). *The practice of social work*. Pacific Grove, CA: Brooks/Cole.

Social Work Practice and Theory

Social workers are prepared through their BSW education to practice as generalist social workers. To be an effective generalist, social workers must be grounded in a broad range of practice theory. To be a generalist social worker means one is able to draw upon many theories or components of theories and pull them together to create a reasoned and comprehensive approach to practice for specific clients in specific contexts. Client problems, values, culture, and belief systems should influence our selection of theoretical frameworks in constructing practice interventions.

From its beginning, social work has been concerned with providing care that is grounded in tested knowledge. Many of our early theories were borrowed from other disciplines such as psychology, medicine, anthropology, biology and sociology. While many of these and other theories continue to inform social work practice, with maturity, the profession has developed empirically tested theories of its own. Today, there are more than 50 theories commonly used in social work practice, and many of these were developed for social work practice by social workers. See Box 3.1 for a list of commonly used theories in social work practice.

Box 3.1 Sampling of Social Work Practice Theories

Attachment	Behavioral	Client Centered
Cognitive	Communication	Constructivism
Crisis	Developmental	Ecological Perspective
Ego Psychology	Existential	Family Centered
Feminist	Functional	General Systems
Gestalt	Human Relations	Life Model
Management	Marxist	Natural Helping Network
Person Centered	Problem Solving	Psychoanalytic
Psychosocial	Organizational	Role
Social Action	Strengths Perspective	Structural
Symbolic Interactionism	Task-oriented	Transactional Analysis

Sources: NASW, 1997; Miley, O'melia, & DuBois,(2001; Sheafor & Horejsi, 2003.

Fundamentally, practice theory is a body of knowledge that has been empirically tested and shown to be effective. Theory then, guides the action of practice, and its evidence of effectiveness becomes our standard of accountability (Turner, 1997). Without the application of tested knowledge, we cannot claim to be practicing professionals. If we did not use theory to guide us in our practice decisions, we would be no different from a kind, warm-hearted person wanting to be of help and doing what he or she felt was the 'right thing to do.' Theory then becomes the basis of our assessments and interventions with clients. We use it to give meaning to situations, to assess the strengths and weaknesses (or barriers) in presenting situations, and to understand our clients' lives and the environments in which they live and function. Usually practice requires that we employ multiple theories when working with a client (which may be an individual, family, group, organization, or community) (Turner, 1997). For example, we may use the person-in-environment perspective to understand the complexity of our client's life, psychodynamic theory to understand her low self-esteem, crisis theory to counsel her through a rape, and grief theory to help her through the recovery process.

Our earliest concern in social work practice was to understand the person in the context of his or her environment. However, initially this understanding of person in relationship to their environment was limited to including important members of the client's family in the initial assessment. For example, it was common to gather information from family members, employers, and even neighbors, but the full understanding of the physical, economic, religious, social and cultural impacts of the environment on clients' lives had not yet evolved. The importance of the role these factors had in influencing clients' lives emerged in the 1970s as new concepts were borrowed from general systems theory and ecology that would eventually lead the profession into the development of ecological systems theory or ecosystems theory (Beckett & Johnson, 1997; Miller, 1978; Germain, 1973; and Germain & Gitterman, 1997).

Ecological perspective provides a broad theory base to social work practice and is used as a context or backdrop for applying more practice-specific theories such as crisis intervention theory or cognitive-behavioral theory. Other broad theories common to social work practice today include the life model theory (drawn from ecological perspective), the strengths perspective, and empowerment base practice theory. This chapter provides an overview of these general theories for social work practice.

SYSTEMS THEORY

Peoples' environments extend beyond their immediate family and encompass the entirety of their lived experiences, including interactions with extended families, friends, neighborhoods, schools, religious centers, public laws, cultural norms, and the economic system. To understand the complex interactions among individuals and all the components of their environment, social work draws upon general systems theory as a framework for understanding people's problems and intervening in their lives. General systems theory was developed in the physical sciences and later expanded for application to the applied professions as a conceptual framework within which diverse theories could be organized. It was also seen as a framework that could bring a common language to practitioners, thus facilitating communications and cooperation (Doggett & Johnson, 1997).

A system is defined as a whole made up of many interacting parts or subsystems. For instance, a person represents an individual subsystem within a larger family system; a family is seen as a subsystem within a larger community system; and a community is a subsystem within a larger societal system. Systems and subsystems have a structural relationship to each other and are separated by boundaries. Boundaries can be either impermeable, creating closed systems that are self-contained and allow few influences from the outside; or permeable, creating open systems that actively exchange with other subsystems and as such, are constantly changing. The interactions or exchanges among subsystems are dynamic processes that keep open systems constantly in flux. As long as systems can readily adapt to change, the system will remain in balance or maintain a state of equilibrium. When major changes occur to a system where adaptation will occur over time, systems may be in a state of disequilibrium until the system can adapt and compensate for the change that has affected the system. For example, when 9-11 occurred in New York City, the change to the city system was so immense that it could not adapt to the massive destruction that occurred. With the response of many subsystems (communities, organizations, individuals) and suprasystems (state, federal and international responses), New York was slowly able to come back into balance or equilibrium. However, this took a long period of time, and many businesses, families, and aspects of the economy are still recovering. These enormous shocks to the subsystem of New York occurred in the context of a nation (suprasystem) that was struggling with the shattering of a long-held belief that in America individuals can count on feeling a sense of safety and security.

In response to insults and disruption to systems, whether they be families, communities, or nations, social workers direct their attention to the total interactions among individuals and the sum of all social forces or systems (Haynes and Holmes, 1994) so that they may "promote or restore a mutually beneficial interaction between individuals and society in order to improve the quality of life for everyone" (Minahan, 1981, p.6). In the case of 9-11, this continues to be an ongoing effort on all levels of practice for the profession as families continue to grieve their losses, cities confront their vulnerability to threats of terrorist attacks, and local and national economies struggle to recover form the impact of this fateful day in the country's history.

Optimal functioning of an individual in the environment requires subsystems that are also functioning at an optimal level, which promote individuals' development toward self-actualization. System dysfunction is understood as functioning that limits or deters from reaching innate potentials. System dysfunctions can occur at the individual, family, community, organizational, or societal level. Regardless of where the dysfunction originates within a system, it can create chaos that can be perpetuated throughout the associated subsystems. Sarah, our client from Chapter 1, disturbed many systems in her crisis around her pregnancy. See Box 3.2 for a description of interactions between Sarah and the multiple subsystems in her environment.

Box 3.2 Sarah

Recall Sarah, our client from chapter one. As a 17-year-old girl who was pregnant, Sarah affected not only her life, but also those around her. Sarah's family became quite distressed, reacted angrily, and expelled her from their home, leaving her to fend for herself. Confused and alone, Sarah dropped out of school in order to pursue employment to financially support herself and her forthcoming child. Sarah's limited education seriously impaired her ability to become self-sufficient and to support her child in the future. The employment and wage system is geared toward promoting people with education and skills, and has few supports for young single parents without an adequate education. The baby that Sarah will give birth to will also face many challenges, such as poverty and under-nutrition, which in turn will have a direct impact on her child's physical, mental, and psychological growth and development. Cultural norms that support a traditional family structure may negatively affect the psychological well-being of both Sarah and her child as they understand themselves to be outside the norms of their family and community. The social worker at the level of direct practice worked with Sarah across a variety of subsystems in order to restore stability to her life. The social worker worked on the individual system through assessment and counseling with Sarah; on the family system by reestablishing relationships with her family; on organizational systems by linking her to a prenatal care clinic and parenting classes and connecting her to an educational program where she completed her GED; with the economic system by assisting her in an employment search; and, with the federal benefits system by helping Sarah apply and receive TANF (Temporary Assistance to Needy Families), housing assistance, and Medicaid welfare services.

As presented in Chapter 1, the goal of direct practice is to assess and improve the interaction of subsystems (the individual, family group, community, and organization) within the context of a larger societal system. The profession recognizes the importance of addressing systems at three levels. The **micro system** is the individual, and encompasses individuals' past history, experiences, unique personality, and accessibility to resources. The **mezzo system** is the small group, such as the family, which has its own complexities and dynamics. Such small groups strongly influence and are influenced by their individual members. Community organizations and agencies also fall under the mezzo system classification. The **macro system** is the large group, such as the societal institutions of work, schools, and the religious community (Zastrow, 2003). To this aim, Zastrow (2003) put forward four goals of social work practice that address all levels of system intervention:

1. To enhance people's problem-solving, coping, and developmental capacities;
2. To link people with systems that provide them with resources, services, and opportunities;

3. To promote the effective and humane operation of systems that provide people with resources and services; and

4. To develop and improve social policy (pp. 25-26).

Micro, mezzo, and macro systems interact along a continuum of functioning with the aim of enhancing system functioning so that healthy functioning dominates and dysfunction is minimized. This environment or ecology of systems plays an important part in the development of individual and family systems. Social work is at its best when the transactions of these systems promote growth and development of the individual, family, and community, and in exchange makes the environment amenable to positive growth among all the subsystems (Ashford, Lecroy, & Lortie, 2006). In Box 3.2, the social worker intervenes at the **micro** level when involved in individual assessment and counseling with Sarah; at the **mezzo** level when working with Sarah's family and linking Sarah to the prenatal clinic, and parenting class; and at the **macro** level when intervening with the educational, employment, and social welfare systems. Practice interventions at all three system levels are necessary to bringing stability to Sarah-'s world.

ECOLOGICAL PERSPECTIVE

The person-in-environment perspective of social work practice expanded and benefited from the transfer of general systems theory concepts in the physical sciences to the application to the living systems of the human family. The work of Germain (1973, 1979) and Germain and Gitterman (1987) further deepened our understanding of the complexities of the human condition in the context of various subsystems in their groundbreaking ecological perspective. Borrowing concepts from ecology (the study of organisms and their relationship with their environment), the ecological perspective provided more concrete concepts for understanding the person in environment than systems theory had been able to do. For example, the notion of 'goodness of fit' between a person and the environment sprang from the ecological framework and provides a lens through which to assess the extent to which a person's adaptive behaviors promote growth and health (a good fit) or support a decline of physical, social or psychological functioning (bad fit). Other important concepts that are part of understanding a person in the environment introduced through the ecological framework are the role of stress and coping measures that individuals bring to their environment, and their ability to relate, or build attachments, friendships and positive family relationships, all of which serve as resources when meeting life's challenges (Germain & Gitterman, 1997).

The ecological perspective also challenges social workers to think in much more complex patterns that capture the mutually shaping back and forth of interactions among individuals, groups, organizations, and institutions (Germain & Gitterman, 1997). Logical thinking tends to be linear, where we assume a cause and effect relationship between two events, whereas 'ecological thinking' requires that we understand the back and forth interactions of a person in the environment. In logical thinking, A causes B, and that's the end of the story. In ecological thinking, A has an impact on B, which changes B, which in turn has an impact on A, which changes A, which in turn changes B and so on. For instance, a mother who views the challenges of toilet training her two year old as a normal developmental stage and major accomplishment for her child will approach the task with greater ease and excitement than a mother who interprets her child's inconsistency in toileting as defiant behavior. The latter mother sees her child as a problem while the first mother does not. Clearly, the mother who views toilet training as a normal part of her child's growth and development will be able to create a more supportive environment for the child (good fit) to complete this critical task than the mother who sees the lack of toileting mastery in her two year old as a discipline problem (bad fit). Each mother's responses shape the child's sense of self and feelings of competence. The extent to which we experience success in shaping our environments, we grow in self-esteem and feelings of competence.

From a social work perspective, both mothers are part of the environment that either enhances or deters their child's developmental potential. The reciprocal nature of the relationship between individuals and their environments means that as individuals, we move and shape our surroundings, and that our surroundings have a profound effect on us as well. For example, the mother who acknowledges and praises her child's mastery of toilet training affects the child's sense of competence and self-worth. As the child responds with pride in his or her accomplishment, the mother feels competence in her role as a mother. Both the mother and the child mutually shape their sense of well-being. Conversely, the mother who sees toilet training as a discipline problem and responds with anger and punishment equally influences her child's sense of self worth. The child may respond with fear, confusion, and a feeling of inadequacy in meeting his or her mother's demands. The child's failure at toilet training may affirm the mother's suspicions of her own inadequacies as a parent. In both cases, the child and the mother mutually contribute to the stress or satisfaction they individually experience around the task of toilet training and the role of mothering. Box 3.3 provides a summary of important concepts central to understanding the ecological perspective in assessing the goodness of fit between a person and the environment.

Box 3.3 Ecological Perspective Concepts

Person:Environment Fit: The relationship between an individual or group and their physical and social environment within a historical and cultural context. When the environment supports growth and health, then a 'good fit' between the person and the environment is said to exist.

Adaptations: Internal or external changes to self or one's environment that maintain or enhance the goodness of fit between an individual and the environment.

Life Stressors: Critical life events or issues that disrupt the goodness of fit between an individual and the environment. Common issues include traumatic events, such as the loss of a loved one, job or one's health; major life transitions such as marriage, divorce, or retirement; or larger issues that impair the goodness of fit and often bring on other life stressors such as poverty and oppression.

Box 3.3 Ecological Perspective Concepts, *continued*

Stress: An internal response to life stressors that produces negative emotions such as guilt, anxiety, depression, despair, or fear, and result in a person feeling less competent, producing a lower level of relatedness, self-esteem, and self-direction.

Coping Measures: Behaviors that individuals initiate to respond to life stressors in ways that restore or heighten the goodness of fit between and individual and the environment.

Relatedness: One's ability to form attachments to friends, family, co-workers, and neighbors and attain a sense of belonging in the world.

Competence: When individuals are provided with opportunities to shape their environment from infancy on, they have the opportunity to develop a sense of efficacy. Ongoing experiences of efficacy accumulate to provide a feeling of competence at shaping and managing one's environment.

Self-Esteem: Represents an assessment of oneself as worthy of love and respect. People with high self-esteem feel competent, valued, and respected. Those with low self-esteem perceive themselves as inadequate, unlovable, inferior and unworthy, and often experience depression. How we feel about ourselves deeply influences our thinking and behaviors.

Self-Direction: The capacity to make decisions, take control of one's life and direct it in desired paths, while taking responsibility for one's decisions and navigating one's life with respect to others' rights and needs. The ability to self-direct is strongly related to feelings of power and powerlessness. If individuals are not provided with opportunities to make decisions and direct their own lives, they will likely feel powerless and lack self-direction. Living in oppressive conditions often robs people of their power and can profoundly influence their ability to self-direct.

Habitat: Refers to the nature and location of the person's 'home' territory or where they feel most at home. Some terms often applied to habitat are nesting places, home range, or territory. For humans it may include home community, school, workplace, or local hang out, and people's behaviors within the spaces.

Niche: Social position or ranking within one's community, or the status one holds within the family, with co-workers or in the community. For example, a man may be a patriarch at home, the boss at work, and a buddy at the local pub, all indicating high levels of status across his habitat. Conversely, a man might be a drifter to his family, undependable at work, and homeless in the community, all of which signify low status across the habitat.

Source: Germain & Gitterman, 1997.

LIFE MODEL OF SOCIAL WORK PRACTICE

In response to changing practice needs in the 1970s, Germain and Gitterman (1997) developed a practice method that implemented the concepts of the ecological perspective into a practice approach. It differed from popular practice approaches in that it did not focus on the deficits of a person, but rather modeled interactions in the practice relationship around life processes and focused on client strengths. The goals of the life model are not to provide remedial treatment, but rather to

> ➢ Promote health, growth, and the expression of one's potentials;
> ➢ Make changes to the environment that will promote and sustain growth and well-being; and,
> ➢ Improve the person:environment fit (Germain & Gitterman, 1997).

The life model application in practice guides the practitioner in assessing life stressors, stress, and coping mechanisms in the client, and seeks to use interventions that restore or enhance relatedness, self-esteem, and self-direction. Specific goals toward these aims are outlined and established with the client. The life model is grounded in the principle of empowerment and as such is particularly sensitive to cultural, physical, and social contexts. Aspects of empowerment that are central to the life model include:

> ➢ Client and social worker as partners in change;
> ➢ Recognizing clients as expert on their lives; and,
> ➢ Sensitivity to the power differential in the client/social worker relationship (Germain & Gitterman, 1997)

The evolving working relationship between the client and social worker within the empowerment practice principles is geared to enhancing clients' access to personal power and in turn promoting a sense of self-worth. When clients have the ability to experience efficacy in their relationship to their environment, they grow in feelings of competence, promoting decision-making that gives direction to clients' lives (Germain & Gitterman, 1996).

PERSON-IN-ENVIRONMENT (PIE) ASSESSMENT AND CLASSIFICATION SYSTEM

A step toward a more structured and uniform application of the person-in-environment (PIE) perspective represented by ecological perspective and systems theory was the development of the PIE assessment and classification system in the 1980s. The system was developed by a NASW task force in response to two trends. First, the Diagnostic Statistical Manual (DSM) III medical model classification systems had become the most used system in the human services, but that system, at best, used only limited environmental factors in understanding human behavior, thus limiting social work practitioners in their analysis of environmental factors contributing to patient problems. Second, the evolution of systems theory, ecological perspective, and the Life Model of practice highlighted the need for practice tools for implementing the constructs of person-in-environment theoretical frameworks (Karls & Wandrei, 1997).

The PIE system is used by practitioners to assess client functioning within their environment, and calls attention to difficulties as well as strengths. It focuses on function and dysfunction or balance and imbalance between the person and their environment. Social functioning is identified and described in terms of social role performance. Social role performance is understood as one's ability to fulfill role expectations across the multiple roles of a client's life. For example, how well does a client fulfill their role of employee, in terms of company policies, such as showing up to work on time and absenteeism, or in relations to meeting the job expectations for which the person was hired. Clients are assessed on all major roles in their lives, such as parent and spouse (Karls & Wandrei, 1994). The PIE system provides a way to analyze the complexities of clients' lives including the biological, psychological, physical, and social aspects. It is best described as a method for understanding the whole problem complex. This descriptive classification system is made up of four factors on which social work practitioners make an assessment (see Box 3.4). In the assessment, the social worker identifies and describes the client's social function across these four factors.

Box 3.4 PIE System Factors

FACTOR I: Client problems in social functioning, and also the client's capacity to resolve problems;

FACTOR II: Problems that arise from the client's environment that affect the client's social functioning;

FACTOR III: Any mental health problem that interferes with the client's social functioning; and,

FACTOR IV: Any physical problems.

Source: Karls & Wandrei, 1994.

The PIE system produces a descriptive statement and coding of social role functioning and environmental problems of clients. Social work interventions are appropriate when the PIE assessment reveals impaired role functioning in the client or an environment that negatively affects the client's social functioning. The client's severity and duration of social dysfunction are also noted, as are his coping skills. Codes are assigned across all four factors, creating a common practice language that communicates across agency settings and practitioners (Karls & Wandrei, 1994). Each factor assesses different dimensions of the client's life, and each dimension is referred to as an 'axis.' For example, an assessment of factor I would produce an axis I code and description of the client's ability to function within their life roles; factor II assessment generates a code and description of people or events in a client's environment that interfere with his or her social functioning, and is known as axis II; factor III assesses the client's mental health status along axis III using the DSM IV, and factor IV or axis IV code and description reflects the client's physical challenges.

The significance of the PIE classification system is that it links the development of social work concepts, theories and models with social work practice by providing an assessment practice tool. Hopefully, familiarizing yourself with this model will lead to the more frequent use of contextualized assessment in practice and less on individual and deficit focused assessments. The PIE classification system is available online and can be downloaded for a free trial. To become more familiar with the PIE system and to practice using it, go to http://www.compupie.org/PIE/about_pie.htm or access the link from the companion website with this book at http://www.ablongman.com/cummins2e.

STRENGTHS PERSPECTIVE

The strengths perspective of social work practice springs from the values that permeate the profession—inherent worth, human dignity, and self-determination. Putting these values into action requires that we believe in the unleashed power that resides in all human beings and the possibility of change. Client strengths become the resources for change that move them forward to growth, mastery, and self-actualization (Miley, et al,, 2001). Box 3.5 summarizes the assumptions that underlie strengths perspective.

Box 3.5 Underlying Assumptions of the Strengths Perspective

1. Everyone is imbued with abilities, capacities, talents and competencies;
2. People have an inherent capacity for growth and change;
3. Life traumas may have a negative impact on peoples lives, but they can also serve as a source of growth;
4. The upper limits of peoples ability to grow and overcome adversity is unknown and unknowable;
5. Problems do not reside within the person, but occur in the transactions within and across systems;
6. People are experts on their own lives;
7. People's friends, families, and communities are reservoirs of resources that are or can be made available;
8. Growth is future focused on what is possible;
9. Mastery and competence is best attained within a supportive process; and,
10. People generally know what will and will not be helpful in overcoming the challenges they face.

Sources: Miley, O'Melia, DuBois, 2001; Sheafor & Horejsi, 2003.

An important aspect of the strengths perspective is that it provides social work practitioners with an alternative framework for practice that is counter to the deficit model that has dominated human services perspectives (Saleebey, 1992). Often social workers find themselves in practice contexts that subscribe to the medical model of practice that focuses on remedial care and 'fixing' what is broken. If social workers are not armed with theoretical frameworks that emphasize the inherent worth of individuals, families, and communities, it is all too easy to slip into a deficit model of practice. Box 3.6 provides a contrast of pathology (inherent in the medical model) with strength.

Box 3.6 Comparison of Deficit and Strengths

Deficit Perspective	Strengths Perspective
Cumulative symptoms = diagnosis	Individual uniqueness, abilities, talents, resources = strength
Interventions focuses on the diagnosis of 'problem'	Interventions focus on possibilities
Practitioner doubts client stories and becomes the 'expert' on client's life	Practitioner views the client as the expert in his/her life and comes to know the person from the inside out
Adult problems are rooted in childhood traumas	Childhood traumas are not predictive of later life events
Treatment is directed by a treatment plan devised by the practitioner	Interventions are directed by client's aspirations
Client's possibilities in life are limited by his pathology	Life possibilities are open
Resources for therapeutic work reside in the knowledge and skills of the practitioner	Resources for therapeutic work reside in client, family, community
Therapeutic work is focused on reducing symptomology and its negative impact on client	Therapeutic work is focused on moving the client forward in living into their possibilities and vision for their life

Adapted from D. Saleebey's comparison of pathology and strengths.
Source: Saleebey, 1996.

When using a strengths perspective in practice, social workers use a wide range of practice principles, ideas, skills and techniques to promote and draw out the resources of clients and those in their environments to initiate change, energize the change process, and sustain change once it has occurred (Miley et al., 2001).

To intervene from a strengths perspective effectively, the practitioner must first examine their own underlying perspective and resulting language about problems in society. Do you fundamentally believe that people are powerful and able to direct their own lives in positive ways, or do you believe them to be powerless and in need of repair? Your perspective will be communicated in your language. For example, do you see people as having 'problems' or facing challenges that while difficult, can transform their lives? Problems have a way of demoralizing us, making us feel like failures, and generally bringing us down. Challenges are viewed as opportunities for growth and inspire us to pull upon our internal and external resources to meet the challenge and attain our goals. Challenges lift us up. For example, an immigrant from Haiti with limited English speaking skills may struggle with finding her place in a new country and community; but the external resource of strong family connectedness of her culture (even from a distance) can be used to move her forward toward stability and creating the life she envisioned when she left her home country. For more information on culture as strength, see Chapter 4.

When you see unusual behaviors do you see pathology or strengths? When social workers focus on pathology as the central point in working with clients, it may block their ability to see the strengths that lie within the client or to use techniques in the helping process that will uncover client strengths. When designing interventions, are you focused on undoing the past or creating a future? A "past" perspective in treatment assumes that something in the past happened that caused the client to be 'not OK' today. Overemphasis on the past prevents the use of the present in exploring resources and option and planning for the desired future. Shifting our focus to the present and future can have the power of releasing the past and giving up negative assumptions about ourselves that keep us stuck in positions we would rather not be in (Miley et al., 2001). Yes, problems exist, as do pathologies and past events that stop us in our tracks. We cannot ignore these realities, but we can redirect our thinking in ways that see beyond these negative and deficit interpretations of clients' lives. Dennis Saleebey (2001) captured the challenge in transition to a vision of strength in practice:

> We are not asking you to forget the problems and pains that people may bring to your doorstep. Rather, we are asking that you honor and understand those dilemmas, and that you also revise, fill out, expand, illuminate your understanding with the realization that the work to be done, in the end, depends on the resources, reserves, and assets in and around the individual, family or community (p. 221).

Applying the strengths perspective requires that the social work practitioner reorient from a deficit or pathology framework to a strengths and possibility perspective. As practitioners, we do not ignore problems, but we focus on client strengths (Sheafor & Horejsi, 2003). In interacting with clients, we must ask ourselves, What is he doing right? What life skills does she possess that she can bring to bear on the challenges at hand?

What untapped resources does he hold within him? What other resources reside in her family, friends and community that can lift her up to meet today's challenges and creating a preferred vision of her future)?

EMPOWERMENT-BASED PRACTICE MODEL

Social work has a long tradition in empowerment practice, dating back to the early settlement houses. In more recent years, empowerment-based practiced emerged from work with women and people of color and built upon the belief that members in groups with limited social and political power suffer personal loss of power and opportunities across systems in mainstream society (Gutiérrez, DeLois, & GlenMaye, 1995). The concept of power in the context of empowerment practice has been defined by Gutierrez et al. (1995) in three ways:

1. The ability to get what one wants;
2. The ability to influence how others think, feel, act, or believe; and,
3. The ability to influence the distribution of resources in social systems such as family, organization, community and society. (p.535).

Power described in this way suggests that practice interventions will need to occur at multiple levels of practice (individual, family, organization, community, and national levels), and that the dimensions of power encompass the personal, interpersonal, and political levels. To have personal power is experienced as a sense of control over one's life and feelings of competence. Individual who experience internal power feel competent in their ability to take care of themselves, to access resources as needed across systems, and to contribute to community and system resources. When we have interpersonal power, we have the ability to influence others and know ourselves to be effective in interactions with others and are highly regarded by others. (Gutierrez & Ortega, 1991; Miley et al., 2001). When people experience political power, their interactions with their environment results in access to and control over resources. Box 3.7 illustrates how the client perceives issues of personal power and how the client uses this to meet her needs.

Box 3.7 Sylvia

Sylvia perceives herself to be self-sufficient and holds an expectation that she can and will take care of herself. She does this by accessing resources from 1) her friends, such as support, socializing and fun, borrowing items when needed; 2) her family, such as information on the pros and cons of owning a home, a place of comfort to return to for visits, referrals to family contacts when trusted information is needed, or a loan for a down payment on her new condo; 3) from the community, such as locating retail stores to purchase her needs, community agencies that will support her in meeting life and role expectations (i.e., a tax preparation firm, or gaining membership into the local YWCA where she develops a exercise routine to support her health). Sylvia may experience interpersonal power in persuading her father to give her a loan, or her knowledge that she is highly regarded by her peers and colleagues at work, which is affirmed by positive feedback and acknowledgments of her contributions to the work community. To the extent that Sylvia can access and gain control over resources in all areas of her life, she possesses political power. For example, Sylvia's ability to negotiate a raise with her boss at work, voice her opinion at a town meeting and influence local policy on how to spend town funds, or sit as a board member on a local social service agency in her community, are just a few ways in which she and others can exercise political power. In each of these examples, access to and control over resources is actualized.

Activating clients' internal power requires that social workers understand the context of clients' lives (person-in-environment) and perceive clients as reservoirs of latent power waiting to be awakened (strengths perspective). Helping clients to attain personal, interpersonal, and political power requires that social work practitioners collaborate with clients and assist them in structuring interventions at the individual, family, and community levels. The work of social work practitioners is to recognize, facilitate, and promote clients' connections with their internal power (resources) and to mobilize it across systems in ways that increase their mastery in shaping their environments in desirable ways.   Look for ways to enhance their feelings of competency and their ability to forge effective relationships. Finally, assist clients in identifying ways to draw upon and contribute to community resource pools. To do this, the focus of practice must be on accentuating potentials and client resiliencies, and minimizing client vulnerabilities (Miley et al. 2001).

REFERENCES

Anderson, R.E. & Carter, I. (1984). *Human behavior in the social environment: A Social systems approach* (3rd ed). New York: Aldine de Gruyter.

Ashford, J., Lecroy, C., & Lortie, K. (2006). *Human behavior in the social environment.* Pacific Grove, CA: Brooks/Cole.

Beckett, J.O. & Johnson, H.C. (1997). Human development. In National Association of Social Work's *Encyclopedia of social work* (19th ed.). Washington DC: NASW Press.

Germain, C.B. (1973). An ecological perspective in casework. *Social Casework, 54* 323-330.

Germain, C.B. (1979). Introduction: Ecology and social work. In C.B. Germain's (Ed.) *Social work practice: People and environments* (pp. 1-22). New York: Columbia University Press.

Germain, C.B. & Gitterman, A. (1997). *The life model of social work practice* (2nd ed.). New York: Columbia University Press.

Germain, C.B. & Gitterman, A. (1997). Ecological Perspective. In National Association of Social Worker's *Encyclopedia of social work* (19th ed.). Washington DC: NASW Press.

Gutiérrez, L.M., DeLois, K.A. & GlenMaye, L. (1995). Understanding empowerment practice: Building on practitioner-based knowledge. *Families in Society, 76*(9), 534-542.

Gutierrez, L.M. & Ortega, R. (1991). Develoiping methos to empower Latinos: The importance of groups. *Social work with Groups, 14*(2), 23-43.

Karls, J.M. & Wandrei, K.E. (1994). *PIE manual: Person-in-environment system: The PIE classification system for social functioning problems.* Washington DC: NASW Press.

Karls, J.M. & Wandrei, K.E. (1997). Person in environment. In National Association of Social Worker's *Encyclopedia of social work* (19th ed.). Washington DC: NASW Press.

Miley, K.K., O'Melia, M. & DuBois, B. (2001). *Generalist social work practice: An empowering approach.* Boston, MA: Allyn & Bacon.

Miller, J. G. (1978). *Living systems.* New York: McGraw Hill.

Minahan, A. (1981. Purpose and objectives of social work revisited. *Social Work, 26,* 5-6.

National Association of Social Workers (1997). *Encyclopedia of social work* (19th ed.). Washington DC: NASW Press.

Saleebey, D. (1992). Conclusions: Possibilities of problems with the strengths perspective. In D. Saleebey (Ed.), *The strengths perspective in social work practice* (pp. 169-179), New York: Longman Press.

Saleebey, D. (1996). The strengths perspective in social work practice: Extensions and cautions. *Social Work, 41*(3), 296-305.

Saleebey, D. (2001). Practicing the strengths perspective: Everyday tools and resources. *Families in Society, 82*(3), 221-222.

Sheafor, B.W. & Horejsi, C.R. (2003) *Techniques and guidelines for social work practice* (6th ed.) Boston, MA: Allyn & Bacon.

Turner, F. (1997). Social workpractice: Theoretical base. In National Association of Social Worker's *Encyclopedia of social work* (19th ed.). Washington DC: NASW Press.

Zastrow, C. (2003). *The practice of social work.* Pacific Grove, CA: Brooks/Cole Publishing Company.

The Cultural Context of Practice:
Using Interviewing Skills Effectively

How well we understand our clients and their problems is, to a large extent, dependent on how well we understand the context of their lives. Nothing influences our values, our commitments, our life practices, and our world views about how our lives 'ought' to be more than the culture we were born into, socialized by, and live in. To this end, multicultural competence is an indispensable part of the social worker's skill set. In different cultural contexts, the same skill can have very different meanings to clients. For example, maintaining eye contact can be perceived as either comforting or threatening, depending on the client's cultural traditions. The social worker's interaction with the client should be informed by knowledge of the client's cultural background and value system, *as well as by the social worker's self-knowledge of any biases or gaps in cultural familiarity he or she may bring to the helping relationship.* The dialogue between social worker and client is thus embedded in a cultural context on both sides, and the social worker must approach the client relationship with this awareness and with the intent and ability to adjust the interview to best meet the client's needs.

In recent years cultural competence has become an increasingly critical factor in the success of any social work intervention. This is due in part to the increased diversity of U.S. society (by 2050, it is estimated that non-Hispanic whites will constitute 50% of the population, down from 69% in 2000), but also to a resurgence of pride in cultures of origin and, in turn, to a new awareness of culture as a positive resource for clients (U.S. Census Bureau, 2004; McGoldrick, Giordano & Pearce, 1996; Saleebey, 1997). The strengths perspective in social work practice places culture at the center of the helping process:

> The assessed strengths of the client's cultural values should determine the design and planning of interventions. If the cultural strength of extended family is assessed, then recommending and implementing individual therapy may be contraindicated. If spirituality is central to the belief system of a culture, to omit or neglect it is no longer acceptable for culturally competent practice. Historically, social workers have ignored cultural values or, at best, we have been asked to 'be aware' or be sensitive' to them….To be culturally competent is to know the cultural values of the client system and to use them in planning and implementing services….This requires culturally competent social work practice to shift to the strengths of the client, extracted from the cultural value system, as a means of identifying resources for empowerment. (Fong & Furuto, 2001, p. 6)

Well-honed interviewing skills are essential to culturally competent practice. Although general cultural knowledge is useful, it is your interaction with the client that will enable you to assess the client's cultural identity and subsequently work toward a culturally congruent intervention.

Developing multicultural competence is an ongoing commitment for the social work professional. Cultures are not static or uniform. They change in response to new circumstances (i.e., economic conditions, technological innovations, demographic shifts, etc.). Cultures often contain *subcultures*, which are cohesive and distinctly different groups that exist within the larger culture. For example, there is a vibrant Latino culture within the United States, and within the broad Latino culture there are a variety of subcultures, such as Puerto Rican American, Mexican American, first versus second generation subcultures, etc. These within-group differences can be as great as the variation between larger cultures. Each culture is also influenced by other cultures. Some groups, such as the Amish, are relatively isolated from the larger society, while others are more assimilated into the dominant culture. At the individual level, clients may identify with more than one culture. For example, a teenager whose mother is a Japanese American and whose father is of German extraction may be comfortable in both of her parents' cultures of origin. Nearly seven million Americans identified themselves as being of two or more races in the 2000 census (U.S. Census Bureau, 2001).

As in the example above, an individual may be able to draw from a number of cultures and subcultures in responding to any given situation. The self-concept is dynamic, involving a "continually active, shifting array of available self-knowledge" (Markus & Nurius, 1986, p. 957). Which "possible self" will the client present? The give-and-take of the interview process is what enables the social worker to identify and best utilize the combination of cultural strengths the client brings to the helping relationship, when planning culturally appropriate interventions.

It is important to understand the impact of oppression and racism on clients' lives. While racism affects all members of society, whether they're discriminated against or not, members of historically disadvantaged groups face formidable challenges in many areas of their lives. Social workers need to understand the institutional barriers to services their clients may face: These can include poor housing; lack of access to good schools, jobs, and public transportation; greater risk of being arrested; and environmental degradation and loss of community due to low-income areas' tendency to serve as sites for heavy industry and freeway development. (See http://www.ablongman.com/cummins2e for examples of institutional barriers faced by historically disadvantaged groups). Box 4.1 introduces some core concepts necessary to understand and apply as one moves toward developing cultural competence.

Box 4.1 Cultural Context: Core Concepts

The following concepts are important in understanding this chapter:

Culture is difficult to define, but broadly stated, it's a quality of all communities of people identified by geographic location, common characteristics, or similar interests. This includes values, norms, beliefs, language, and traditions. For example, there is a rural culture, a drug culture, a homeless culture, a teenage culture, an Italian culture, and a white supremacist culture, to name a few.

Cultural diversity refers to human differences as generated by membership in various identifiable human groups. Cultural diversity includes not only race, ethnicity, and gender, but also sexual orientation, persons with physical or cognitive impairments, religion, socioeconomic status, and age.

Social workers strive to avoid **stereotypes**, or oversimplified mental representations of people and cultures. Stereotypes reflect prejudiced attitudes and are not based on a reasoned, thoughtful analysis.

Social workers possess **cultural sensitivity** when they have an attitude of acceptance, respect, and appreciation for each client's cultural uniqueness, and a willingness to learn about each client's unqeness.

Cultural sensitivity is the foundation for **cultural competence**, which is a social worker's ability to acquire and utilize extensive knowledge about a cultural group and more specifically, an individual member within a cultural group.

The next level of ability is **cultural responsiveness**, which is the ability to use client-perspective-centered practice skills as a method to achieve true multicultural competence. An example of cultural responsiveness would be knowing which interviewing strategies would be most effective in communicating with a Somali immigrant.

Multicultural competence is the ability to pull it all together, integrating cultural knowledge, values, and skills into practice in order to relate to clients in culturally relevant and appropriate ways.

The National Association of Social Workers (NASW) provides ten *Standards for Cultural Competence in Social Work Practice* to guide social workers toward developing a culturally competent practice (see Box 4.2). For the beginning social worker, these standards are an invaluable resource While all of these standards are important to know and apply to social work practice, in this chapter we will focus on the following three standards: 1) self-awareness; 2) cross-cultural knowledge; and, 3) cross-cultural skills.

Box 4.2 NASW Standards for Cultural Competence in Social Work

Standard 1. Ethics and Values
Social workers shall function in accordance with the values, ethics, and standards of the profession, recognizing how personal and professional values may conflict with or accommodate the needs of diverse clients.

Standard 2. Self-Awareness
Social workers shall seek to develop an understanding of their own personal, cultural values and beliefs as one way of appreciating the importance of multicultural identities in the lives of people.

Standard 3. Cross-Cultural Knowledge
Social workers shall have and continue to develop specialized knowledge and understanding about the history, traditions, values, family systems, and artistic expressions of major client groups that they serve.

Standard 4. Cross-Cultural Skills
Social workers shall use appropriate methodological approaches, skills, and techniques that reflect the workers' understanding of the role of culture in the helping process.

Standard 5. Service Delivery
Social workers shall be knowledgeable about and skillful in the use of services available in the community and broader society and be able to make appropriate referrals for their diverse clients.

Standard 6. Empowerment and Advocacy
Social workers shall be aware of the effect of social policies and programs on diverse client populations, advocating for and with clients whenever appropriate.

Box 4.2 NASW Standards for Cultural Competence in Social Work, continued

Standard 7. Diverse Workforce
Social workers shall support and advocate for recruitment, admissions and hiring, and retention efforts in social work programs and agencies that ensure diversity within the profession.

Standard 8. Professional Education
Social workers shall advocate for and participate in educational and training programs that help advance cultural competence within the profession.

Standard 9. Language Diversity
Social workers shall seek to provide or advocate for the provision of information, referrals, and services in the language appropriate to the client, which may include use of interpreters.

Standard 10. Cross-Cultural Leadership
Social workers shall be able to communicate information about diverse client groups to other professionals.

While the multiculturally competent social worker is able to meet all ten of these standards, cultural self-awareness, knowledge, and skills provide the foundation for developing the culturally effective use of social work interviewing skills.

SELF-AWARENESS

NASW Standard #2: Social workers shall seek to develop an understanding of their own personal, cultural values and beliefs as one way of appreciating the importance of multicultural identities in the lives of people.

When you are born into a culture, your worldview is conditioned by the values, norms, beliefs, language, and traditions of that culture. You are raised to value the things that the culture values, and it can be difficult to see the ways in which your attitudes, beliefs, and behavior are specific to your culture. People tend to be conditioned into specific roles in their home culture. These roles can be related to gender, age, or class status. It is easy to conclude that values and actions arising from a culture other than their own can somehow be 'wrong' or 'deviant,' especially if they are foreign to us or fall outside mainstream societal values and practices.

It is particularly difficult to develop a broader perspective when you are a member of a dominant cultural group. In U.S. society, members of historically disadvantaged groups such as African Americans can and must function both in their own culture and in the dominant culture—a survival strategy reflected in the phenomenon known as 'code switching," in which African American speakers switch from Standard English to Afrian

American Vernacular depending on the setting. (Cooper et al., 2002; Turner, Wieling & Allen, 2004). White European-Americans, however, have not had to develop such bicultural expertise, and this more limited worldview can lead to the minimization of others' ongoing experience of oppression (Frankenberg, 1997). Taking a global view, it is difficult for us to find ways to experience other cultures authentically. The widespread use of the English language and U.S. cultural, military, and economic dominance all work against the goal of meeting the 'other' as an equal.

Evolving Self-Awareness

Becoming culturally self aware is a quality that can evolve over time, but only with a commitment to periodically taking a personal cultural-awareness inventory; identifying one's own cross cultural limitations; and intentionally taking action to become culturally competent. When completing a personal cultural-awareness inventory, we assess where we fall on the continuum of cultural competence. One way to gage one's level of cultural competence is to apply the Developmental Model of Intercultural Sensitivity (DMIS) to oneself. The DMIS provides a progression of cross-cultural awareness along a continuum, moving from an ethnocentric worldview to an ethnorelative perspective. In ethnocentric perspectives, the individual's culture dominates their thinking, to the exclusion of other cultural perspectives (Bennett, 1986, 1993). Ethnocentric individuals will often deny or minimize the value of other cultural views. Conversely, individuals who hold ethnorelative worldviews experience their culture in the context of, or relative to, other cultures. They have greater awareness of and appreciation for other cultures. At the ethnorelative stages of cross-cultural experience there is acceptance of other cultures, and individuals are able to function effectively within another culture. The following graphic illustrates the developmental stages that individuals move through in acquiring intercultural sensitivity.

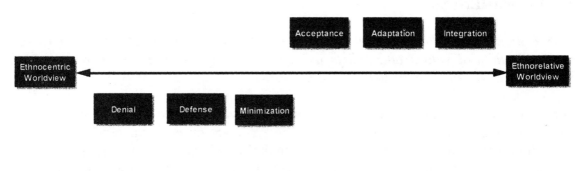

Bennett's Developmental Model of Intercultural Sensitivity

Each developmental stage has a unique worldview, or perspective, that influences the attitudes, values, and behavior of individuals holding that worldview. As one moves from the left to the right side of the spectrum, there is increasing intercultural sensitivity, or awareness and appreciation of cultural difference.

The first three DMIS stages are ethnocentric (i.e., the individual's culture dominates thinking about other cultures).

Denial. Individuals at the first stage of ethnocentrism, denial, do not have any meaningful experience of cultures other than their own. Cultural avoidance is the norm and is achieved by strategies of isolation or separation (Bennett, 1986). An example of denial would be a religious group that strongly emphasizes socializing within the group, home schooling, and avoidance of mainstream culture as expressed on television.

Defense. The second stage of ethnocentrism, defense, is characterized by a very limited engagement with other cultures—an interaction that takes the form of a vigorous defense of the individual's culture as the only 'true' culture. An individual who can argue about the superiority of her culture by citing the ways in which her own culture is better than another culture is at the defense stage (i.e., a neo-Nazi who defends his views by citing alleged 'weaknesses' in Jewish culture).

Minimization. When individuals relate to cultural difference by minimizing those differences, generally under the umbrella of 'we're all the same on the inside,' they're at the minimization stage. This seemingly positive worldview is, in reality, rooted in a refusal to explore the implications of cultural differences. This worldview assumes that what's the 'same' is generally in line with the individual's home culture. On one level, it is true to say that "we all have ceremonies to celebrate marriage"—but if we stop at that level of generality, we miss underlying differences—in one culture, marriages may be arranged, based on an economic match between two families—in another, it may be based on love between the two partners. These two perspectives can lead to very different behaviors, something that is not accounted for in the minimization stage. When an individual is able to move beyond the minimization stage of the ethnocentric world view, they emerge at acceptance, the first stage of the ethnorelative worldview.

Acceptance. Individuals at the acceptance stage acknowledge that cultural differences are real and should be respected. Cross-cultural knowledge is implicit in this stage. For example, a grade school teacher who realizes that not every culture socializes children the same way and seeks out information to enhance her understanding of her students is at the acceptance stage.

Adaptation. The second stage of the ethnorelative world view is adaptation. At this stage, individuals use their cross-cultural knowledge and skills in their interactions with members of other cultural groups. To extend the previous example, a grade school teacher who adapts her teaching strategies based on knowledge of her students' culture is at the adaptation stage of intercultural sensitivity.

Integration. The third ethnorelative stage, integration, is characterized by a high degree of fluency in more than one culture, to the point that an individual can fully adopt different worldviews, depending on the cultural setting. "This stage is not necessarily better than Adaptation in most situations demanding intercultural competence, but it is common among non-dominant minority groups, long-term expatriates, and 'global nomads'" (Bennett & Hammer, 1998). An immigrant who has learned to function in both her own subculture and in mainstream society and who can think in both English and her native language could be said to have reached the integration stage of intercultural sensitivity.

Self-awareness of your cultural identity is a prerequisite to building cross-cultural skills and knowledge. You can start by assessing the frame of reference you bring to the helping process. Take a moment to assess yourself on your cultural self-awareness by completing part I of the Cultural Inventory in Box 4.3. Think about your own world view; your values and traditions; your cultural experiences and your understanding of other cultures. After completing the self-awareness inventory, locate yourself on the DMIS continuum. Where do you find yourself? There is no right or wrong placement. Most important is that you become aware of where you fall on the continuum of cultural awareness....then you are in a good position to move forward toward cultural competence.

Box 4.3 Cultural Self-Inventory Part 1: Self-Awareness

Personal Identity
> What are your ethnic identities?
> Of which other cultural groups are you a member?
> Which cultural memberships are most influential in the way you define yourself?
> What characteristics or behaviors do you display that indicate the influences of these cultural identities?
> What values are associated with these cultural memberships?
> Do you feel positively or negatively about these identities?
> Have you ever experienced discrimination based on your cultural memberships?
> What privileges do your cultural memberships afford you?

Spiritual Beliefs
> What are your spiritual beliefs?
> What led you to these beliefs?
> How important are spiritual beliefs in your daily life?
> How do these beliefs influence the way you perceive others who hold different beliefs?

Source: Miley, O'Melia & DuBois, 2001 p.68

As you reflect on your responses to the self-inventory, step back from yourself and try to observe your life from a distance. Acknowledge your own biases, which, depending on your background, may arise from white privilege, ageism, sexism, weight bias, religious affiliation, where you grew up, where you went to college, or your peer group.

Developing self-awareness is the foundation for growing in cultural competence. The following case study demonstrates how a new social worker's increased self-awareness can lead to a deeper understanding of her clients.

Box 4.4 Jennifer

Jennifer is a white 23-year-old female who is just starting out on a career in social work. She grew up in a rural area, attended a state university, and is now a Family Transition Facilitator in a community-based family transition program, working with incarcerated women to help them prepare for their release from prison. Although the prison is located in a small town near where Jennifer grew up, the population she works with is largely from the state's urban center. In her first months on the job, Jennifer found herself getting frustrated with what she perceived as an unrealistic attitude on the part of her clients. In discussing career options, clients sometimes talked of becoming doctors, actresses, or of finding a man who would take care of them. She felt that, in many cases, clients either did not understand the extent of preparation and training for some careers or were pinning their hopes on things that were very unlikely to happen. As part of the training for her position, Jennifer took a workshop on cultural competence and did an inventory of her beliefs and values. Here are the results:

Ethnic identity: German and Swedish

Cultural group memberships: 'American'—no strong roots in heritage other than holiday traditions; part of a farming community; identifies with being an 'alum' of her university and with other people who participate in her favorite hobbies—horseback riding and camping

Behaviors and values derived from these memberships: belief in self-reliance→working her own way through school; sense of community, of belonging to something larger→has a network of people she draws on for support and is optimistic—has made concrete plans for the future with the expectation that things will work out for the best.

Feels positive about her cultural identity and has never, to her knowledge, experienced overt discrimination (but wonders why her father did not teach her more about farming, given her love of animals and the outdoors—is it because she's female?) Has also encountered stereotypical thinking about being a 'hick,' but doesn't see it as affecting her life in any way.

Privileges: access to support networks, financial stability, access to good health care, education, knowledge of possible career paths

Spiritual beliefs: Has attended a fundamentalist, Bible-based church all her life

Influences on the way she perceives others who hold different beliefs: while her church does not actively 'preach' intolerance, neither does it encourage exploration of other faith traditions

After thinking about these results, Jennifer realizes that nothing in her upbringing has prepared her to work closely with people from other cultural backgrounds. Although she learned about cross-cultural competence in her Social Work courses, she did not take the initiative to practice these skills. As she compares her personal history with the very different life experiences of her clients, Jennifer is beginning to sense that it is an urgent priority for her to learn more about who her clients are in order to understand the 'why' underlying their actions.

CROSS-CULTURAL KNOWLEDGE

NASW Standard #3: Social workers shall have and continue to develop specialized knowledge and understanding about the history, traditions, values, family systems, and artistic expressions of major client groups that they serve.

Acquiring cultural knowledge and skills is an ongoing effort that cannot be achieved by reading a short list of "cultural do's and don'ts." Although this chapter uses examples and case studies, it does not outline comprehensive strategies for interviewing members of specific cultural groups. Instead, we provide markers of multicultural competence that will help you gauge how much progress you are making toward this goal, and we offer strategies on 'learning how to learn' about other cultures.

In acquiring cultural knowledge, the following traits can serve as indicators that you are on your way to building an ample cross-cultural knowledge base.

- **Cultural empathy**: "The ability to empathize with the feelings, thoughts and behaviors of members from different cultural groups" (Van der Zee & Van Oudenhoven, 2000, p.296). Having empathy means that you can internalize what's happening to a client. For example, a social worker who is working with a Latina girl whose father is in prison would understand the significance of the client's father not being there for the father-daughter waltz at the Quinceanera coming-of-age celebration that many Latina girls experience at age 15. Note that the 'feeling' part of empathy rests on a base of knowledge. Cultural empathy is not simply wanting things to be better for the client—it's rooted in knowledge about the client's cultural traditions.

- **Intercultural sensitivity**: A multiculturally competent social worker takes into account the client's norms and values, understanding that the client's value system may be quite different from her own. For example, cultures deal with death in different ways. In a situation in which a social worker has the norm of 'moving on' to recover from grief, but the client's culture stresses a formal, extended mourning period, an interculturally sensitive social worker will set aside her own cultural norms to work within the client's norms.

- **Open-mindedness**: Defined as an "open and unprejudiced attitude toward different groups and toward different cultural norms and values" (Van der Zee &Van Oudenhoven, 2000, p.296). Difference can be exciting and fascinating, but it can also be threatening or be perceived as inferior. A client whose culture values faith healing, for example, might hold beliefs that members of a more science-oriented culture find 'quaint.' To understand the client's needs, the social worker who finds herself across a cultural divide such as this must strive to comprehend a worldview with different foundational assumptions than her own. Clients will sense when they're being patronized—you don't need to adopt the client's cultural practices, but as a social work professional you should be able to learn about them with an open mind and a nonjudgmental attitude.

Being open-minded is easy to achieve in principle. In actuality, our thinking processes often rely on making snap judgments (Chaiken, 1980). Mental shortcuts such as making an immediate association between two people or events based on superficial similarities result in stereotypical thinking. In the context of a social work interview, stereotypical thinking leads to the pitfall of judgmental response (see Chapter 7). Overcoming the implicit associations we make between people is difficult, but being aware of these tendencies is a first step toward reducing their power. One way to assess our tendencies toward cultural biases is to test ourselves. Greenwald and Banaji (1995) developed an interactive web-based assessment tool to help people understand the extent to which they have conscious and unconscious cultural biases. The assessment tool, call the *Implicit Association Test* (IAT), assesses one's tendencies to associate certain attributes and qualities to different groups of people (Poehlman, Uhlmann, Greenwald, & Banaji, 2005). Since 1998, more than one million IATs have been completed on the Project's website (Greenwald, Banaji & Nosek, 2003). Try taking the Implicit Association Test, which is available on line at https://implicit.harvard.edu/implicit/demo/index.jsp (Greenwald & Banaji, 1995), or the link can be accessed through the companion website for this book at http://www.ablongman.com/cummins2e

Building a cross cultural knowledge base occurs more readily in people who are excited about acquiring knowledge about other cultures, and who are open-minded about values and practices different from their own. Assess your cultural knowledge and open-mindedness by completing Part 2 of the Cultural Self-Inventory in Box 4.5.

Box 4.5 Cultural Self-Inventory Part 2: Cross-Cultural Knowledge

- What other cultural groups are present in your community?
- What do you know about the beliefs, values, and customs of members of these other cultural groups?
- What is the source of this knowledge?
- Have your interactions with people from these cultures reinforced or altered this knowledge base?
- What stereotypes or prejudices do you hold about other cultural groups?
- What is the source of your biases?
- What are you doing to increase your knowledge about people who are culturally different from you?

Source: Miley, O'Melia & DuBois, 2001, p.68

As you reflect on your responses, assess the extent of your cultural knowledge. Have you had very little exposure to other cultures? Then start exploring—some strategies for expanding your cultural knowledge are presented in Box 4.6. If you possess more cross-cultural knowledge, is that knowledge base broad but relatively shallow? If so, start exploring one or two cultures in depth. Or is your knowledge deep but narrow, concentrated on one other culture? Then branch out to other cultures.

Authors and educators in the areas of cultural diversity and practice have suggested a number of activities that you can engage in to help you build your cross-cultural knowledge base. Some of these are listed below. Indicate whether you have engaged in each activity by checking 'yes' or 'no' at the end of each item. If you find that you have not been very proactive in acquiring cross cultural knowledge, you can choose to increase your knowledge of other cultures by implementing some of these actions in your daily life. For those who have had limited exposure to cultures other than your own, some of these suggestions might feel a bit intimidating. Consider trying them with a friend, and remember that this is a lifelong learning process. Move at your own pace.

Box 4.6 Building Cross-Cultural Knowledge: Activities

	Activity	Tried It?	
1	Include-diverse perspectives in writing assignments.	Yes___	No___
2	Be–an active listener in class discussions. Attend closely to comments from students who are culturally different from you.	Yes___	No___
3	Talk with students of a different race or ethnicity than your own.	Yes___	No___
4	Talk with students who are very different from you in terms of their religious beliefs, political opinions, or personal values.	Yes___	No___
5	Make-friends outside your group	Yes___	No___
6	Take a service learning class.	Yes___	No___
7	Take-courses on other cultures.	Yes___	No___
8	Study abroad, either for a semester or during a short-course period.	Yes___	No___
9	Go on an alternative spring break.	Yes___	No___
10	Get involved with the international student office at your university.	Yes___	No___
11	Read-widely—look for novels set in other cultures.	Yes___	No___
12	Use–the Internet as a resource to learn about other cultures. (see the "Explore Other Cultures" link on the *Social Work Skills Demonstrated* companion website)	Yes___	No___
13	Seek out a mentor who is a member of the culture you want to learn-about.	Yes___	No___

Box 4.6 Building Cross-Cultural Knowledge: Activities, *continued*

	Activity	Tried It?	
14	Visit a mosque, synagogue, African American church, a Buddhist temple	Yes___	No___
15	Host a dinner, ask guests to provide foods from their culture with the recipe.	Yes___	No___
16	Participate in your campus' Safe Zone program for people who are supportive of gay, lesbian, and bisexual people	Yes___	No___
17	Learn another language	Yes___	No___
18	Attend workshops and trainings on developing multicultural competence	Yes___	No___
19	Attend university and community lectures given by individuals from other countries	Yes___	No___
20	Visit museums (i.e., the Holocaust Museum, The Native American Museum and Resource Center in Washington, D.C.)	Yes___	No___
21	Visit an independent living center, sheltered workshop group home, or a homeless shelter.	Yes___	No___

Consider what you have learned from these experiences; how can you use these experiences to enhance your understanding of others? How have these experiences affected the way you see your world and interact with others? What other activities have you tried or can you think of that could facilitate building your cross-cultural knowledge base?

As you pursue knowledge of cultures and subcultures, recognize that there are some key dimensions along which cultures vary. If you know where to look, you will be a more efficient learner (see Box 4.7).

Box 4.7 Key Areas of Cultural Difference

- ➢ whether the culture tends toward individualistic or collectivistic values
- ➢ gender roles
- ➢ orientation to authority/presence or relative absence of hierarchies
- ➢ family structure
- ➢ perceptions of time and space
- ➢ attitudes toward the future and life planning
- ➢ sense of personal control over one's life circumstances
- ➢ humor
- ➢ speech norms (including the use of silence)

> ┌───┐
> │ **Box 4.7 Key Areas of Cultural Difference,** *continued*
> │
> │ ➢ degree of openness toward members of other cultures
> │ ➢ preference for direct versus indirect communication
> │ ➢ level of formality in communication
> │ ➢ the extent to which meetings are focused on completing tasks or
> │   building relationships
> │
> │ *Source*: Fong & Furuto, 2001.
> └───┘

Using the key areas of cultural differences listed in Box 4.7—how would you describe your own culture? To get you started on how you might use these key areas in describing your own culture (or cultures), here are some examples that illustrate how some of these factors vary across cultures:

- The extent to which a culture stresses **individualistic or collectivistic** values is an important difference between cultures (Guss, 2002). In the United States, for example, the dominant culture has historically valued the individual over the group. This cultural trait is evident in many facets of American culture. For example, in one study, Ohbuchi, Fukushima and Tedeschi (1999) found that American college students favor assertive tactics in decision making (i.e., the group gets everything 'out in the open'), while Japanese students prefer indirect strategies that minimize open conflict, which might disrupt group harmony. In the context of the social work interview, tactics such as confrontation that might seem healthy from an individualistic perspective may be perceived as a threatening disruption of the social order from a collectivistic perspective.

- **Gender roles** are culturally constructed. Within the United States, for example, the experience of gender is different for women in Appalachia than it is for American women in general. In areas of Appalachia such as rural West Virginia, gender roles are traditional (Borman, Mueninghoff, and Piazza, 1988). Girls grow up expecting to 'put family first,' which can mean deferring or not pursuing education and staying close to home, not moving away to pursue richer life opportunities. In contrast, national trends in family attitudes and values have moved more toward individual autonomy and equality in marriage (Thornton and Young-DeMarco, 2001).

- Cultures (and subcultures) vary with respect to **attitudes toward the future and life planning**. While there are commonalities across cultures (i.e., adolescents tend to focus on education, career and family in thinking about the future), there are also culture-specific differences (Kagitchibasi, 1996). In working class culture, for example, adolescents have a relatively short future-time horizon (defined as how far into the future an individual makes plans). Adolescents from more affluent backgrounds have longer future-time horizons. Limited access to a university education reduces the likelihood that individuals will be inclined to make long-range life plans (Nurmi, 1987).

- Perceptions of time are culture bound as well. In their influential book *Metaphors We Live By* (1980) George Lakoff and Mark Johnson analyze how our thinking is reflected in and shaped by the use of metaphor. They identify a cluster of metaphors in Western culture around the 'Time is Money' concept:

   How do you spend your time these days?

   That flat tire cost me an hour.

   I've invested a lot of time in her.

   You need to budget your time. (Lakoff and Johnson, 1980, p. 8)

   Underlying the 'Time is Money' metaphor is an understanding of time as a limited resource and a valuable commodity that is characteristic of the industrialized world. In non-Western cultures, people are more attuned to looser agricultural time cycles. These differences can affect the social worker-client relationship when the social worker and the client have different expectations regarding meeting times and timelines for meeting goals.

Note that every culture expresses meaning through metaphor—take the time to observe how members of other cultures use metaphors. You may learn, for example, that in China food-based metaphors are common, which could be important in understanding what is deeply valued in Chinese culture (Yu, 2003). In Mexican culture, there are many traditional *dichos*, or proverbs, that convey core cultural concepts. For example, there is a cluster of metaphors around the concept of self-responsibility:

   The person whose tooth is causing pain should pull it out.

   The person whose shoe is too tight should loosen the shoe strings (Zuniga, 1992)

Knowing and using metaphors that are rooted in the client's culture can help you connect with the client. In the case of the *dicho*, it "offers the clinician the opportunity to use the client's culture to motivate the clients. This validates the clinician's approach, which is less foreign to clients because it is interwoven with figurative speech that they recognize" (Zuniga, 1992, p. 58).

The cultural differences discussed above are generalizations. Remember, though, that cultures have subcultures, or within-group variations. What holds true for most or many members of a culture may not be the case for your client. On a personal level, knowing a few members of a group does not confer expert knowledge about the group in general.

Approach each client as a "culture of one," informed by cultural knowledge, but open to discovery.

The breadth of cultural diversity, and thus the breadth of knowledge that you would need to be considered multiculturally competent, is striking. As previously defined, cultural diversity includes not only race, ethnicity, and gender, but also sexual orientation, persons with physical or cognitive impairments, religion, socioeconomic status, geographic location (urban versus rural), and age. Social work practice takes a 'person-in-environment' approach that situates the individual within her or his ecosystem, which is shaped by all of these factors (Bronfenbrenner, 1979). The NASW *Standards for Cultural Competence in Social Work* treat the acquisition of cultural knowledge as a lifelong learning commitment on the part of the social worker ("Social workers shall have and *continue to develop* specialized knowledge and understanding…" [emphasis added]). As one intercultural researcher notes, "cultural competence is a process, not an event" (Campinha-Bacote, 2002, p. 181). In a process-oriented model of cultural competence, professionals ideally "see themselves as *becoming* culturally competent rather than already *being* culturally competent" (*ibid.*, p.181). As you work toward cultural competence, it is important to realize that you will make mistakes. This is to be expected…..you're human. If problems arise from a judgmental attitude, use some of the recovery techniques discussed in chapter seven. Whether our errors are culturally grounded or come from some other source, we all experience pitfalls in the interview process from time to time. Use these moments to acquire cultural humility, and to learn about your client's culture of one (Tervalon & Murray-Garcia, 1998).

The strengths perspective in social work practice regards clients' cultural traits as assets in the helping process. Viewing the client as a cultural teacher can bring more balance to the social worker-client relationship. The social worker does not possess all of the resources needed to address the client's needs—instead, the client's own culturally endowed protective factors are a rich resource for strategies and solutions (Turner et al., 2004). That being said, we also want to caution against using our clients as learning laboratories. Differentiate between a need to know in order to advance the helping process and your client's quality of life versus pure curiosity on your part. The focus of the interview should always be on the client.

Box 4.8 Frederick

Frederick, is a hospital social worker in a large metropolitan area. He grew up in San Francisco, CA living in a middle-class community that was predominantly Protestant. Many of the patients receiving medical care at the hospital are of Chinese ancestry. Mrs. Wang, a widow, was seen in the emergency room for stroke symptoms. Mrs. Wang has three children, all of whom accompanied her to the emergency room. Mrs. Wang does not speak English, so her children served as the translator. The oldest daughter, Ying, plans to have Mrs. Wang move in (at least temporarily) to her home upon her release from the hospital. The other siblings are very supportive, as the thought of a nursing home (or any other out of home care) is not an option.

It was through Frederick's college education and internship that he began to develop an interesting other cultures. He has studied a wide variety of cultures and religions and sees himself as fairly open minded and flexible in his work with clients. Because of his understanding of the Chinese culture and norms, he knows that any effective intervention will have to include all the family, including Mrs. Wang's extended family. He knows that Mrs. Wang is highly regarded and valued by her children. He also knows that she may have some suspicion and fears regarding Western medical practices.

Points for reflection:

If you were Frederick's supervisor, what might you suggest to help him further his cultural competence? What does he need to consider to better understand his client's environment and barriers to services? How (or how do you anticipate) that Frederick might respond to this family if he were of Chinese descent as well? Finally, what do you need to learn about Chinese culture in order to be more competent in your work with Chinese clients?

CROSS-CULTURAL SKILLS

NASW Standard #4: Social workers shall use appropriate methodological approaches, skills, and techniques that reflect the workers' understanding of the role of culture in the helping process.

As you read subsequent chapters and as you progress through the CD-ROM that accompanies this book, you will learn about interviewing skills, attending behaviors and common pitfalls in the interviewing process. It is important to realize that all of the material covered is affected by the cultural context in which practice occurs. The attending behavior of maintaining eye contact, for example, will be more effective when working with clients for whom direct eye contact is the cultural norm, such as European Americans. For clients who are members of a culture that favors indirect communication, such as many Asian cultures, direct eye contact may be intimidating. Similarly, the use of silence can be comforting in some cultures and cause tension in others. The optimal amount of personal space and acceptability of touch also vary widely across cultures. An interviewing skill may be applied correctly from a technical perspective, but it can turn into a pitfall if cultural appropriateness is lacking.

Assess your cross-cultural skills by completing Part 3 of the Cultural Self-Inventory:

Box 4.9 Cultural Self-Inventory Part 3: Cross-Cultural Skills

- Are you currently involved in relationships or activities in which you have ongoing interactions with people from other cultures?
- What is your comfort level while interacting with people who are culturally different from you?
- Are you able to talk with people who are culturally different from you about these differences?
- What languages do you speak other than your own primary language?
- What words, phrases, or nonverbal behaviors do you know that have different meanings in different cultures?

Source: Miley, O'Melia & DuBois, 2001, p.68

As you reflect on your responses, think about how you can build on your skills—set a challenge for yourself to advance your cross-cultural skills to the next level. This might mean moving from a surface knowledge of another culture to a deeper, more nuanced understanding. It might mean committing to taking a language course, or advancing from observing cultural differences to talking about them with people who are culturally different from you.

A sound cross-cultural knowledge base is essential for the culturally appropriate application of social work interviewing skills. Within this context, the use of interviewing skills can help you adjust to a variety of cultural contexts. Open-ended questions such as "What do you mean by that?" and the skill of clarification can be used to learn about the client's culture (for more on social work interviewing skills and attending behaviors, see Chapter 6).

In addition to social work skills, there are some general characteristics and skills that will increase the likelihood of your success in working with members of other cultures.

Individuals who are effective in multicultural settings are **flexible.** They possess the "ability to switch easily from one strategy to another…[with] a tendency to feel attracted to new and unknown situations, experiencing them as a challenge rather than as a threat" (Van der Zee & Brinkmann, 2004, p289). Flexibility means that you learn from your mistakes, and adjust your behavior accordingly.

A quality related to flexibility is **tolerance of ambiguity** (Van der Zee & Brinkmann, 2004). The cross-cultural encounter is inherently a situation in which your engrained expectations are continually overturned. Instead, expect to be surprised, and have confidence that any confusion can be resolved. The phenomenon of 'culture shock' is real. When you first immerse yourself in another culture, you may not know why someone is laughing, why someone *isn't* laughing, or why you feel like you're somehow involved in a joke you don't understand! With greater familiarity and cross-cultural knowledge, you will acquire insider knowledge. Until then, though, your best coping strategy is to simply accept that the situation is ambiguous.

Another marker of multicultural competence is the ability to take the **social initiative**. Defined as "a tendency to actively approach social situations and to take the initiative rather than to wait and see" (Van der Zee & Brinkmann, 2004, p. 289), social initiative enables an individual to reach out to members of other cultures. Developing cultural competence takes effort—having the desire to interact with members of another culture makes the effort seem less like work and more like an opportunity for personal growth. Also, the act of reaching out, of being culturally humble and open to new experiences, sends the positive message that you are interested in the culture.

CONCLUSION

The central theme of this chapter is that the social worker's cultural knowledge is a mixture of general cultural information and unique-to-the-client information that results from interacting with the client. The interviewing skills presented in this textbook and CD-ROM will help you learn from the client, and thus help you be effective in a variety of cultural settings. As a social worker, you will come into contact with a wide range of people. The reward for successfully applying your interviewing skills in working with members of another culture is the moment of true contact. When your client opens up and tells you why her problem is causing her so much pain; when you 'get' why a client is tensing up and you know how to change your interviewing strategy so that he is more comfortable; when a client nods and repeatedly says "yes" as you interpret what's just been said—those moments of true contact are what leads to interventions that emerge from the client's culture and are therefore more likely to be fully embraced by the client. Multicultural competence enables you to truly work *with* the client's culture.

REFERENCES

Bennett, M.J. (1986). A developmental approach to training for intercultural sensitivity. *International Journal of Intercultural Relations 10*(2), 179-95.

Bennett, M.J. (1993). Towards ethnorelativism: A developmental model of intercultural sensitivity. In M. Paige (Ed.), *Education for the intercultural experience.* Yarmouth, ME: Intercultural Press.

Bennett, M.J, & Hammer, M. (1998). The developmental model of intercultural sensitivity. Retrieved January 10, 2005 from http://www.intercultural.org/pdf/dmis.pdf.

Borman, K., Mueninghoff, E., & Piazza, S. (1988). Urban Appalachian girls and young women: Bowing to no one. In L. Weis (Ed.), *Class, race, and gender in American education* (pp. 230-48). Albany, NY: SUNY University Press. .

Bruns, D.A. & Corso, R.M. (2001, August). Working with culturally & linguistically diverse families. *ERIC Digest 455972, 1-7.*

Campinha-Bacote, J. (2002). The process of cultural competence in the delivery of healthcare services: A model of care. *Journal of Transcultural Nursing, 13*(3), 181-184.

Chaiken, S. (1980). Heuristic versus systematic information processing and the use of source versus message cues in persuasion. *Journal of Personality and Social Psychology, 39,* 752-766.

Cooper, C. R., Cooper, R. G., Azmitia, M., Chavira, G., & Gullatt, Y. (2002). Bridging multiple worlds: How African American and Latino youth in academic outreach programs navigate math pathways to college. *Applied Developmental Science, 6,* 73-87.

Fong, R. & Furuto, S. (2001). *Culturally competent practice: Skills, interventions, and evaluations.* Boston: Allyn and Bacon.

Greenwald, A. G., & Banaji, M. R. (1995). Implicit social cognition: Attitudes, self-esteem, and stereotypes. *Psychological Review, 102*(1), 4-27.

Greenwald, A.G., Banaji, M.R. & Nosek, B.A. (2003). Understanding and using the Implicit Association Test: An improved scoring algorithm. *Journal of Personality and Social Psychology, 85*(2), 197–216.

Gudykunst, W.B., Ting-Toomey, S., & Nishida, T. (1996). *Communication in personal relationships across cultures.* Thousand Oaks, CA: Sage.

Guss, C.D. (2002). Decision making in individualistic and collectivistic cultures, in W.J. Lonner, D.L. Dinnel, S.A. Hayes & D.N. Sattlet (Eds.). Online readings in psychology and culture. Retrieved January 10, 2005 from http://www.wwu.edu/~culture.

Frankenberg, R. (Ed.). (1997). *Displacing whiteness: Essays in social and cultural criticism.* Durham, NC: Duke University Press.

Kagitchibasi, C. (1996). *Family and human development across cultures.* Mahwah, NJ: Erlbaum.

Lakoff, G. & Johnson, M. (1980). *Metaphors we live by.* Chicago: University of Chicago Press.

Markus, H. & Nurius, P. (1986). Possible selves. *American Psychologist, 41,* 954-969.

McGoldrick, M., Giordano, J. & Pearce, J. (Eds.) (1996). *Ethnicity and Family Therapy.* New York: Guilford Press.

Miley,K.K., O'Melia, M.,& DuBois, B. (2001). *Generalist social work practice: An empowering approach.* Boston, MA: Allyn and Bacon.

Nurmi, J.E. (1987). Age, sex, social class, and quality of family interaction as determinants of adolescents' future orientation: a developmental task interpretation. *Adolescence, 22*(88):977-991.

Ohbuchi, K.I., Fukushima, O. & Tedeschi, J.T. (1999). Cultural values in conflict management: Goal orientation, goal attainment, and tactical decision. *Journal of Cross-Cultural Psychology, 30,* 51-71.

Poehlman, T. A., Uhlmann, E., Greenwald, A. G., & Banaji, M. R."Understanding and using the Implicit Association Test: III. Meta-analysis of predictive validity. Retrieved January 10, 2005 from http://faculty.washington.edu/agg/pdf/IAT.Meta-analysis.15Nov04.pdf

Saleebey, D. (Ed.) (1997). *The strengths perspective in social work practice.* (2nd ed.) White Plains, NY: Longman.

Tervalon, M. & Murray-Garcia, J. (1998). Cultural humility versus cultural competence: A critical distinction in defining physician training outcomes in multicultural education. *Journal of Health Care to the Poor and Underserved, 9*(2), 117-125.

Thornton, A. & Young-DeMarco, L. (2001). Four decades of trends in attitudes toward family issues in the United States: The 1960s through the 1990s. *Journal of Marriage and Family, 63*(4), 1009-1037.

Turner, W.L. & Wieling, E. (2004). Developing culturally effective family-based research programs: Implications for family therapists. *Journal of Marital and Family Therapy, 30*(3), 257-270.

U.S. Census Bureau News. (2004). Census Bureau Projects Tripling of Hispanic and Asian Populations in 50 Years; Non-Hispanic Whites May Drop To Half of Total Population. Retrieved January 10, 2005 from http://www.census.gov/Press-Release/www/releases/archives/population/001720.html

U.S. Census Bureau News. (2001). Census 2000 Shows America's Diversity. Retrieved January 10, 2005 from http://www.census.gov/Press-Release/www/releases/archives/race/000482.html

Van der Zee, K.I. & Brinkmann, U. (2004). Construct validity evidence for the intercultural readiness check against the multicultural personality questionnaire. *International Journal of Selection and Assessment, 12*(3), 285-290.

Van der Zee, K.I. Jaal, J.N. & Peikstra, J. (2003). Validation of the multicultural personality questionnaire in the context of personnel selection. *European Journal of Personality, 17*(Supplement 1), S77-S100.

Van der Zee, K.I. & Van Oudenhoven, J.P. (2000). The Multicultural Personality Questionnaire: A multidimensional instrument of multicultural effectiveness. *European Journal of Personality, 14*, 291-309.

Yu, N. (2003). Chinese metaphors of thinking. *Cognitive Linguistics, 14*–2/3, 141–165.

Zuniga, M.E. (1992). Using metaphors in therapy: *Dichos* and Latino clients. *Social Work, 37*(1), 55-60.

CHAPTER FIVE

The Engagement Process

The Professional Relationship

When people experience difficulties in their lives, they can select from a wide variety of ways to overcome them. Some turn to family and friends, others look within and pull upon internal resources. When they select to see a professional social worker, they are seeking specific knowledge and skills that are usually not available to them through informal helping relationships. Most likely, they have been unsuccessful in resolving their problems through informal means and now seek the assistance of a well trained and experienced professional social worker who can assist them in dealing with their life problems. The purpose and goals of a professional relationship between a client and a social worker "are conscious and deliberate and come within the overall purpose and value system of the profession" (Compton & Galaway, 1999, p. 226). Implicit in this definition is the belief that clients will experience some type of improvement in their life and will be empowered to make changes to their liking as a direct result of working with the social worker in a professional therapeutic relationship. As discussed in Chapter 1, the relationship between the social worker and client is a purposeful one that includes the systematic process of beginning, middle and ending phases. This chapter will discuss engagement process, which occurs in the initial phase of the relationship between the client and social worker.

The relationship between the client and the social worker is unique. Both come into the relationship with a distinctive set of circumstances and life experiences. As social workers, we consider ourselves to be trained helpers and problem solvers. Social workers operate from an established knowledge base and a set of professional values, skills, and techniques. To affect a client's life, we draw upon this professional knowledge and use it as the keystone for building the professional relationship between the client and ourselves.

Clients come to the helping relationship uncertain about what to expect and what is required of them. It is likely that many of our clients have never interacted with a social worker. At most, they may have seen a news report or an episode on TV depicting a social worker, taking children from their home or "losing" children within the state's foster care system. As you know, this characterization is rarely accurate, and at best limits the role of the social worker to the child protective worker role. In reality, social workers work across the continuum of human needs with clients of all ages, cultures, and walks of life, who often are seeing a social worker for the first time. Sometimes, clients have had previous interaction with a social worker as a result of being a court "mandated" into treatment and as such, are involuntary clients. Under this set of circumstances, our job of engaging a client in the helping process can be a very challenging one.

What does it mean to engage a client in the therapeutic helping process? It is important to understand the circumstances under which a client is referred to you or coming to you for help. Many clients are scared about being "shrunk," that the social worker will qualitatively "change them" or take their children away. Although as a profession, we are sometimes sanctioned to intervene in our clients' lives, we must do so with the utmost respect and care. A challenge that we face however, is helping our clients to understand the true nature of who we are as professionals and what we do (see Chapter 1 on social worker roles.)

The setting of a social worker's practice will, in part, determine the types of clients and the range of problems that we will be addressing. A client may be referred to your agency by a teacher, a probation officer, an outreach worker, a physician, a public health official, a judge, or a public housing employee. You may also have clients who seek out services from your agency because they recognize their need for help.

One important aspect of engaging the client is establishing rapport. Rapport is the entry point to the relationship (Hackney & Cormier, 2001) and is the intangible goal of connecting at a central or core level with your client. It is more than comfort, receptiveness, and respect. It is a commitment to stay with the client, to display warmth, interest, and care in a way that encourages trust and confidence. When clients feel understood, honored and valued, they are more likely to open up. It is through the relationship that client's anxiety over time diminishes as their self-esteem and self-worth are enhanced (Hill & O'Brien, 2004).

Rapport connotes a relationship of mutual understanding and trust between two people and requires the ability to put yourself in the position of another. Empathy is an important skill in developing rapport with a client. It is trying to understand your client's life experiences without having to experience them yourself. Small talk, such as a few comments about the weather, traffic, or how the children are feeling is one aspect of rapport, but building rapport is a much more complex and methodical skill. Small talk is never a substitute for genuine rapport.

As a social worker, you may find yourself in situations that are far outside your "comfort zone" or beyond anything you can imagine. Although some of these situations may be scary or uncomfortable, it is our responsibility to put our discomfort aside. However, don't ignore clear warning signs of real danger. In cases of imminent harm to yourself, either leave immediately and/or contact the police. Social workers can also use these experiences to understand and empathize with a client regarding how frightened or overwhelmed they may feel when entering into unknown or foreign territory.

It is always wise to expand your life experiences (without taking unnecessary risks), by reading, asking questions, and educating yourself about other cultures, practices and lifestyles that you are unfamiliar with or that challenge your value system (see chapter 4).

We can all relate to experiences of being disappointed, rejected, happy, or sad. So, as you are trying to relate to your client's situation, remember, even if you haven't experienced something similar, emotions are universals. For example, you are an undergraduate student completing your internship at a nursing home. A 78-year-old resident is on your caseload. You knock on his door and ask if you can come in and talk for a few minutes. He angrily states, "You're just a child, what can you possibly do to help me! I'm stuck here, no one ever visits me. You can do anything you want. I have to wait in my room for my food, my mail, being helped to the bathroom. And no, I don't want your help!" Putting yourself in his place, what feelings come to you as you attempt to absorb the meaning of his message? Probably, you too, have felt lonely and frustrated in life. You know what it feels like to have little control over your life; you may even have experienced a situation where you have lost your own autonomy and independence. Even though you are not a resident of a nursing home, (nor are you in your late seventies) you can relate to his feelings of loss, isolation, and powerlessness. This is the first step in developing empathy and engaging the client.

Actively seeking to understand clients' values, their needs, and purpose, and seeing them as unique human beings, doesn't mean we always agree with them. Empathy is entering into the feelings and experiences of another without losing oneself in the process: "feeling not as the client, but as if the client" (Compton & Galaway, 1999, p. 227). It is important to give up stereotypes when working with a diverse client population. Gaining full understanding of a client's life experiences can only be approached but not achieved. Social workers do, however, provide a safe place to assist clients in exploring thoughts, feelings and come to new understandings of the issues. It is through this process that clients try out new behaviors and make life-enhancing changes.

According to Ragg (2001), the elements of empathic response are:

- *Client disclosure*—The social worker listens, hears and observes a client disclosure by their questions or reactions about some event, person or situation. (What did the client say?)

  Example: As a court service social worker, you are meeting with Yvonne, a 22-year-old female client, who was recently release from prison after a 24-month sentence. Prior to her incarceration, Yvonne was selling drugs and working as a prostitute. The social worker will need to consider the obstacles the client may face, such as living arrangements, job opportunities (or lack thereof), relationships with family members and other people on the inside and outside of prison. You want to ask questions about training and opportunities provided while she was incarcerated, and how she coped and managed to live day to day (assessing her strengths throughout the session). In addition, it is important to understand where the client is in the moment and what issues are relevant to her. Pay attention to her nonverbal body language. For instance, how she is sitting (erect, slumped, not facing you), her verbal tone, and choice of words.

- *Identification of action element*—The social worker listens to the client's statements and identifies what people are doing or saying that contributes to the disclosing feeling. (What are the things that people are saying and doing?)

  Example continued: Yvonne discloses that she has become very religious while incarcerated. She attended prayer meeting daily (including Alcoholics Anonymous meetings) and feels a strong pull toward her faith. Yvonne will disclose more about her religious experiences and what is important to her if the social worker attends to the significance of her new discovery and the strength it provides to her on the "outside." She shares with the social worker that her family and friends never attended church and have been making very negative comments about her new-found religion. Yvonne has maintained close telephone contact with the prison chaplain since her release.

- *Identification of processing elements*—While listening and observing, the social worker reflects on the client's statements and mentally labels the important thinking and feeling themes. (What are the beliefs, thoughts, and feelings that seem to be important?)

  Example continued: As you listen to Yvonne talking about her faith, you begin to realize that she is worried about her family's negative reactions. She begins to distance herself from the family by stating, "They don't get me anymore, and I can't count on them. I knew this was going to be a problem; they are a bunch of heathens. But God will take care of them and me. If they don't start going to church and praying, they will pay the price". Yvonne also had indicated that she wants to start over and maybe get her GED (Graduation Equivalency Degree).

- *What are the core concerns*—From the action and processing elements of the client statement, the social worker identifies what appears to be most important to the client. (What are the critical concerns?)

  Example continued: As the social worker, you understand that her family has been a very important part of her life. Her experiences in prison have changed her in significant ways. Yvonne is determined to make a new life for herself, even if it means no longer maintaining as close a relationship with her family. You also want to attend to Yvonne's goal of getting her GED. A high school education will open up more job and training possibilities for her.

- *Validation and exploration*—When the worker has tuned into the concerns and questions that might be evident for the client, the challenge is to get the concern out in the open and address it. (How can I validate this concern? Where do I take this to explore the experience of the client?)

  Example continued: You can explore with Yvonne ways that she can still maintain a relationship with her family. As a social worker, you understand the need and value of support, be it financial or emotional. You can confirm and acknowledge her choices and beliefs, but also validate the value of her family. Be careful not to judge her past experiences and troubles, while at the same time provide a sense of hope and certainty that she can use those strengths and skills to turn her life around, while also maintaining a belief in her family too. The struggles to stay clean and off the streets may be a challenge for Yvonne. Help her to anticipate some of the obstacles and barriers she may face.

Rapport building and empathy go hand in hand. It is important to remember that you may establish rapport with your client in a relatively short period of time, but it is the conveying of empathy, through the repeated application of basic interviewing skills such as paraphrasing, reflection of feeling, furthering responses and attending behaviors, upon which you ultimately build the helping relationship over time.

By the time clients come to seek the services of a social worker, often they have exhausted other sources of help and have experienced considerable emotional pain (Kottle, 2000). As the social worker listens to their story, it becomes apparent that the client has given quite a bit of consideration to the problem prior to your first session with them. It is important to listen to the story, as relevant pieces of information come to light. You can ask questions that relate to your understanding of the situation, gaining insight into the client's perceptions. As the social worker begins this helping process, it is imperative to understand clients from their unique vantage point, taking into account personal and family background, culture, education, developmental stage, environmental factors, and health status. Egan, (2002) suggests understanding clients in three ways: 1) understand them from the client's point of view, including feelings surrounding this point of view; 2) understand them through the context of their life; and, 3) make a commitment to understand the dissonance between the client's point of view and objective reality.

Social workers are equipped to deal with many different challenges on the client's journey toward self-determination, but a road map can be helpful. This map consists of the profession's knowledge, information, and skills (Egan, 2002). We are called upon to assist our clients in problem solving, resource acquisition and management, and advocacy. The social worker's ability to use basic interviewing and assessment skills is an important aspect of conveying competency. As the helping relationship evolves, the responsibility is clearly more shared and the collaborative nature of the relationship becomes an essential building block.

Fortunately social workers always have the NASW Code of Ethics to refer to as a framework or road map for professional behavior and practice. Social workers can consult the Code of Ethics as a way of helping to make decisions that put clients' best interests before their own. Although the NASW Code of Ethics covers topical areas in a general way, such as resolving disputes involving colleagues, the Code does not identify specific remedies or directions for each situation in which you may be involved. The code is a guide, of values, standards, and principles of professional practice and conduct we strive to meet. When unsure of how to proceed, consulting a trusted supervisor or co-worker is always a good place to start. (NASW Code of Ethics: http://www.naswdc.org/)

Box 5.1 is an excerpt taken from a BSW student's field log entry. This example demonstrates a conflict the student is experiencing between what she believes to be her professional obligation using the NASW Code of Ethics as her guide and the reality of day-to-day practice.

Box 5.1 Excerpt from a BSW Student's Field Log

The basic situation has to do with Mrs. Florence W. She's 83 years old and lives alone. Both her children live out of state. She has a broken hip. Typically the discharge plan is for patients without social support to go to the nursing home, with the hope that they can be rehabilitated well enough to go home.

I have come to know Mrs. W. a little better than many patients because she's been in the hospital for almost two weeks. I see her every day. When I began discussing discharge with her, I assumed that she would want to go to the nursing home. She made it clear that she would not consider it. I discussed this from many different angles (I wanted to make sure she understood her options!) but still – no deal. I began talking with her about home health services and "Meals on Wheels" and other things that would help her at home. I did express on several occasions that I was very worried about her ability to care for herself at home given her hip fracture. She is a very independent woman and she was clear that she wanted to go home, period. OK – so I'm honoring client self-determination, right? I listened carefully to her, I tried to explore the nature of her concerns about going to a nursing home (basically she loves her own home, she's very independent, and she's seen friends "go downhill" in nursing homes) and I shared my concerns about her choice while also giving her information about what kind of support she can (and can't) have at home. Good social work!

Well…the doctor pulled me aside to ask what's been done about discharge. I told him about my efforts and he hit the roof! He says there is no way she can go home and that he will tell her she has to go to the nursing home before she can go home and that I should make arrangements. Meanwhile her daughter showed up from Michigan and made it clear the nursing home is the only plan the family will support. I tried to advocate for Mrs. W's position but the daughter doesn't hear me. As things stand right now, Mrs. W. will be in the hospital a few more weeks. Where does our commitment to self-determination fit with a system that seems to hold other values? How does the social worker (especially a student social worker) advocate for a client in the face of a physician who has lots of authority, power and influence?

So, the issue here is honoring client self-determination. The client is making, maybe not the best choice, but a reasonable choice. She's competent and determined. Who are we to make choices for clients who are able to make them for themselves? The NASW Code of Ethics says "Social workers respect and promote the right of clients to self-determination and assist clients in their efforts to identify and clarify goals." The clash here comes because my professional values tell me to honor this and the physician's values tell him to protect her health and well-being first and foremost.

Box 5.1 Excerpt from a BSW Student's Field Log, *continued*

I can't see that physical health should *always* be put above emotional health (protecting a sense of autonomy and personal power). As a student I certainly feel less powerful in this situation than the physician, who the family will listen to, especially because they agree with his perspective. I'll keep advocating for Mrs. W's position but I'm afraid they'll wear her down. And part of me thinks that she belongs in the nursing home anyway, so...this work is so hard sometimes!

Source: BSW Field Manual, School of Social Work, Illinois State University, 2004

In the example, the student is able to articulate her frustration with the physician, Mrs. W.'s daughter, and the system that doesn't necessarily view client self-determination as a first priority. The student feels powerless in a similar way that Mrs. W. feels powerless.

Social workers can feel very strongly about a situation, client, or circumstance. We may find ourselves experiencing a personal or emotional reaction to a situation (referred to as countertransference). Countertransference is an emotional reaction to clients, where the social worker sees the clients as a sexual object, friend, is overly involved in the client's life, an adversary or even an extension of themselves (Shebib, 2003). It is important to respond to our clients in a non-defensive manner, meaning being able to respond to the client without feeling a need to guard or justify your decisions, positions, actions, feelings, or perceptions. Below are some warning signs that countertransference is occurring (Miley et al., 2001; and Timberlake et al., 2002).

Box 5.2 Signs of Countertransference

- Having intense feelings (i.e.: irritation, anger, boredom, sexual attraction)
- Feeling of attraction or repulsion
- Reluctant to confront or tending to avoid sensitive issues or feelings
- Continually running overtime with certain clients and wishing that other clients would not show up for appointments.
- Acting with rescuing behaviors, such as lending money, adopting abused children or protecting clients
- Being reminded by clients of other people you know
- Dealing with clients who have similar histories or problems as yours
- Employing unnecessary or excessive self-disclosure (see chapter 5 for more about self-disclosure)
- Feeling reluctant to end the helping relationship

Source: Shebib, 2003, p. 87

As a social worker, you will be exposed to many details and facets of your client's life. You are sanctioned as a professional to provide services to clients via your position within an agency or mandated by law. Because of this power differential between the client and the social worker, we must always be mindful of the power we hold, not only sanctioned power through the positions you hold within our society, such as reporting a suspected case of child abuse or determining services and benefits, but also the power within the relationship. Clients will look to the social worker as the expert and may feel intimated by their perceptions or beliefs of who you are. These perceptions can be based on the reality of the relationship as well as subjectively viewed by the client.

Clients may respond differently depending upon the social worker's age, gender, socioeconomic status, martial status, position within the agency, experience, gender, physical appearance, intelligence, social demeanor and attitude, ethnicity, race, or religion (Shebib, 2003). Some clients will wait for the social worker to assume leadership or power within the relationship based on their perceptions of the worker and the worker's role. For example, clients may be used to having others do things for them, or may see themselves as victims with no power to change anything in their lives. In this instance, the social worker must "start where the client is," but should also focus on the needs of the client by imparting information and knowledge to assist in confidence and self-esteem building. Once the client believes that he or she is capable of making positive changes, a sense of worth and a belief in their own ability can serve as the guide and motivator throughout the helping relationship and throughout their lives (See Chapter 3, strengths perspective model).

Box 5.3 illustrates how a social work intern, Danielle, allows her own personal views and discomforts to interfere with the helping relationship. She abdicates her professional (intern) role to the client.

Box 5.3 Danielle

Danielle is a 21-year-old female social work intern. She has been in her internship placement for 5 weeks. She has completed all the required orientation and training. Danielle and her 15-year-old female client, Chaney, have met three times before (see information later in this chapter regarding confidentiality and home visits.) Today, Danielle meets Chaney at the group home and she suggests that they go out for ice cream. Danielle asks Chaney what has been happening in the group home since the last time they met. Chaney discloses that she and Jimmy, who is also a group home resident, have started eating together every day at school. She then whispers to Danielle, that they have had sex while in the group home (this is a violation of the rules) and she doesn't like it. Danielle responds by saying, "You shouldn't be having sex with Jimmy, it is wrong and you will get kicked out of the group home. Don't tell me anymore about this. Let's forget you said anything at all."

Box 5.3 Danielle, *continued*

Analysis 1: In this case, Danielle in uncomfortable talking about sex, the violation of group home rules, and the possible consequences of Chaney's decisions. Because of Danielle's discomfort about the situation, she puts her own needs and feelings ahead of Chaney's. She uses her position as the intern to communicate disapproval as well as demonstrating "breaking the rules and trying to cover it up" as her problem-solving strategy. Danielle also communicates that she can't handle the reality of Chaney's situation. She cuts off communication because of her own nervousness and anxiety. This intervention is not helpful to Chaney in any way.

In Box 5.4, Danielle responds to Chaney as a good friend might. She has difficulty remaining professional, as her interest is piqued.

Box 5.4 Danielle, part 2

Danielle is a 21-year-old female social work intern. She has been in her internship placement for 5 weeks. She has completed all the required orientation and training. Danielle and her 15-year-old female client, Chaney, have met three times before. (See information below regarding confidentiality and home visits.) Today, Danielle meets Chaney at the group home and she suggests that they go out for ice cream. Danielle asks Chaney what has been happening in the group home since the last time they met. Chaney discloses that she and Jimmy, who is also a group home resident, have started eating together everyday at school. She then whispers to Danielle, that they have had sex while in the group home (this is a violation of the rules) and she doesn't like it. Danielle responds by saying, "Oh, do I know what you mean. My boyfriend wants to have sex all the time. I wish he would back off, but I don't want the relationship to end."

Analysis 2: In this case, Danielle is inappropriately self-disclosing information that reflects a friendship rather than a professional relationship. She also takes the focus off Chaney and her situation as she begins to share her own story. Chaney is likely to misinterpret the role of the intern, as she feels obligated to respond to Danielle's struggles with her sexual relationship as well as her own.

In Box 5.5, Danielle responds more appropriately to Chaney by remaining professional and using her role as an intern to educate and support her client.

Box 5.5 Danielle, part 3

Danielle is a 21-year-old female social work intern. She has been in her internship placement for 5 weeks. She has completed all the required orientation and training. Danielle and her 15-year-old female client, Chaney, have met three times before. Today, Danielle meets Chaney at the group home and she suggests that they go out for ice cream. Danielle asks Chaney what has been happening in the group home since the last time they met. Chaney discloses that she and Jimmy, who is also a group home resident, have started eating together everyday at school. She whispers to Danielle that they have had sex while in the group home (this is a violation of the rules). Danielle appears calm and asks Chaney to further describe her relationship with Jimmy. She listens quietly, as Chaney discloses that they are not using any kind of birth control and that she feels pressured to have sex with him. She talks with Chaney about breaking the house rules and ways that she can communicate with Jimmy about her fears and concerns. Danielle offers that unprotected sex can lead to pregnancy and STIs (sexually transmitted infections). She also empowers her with information about how to assertively communicate to Jimmy that she doesn't want to have sex with him right now. Simultaneously, Danielle also affirms Chaney decision to be honest.

Analysis 3: In this revised example, Danielle, realizes this information is very important to share with her internship supervisor and the group home staff but she is unsure how to proceed. Danielle wants to be helpful to Chaney, but also realizes the potential consequences to her behavior. Rather than condemning Chaney and shutting her up, Danielle explored more about the circumstances surrounding her relationship with Jimmy without being judgmental. She provided useful information about birth control, STIs and saying "no" to his sexual advances. Chaney also encouraged her to tell the group home supervisor about what is happening. Danielle puts her client's well-being above her own discomfort. She responded appropriately within her role as an intern. Danielle provided support and understanding as well as some direction for what might happen next.

Finding the balance (or maintaining the boundaries) between a friendship and a professional relationship can be challenging, in part because so many of the qualities we find in a good friend are similar to those qualities needed in the helping relationship. For instance, trust, care, honesty, and genuineness are essential characteristic of both a friendship and a professional relationship. Box 5.6 is a list of some similarities and differences between these two types of relationships.

Box 5.6 Friendship versus Professional Relationships

Friendship	**Professional Relationship**
Caring and concern	Caring and concern
Warmth and genuineness	Warmth and genuineness
Supportive and safe	Supportive and safe
Investment of self	Investment of self
Trust	Trust/Confidentiality as defined by the NASW Code of Ethics
Shared interests	Similar or different interests
Comparable levels of disclosure	Unequaled levels of disclosure
Similar or compatible values	Social Work Values guide the relationship
Physical intimacy/space	Physical proximity and touching is regulated by the NASW Code of Ethics
Friendship has no "Fee" attached	Client or other entity pays for services
Roles are fluid	Roles are constant, i.e., the client is always the client
Natural progression of the friendship	Beginning, middle and ending phase of the relationship/time limited/termination
No set agenda or purpose to the meeting	Each session has an agenda/plan for work toward problem resolution/purposeful
Feedback/advice is open and unsolicited	Feedback is specific to the problem area
Offering opinions	Offering options
Reciprocal (two way communication and disclosure/focus is on both parties)	Non-reciprocal (focus is on the client)
Power differential is determined by parties	Power differential is determined by authority of the position
No formal education or training required	Degreed professional, on-going training and education, seeks consultation

Sources: Egan, 2002; Brill & Levine, 2005; Shebib, 2003

Several social work educators and authors (Compton & Galaway, 1999; Egan, 2002; Hackney & Cormier, 2001; and Kottler, 2000) offer building blocks for creating a strong foundation for your professional therapeutic relationships with your clients:

- Be warm, authentic, genuine, down to earth, and engaging—be approachable and friendly (smile). Be spontaneous. Let your humanness come through. Explore the client's expectations of the process and determine if it is realistic. Avoid social worker defensiveness and stay open and responsive to your client.

- Strength and confidence—appear to be knowledgeable and capable even if you don't always feel that way. Clients want to believe that there is hope. It is through the safety of the relationship that the client is most likely to take risks. Always be mindful of the power differential in the relationship. Serve as a partner and collaborator. Form a working alliance with your client. Making an appropriate referral to a more experienced professional and/or consultation with your supervisor may be necessary if you are in too deep or over your head.

- Be consistent and dependable—Trust is built over time and easy to break. For example, if you say you will check into housing options for your client, do it. Otherwise, trust is broken and the relationship will suffer. Be on time, respectful of confidentiality, follow- through with promises and commitments.

- Model honesty, frankness and integrity—Through your own actions, clients can see and learn to respond similarly. The helping relationship can serve as a guide throughout the client's life, be frank, respectful, consistent and considerate. Always follow the NASW Code of Ethics in all professional interactions. (www.naswdc.org/)

- Stay with client needs, not your own—Deal with your own issues, so they do not cloud or color the relationship or your judgment. It is important to focus and attend to the needs of the client, putting your own issues and struggles aside during the session. Convey a nonjudgmental attitude and actively seek to understand your client from their point of view. Stay objective, so that you can give the client a new way of looking at an old problem. Keep your eye on the long view of the problem, remembering that change takes time. Consider, which feelings are yours, which feelings are the clients? Go beyond yourself to help a client. Know your agency's policies and procedures, for example how and what can be done to assist a client.

- Focus on the client's nonverbal messages and the immediacy of the interview (what is happening within the session itself)—Be aware of your own attending behaviors. Are you fully present; are you maintaining a relaxed demeanor, intermittent eye contact, mirroring the client's emotional reactions?

- Go with the flow—Be willing to shifting gears, from one strategy to another, mid-session if necessary. Consider what is and what isn't working between the client and social worker and adjust accordingly. Remember that relationships do change over time, through this interaction and during the helping process itself. Be tolerant of ambiguity. View new situations as a challenge rather than a threat. Expect to be surprised and believe that you have the confidence to figure out whatever may come your way.

- Stay flexible—As you get to know your clients and what makes them tick, be careful not to 'pigeon hole' them, based on information about their culture, religion, family background, spirituality, socioeconomic status, etc. Avoid stereotypes. Be open minded. This allows the social worker to work with a wide variety or range of clients. Clients often feel, "if the social worker accepts me, then I must be okay."

- Respond therapeutically—There are many ways to respond, but pick one that is helpful and does no harm to the client. With enough goodwill between the client and the social worker, regrouping and moving ahead is possible. Put aside your own concerns to fully engage with the client, however, connectedness and shared understanding are critical aspects of the helping relationship. Learn from your mistakes and respond accordingly.

- Show care and concern—Use all the social work interviewing skills as a way of communicating that you value your clients as human beings. Communicate this concern through the relationship. The best predictor of outcome of the helping process is the relationship between the social worker and the client. (Hill & O'Brien 2004)

Getting Down to the Basics: Know Yourself

It is important to elaborate on the necessity of knowing yourself as a person and as a professional. Brill and Levine (2005) describes the process of becoming knowledgeable and disciplined in relationships and the importance of developing a personal objectivity based on qualities such as self awareness. Below is a series of questions to help you begin the self-reflection process.

1) Awareness of self and personal needs, weaknesses and strengths:

- What factors contributed to your decisions to become a social worker?
- What makes you tick and contributes to who you are?
- How do you communicate to others regarding your needs, wants and interests?
- What is your understanding of how your family and life experiences contribute to who you are today?
- What strengths do you posses? Are others aware of these strengths?
- What defense mechanisms do you use to protect yourself, your feelings and self-esteem?
- What are some of your anxieties and fears?
- What would others who know you well say are your strengths? Weaknesses?

2) Awareness of and ability to deal with our own personality patterns, and with the "stuff" that tends to cloud our perceptions.

- What are some of the patterns or ways that you conduct your life that work well for you?
- What are the barriers that get in your way?
- What does your "inner voice" say to you? (Negative or positive self-talk?)
- How do you view "power" within a relationship?
- What is your view on stereotypic roles within the family?
- What is your view on childrearing and discipline?
- How do you handle conflict? Change?
- What relational issues (between you and close family and friends) seem to come up time and time again?

3) Openness and freedom to perceive with clarity and relate with honesty-regardless of differences and similarities.

- What are your religious and political beliefs and values?
- How are these beliefs and values reflected in your daily life?
- How do you convey these beliefs and values?
- What personal needs do you have that might interfere with the helping relationship?
- What personal values guide your decisions?
- How do you conduct yourself when disagreeing about religion or politics?
- What do you consider to be the most important social issue today?

4) Ability to perceive and evaluate values, attitudes and patterns of behavior of which group the client considers themselves a part.

- How open are you to people who are different from you?
- Consider ways in which you feel (or have felt) vulnerable, disempowered or oppressed
- How do you feel about interacting with people from other cultures?
- What group(s) of people do you think are most like you?
- Are there any groups of people you feel as though you could not interact with
- If you dig deep, what are your stereotypes and prejudices?

5) Ability to differ and stand alone.

- How do you handle differences of opinion?
- What issues in your life do you feel most passionately about?
- If you had the opportunity to stand up for one social issue or social value, what would it be?
- What is your greatest fear about going out on a limb for a cause?

- What would you hope to gain or lose by advocating for an unpopular position?
- How do you receive feedback from others and what do you do with it once you get it?
- What are your views on power and authority?

Hackney and Cormier (2001) address the importance of social workers knowing their own needs (i.e., need for control, need for approval etc.), motivations for helping others, awareness of personal feelings, strengths, limitations, triggers, and coping skills. This kind of self-awareness is important for several reasons. First, objectivity in dealing with a client is a crucial component in avoiding 'blind-spots,' or perceptions, behaviors, or ways of being that the social worker is unaware of, but that may detract from building a professional and therapeutic relationship with clients. For example, if the social worker has unresolved issues around being abused as a child, the worker will see every client's life experience through this lens. Consequently, the social worker can project onto the client his or her own issues, perceptions and experiences, rather than dealing with the client's concerns. The relationship becomes focused on the social worker's needs instead of the client's needs. The social worker may be unaware of these perceptions; indeed this can contribute to the client not feeling understood and the social worker remaining "stuck." Unresolved personal issues can also lead social workers to feel angry and defensive because the social worker feels attacked. In this situation, the focus is on self rather than the needs of the client.

Before moving on, it is important to note that when a social worker inadvertently uses pitfalls, such as advice giving or being judgmental, the client can become disengaged from the helping process. The frustration a client may experience when the social worker is not listening or is generally not attending to the client's needs, can cause extreme frustration and disillusionment. Repairing the "damage" of unintentionally using a pitfall is discussed Chapter 7.

Confidentiality

It is essential to create an atmosphere of trust in order for the client to feel secure enough to share personal information. The NASW Code of Ethics, Ethical Standard, 1.07 (1999) requires that social workers respect clients' right to privacy. Information should only be solicited when it is essential to providing services that address clients' problems and possible resolutions. To maintain confidentiality, social workers must refrain from disclosing information about a client to others. It is because of this expectation that trust can be developed between the client and the social worker over time (Miley et al., 2001).

There is a distinction between adhering to client confidentiality and privileged communication. Privileged communication provides the legal grounds for confidentiality, meaning clients can claim legal privilege and ethical social workers maintain confidentiality. Legal privilege protects the client's private communication with a social worker by prohibiting the social worker from revealing information in court (Miley et al., 2001). According to Miley, O'Melia and DuBois, establishing privilege involves the following: 1) the client can invoke privilege to prevent the social worker testimony or records from being used as evidence in court, 2) the social worker can assert privilege at the client's request, and 3) the judge considers relevant laws and the client waiver and entitlement to determine whether privilege applies. By invoking privilege, clients can restrict the social worker from revealing confidential information in a court of law. Without the client invoking privilege, the social worker can be compelled to testify and provide documentation to the court. Rules of privilege vary from jurisdiction to jurisdiction; therefore, a social worker must determine whether privilege is available in the state in which the professional practices (Hackney, 2000). It is important to determine whether privilege is available in your state and to determine what information is protected and in what situations privilege applies (Hackney, 2000).

Minors (typically 12 years and younger) are generally incapable of giving consent to health care treatment and a parent or guardian will need to consent on the minor's behalf. Exceptions to the general rule vary from state to state. Commonly, a full explanation (or informed consent) is given to the child, parent, or guardian. If the child does not object or the social worker doesn't identify any compelling reason to deny access to information, he or she may do so. When the social worker provides a full explanation of confidentiality and its limits, the possibility of being caught between a parent and a child is reduced. As always, when you are unsure about how to proceed, consult your supervisor. In some cases legal counsel may be required.

It is also important to note that there are two types of confidentiality, one is *absolute* and the other is *relative*. According to the NASW Social Work Dictionary (1999), absolute confidentiality means the professional never shares information in any form with anyone. There would be no written record of any interaction and no oral transmission of data. The principle of relative confidentiality allows for the sharing of information within the agency (such as in supervision or team meetings) but not with outside agencies or collateral contacts unless the client has given consent in writing.

There are some exceptions to confidentiality, such as evidence of child and/or elder abuse or neglect, threats by a client to harm self or others, the need for emergency services, guardianship hearings, lawsuits filed against a social worker, consultation with colleagues, attorneys, and for purposes of internal quality assurance reviews (Miley et al., 2001). Be careful not to discuss your clients with family and friends (even if you do not give any identifying information), or talk about clients in public spaces where others may be within earshot. Also always follow the agency's procedures concerning the safeguarding of client records. Social service agencies are firmly entrenched in the computer age, and client records are now computerized. It is extremely important that these records be password protected or otherwise secured to protect the confidentiality of the client.

Clients can give the social worker permission to share information about their case with others. This is often important when a client is using multiple service providers and the need to coordinate client services across agencies exists. For the client to give "informed consent for releasing information," the worker must share with the client the conditions, risks, and alternatives to sharing this information. Should the need for sharing information occur, be sure to have the client (or in the case of a child, the parent or guardian) sign a consent form that includes the information will be shared, with whom, for what purpose, and within what time frames.

Some communities are now using software that allows multiple agencies serving the same client to share client information online (with the client's permission). This provides an easy way of coordinating client services along a continuum of care. For the client, this often means that they only have to tell their story once to the primary service agency, rather than repeating it for social service workers they see at each separate service agency. For such software to be used safely and ethically, it must contain multiple layers of security to ensure that client information remains secure and confidential. It is important that when talking with a client about parameters of confidentiality you discuss the details upfront and acquire the consents for information sharing as soon as possible. This will reduce the likelihood of misunderstanding should the client situation require the social worker to limit the boundaries of confidentiality (see an example of a consent form at http://www.ablongman.com/cummins2e).

Finally, the Privacy of Health Information/Health Insurance Portability and Accountability Act of 1996 (HIPPA) provides clear guidelines for health care providers. Social workers have a strong tradition of safeguarding information. However, in today's world, the old system of paper records in locked filing cabinets is not enough. With information now broadly held and transmitted electronically, HIPPA provides clear standards for the protection of personal health information. To learn more about HIPPA, check out these websites: http://www.hipaa.org/ and http://www.hhs.gov/ocr/hipaa/.

Preparing for the First Meeting

Probably one of the scariest things a novice social worker faces is how to prepare for the first visit with a client. As mentioned above, the client is already preparing to meet you, thinking about what to say, and how to present him- or herself. As you plan for the first visit, whether a home visit or an office visit, be sure to have reviewed any material about the client that may be available. For instance, the client may have completed an intake form or perhaps information was collected over the telephone about the client's needs. You may have received a formal referral letter from another social worker, a teacher, a physician, or some other helping professional. Generally, some basic data accompanies the client as an introduction. Through this introductory information you may learn how the client came into contact with services. An important piece of information to know is whether the client is voluntary or involuntary.

Additionally, if you have some background information regarding the referral, it can be helpful to do some preliminary informal and formal research about that particular topic, issue or circumstance. In keeping with social worker's obligation to develop multicultural competence, if your client is a member of a group that you have little familiarity with, this is a great opportunity to learn more (see Chapter 4 for ideas and suggestions for building cultural competence).

Conversely, you may be working on a 24-hour hotline and the nature of the call is unknown. You have very little time to prepare for the interview other than to introduce yourself and ask the client how you may be of assistance. What you do know, however, is that the person is experiencing some type of distress. Mastery of basic interviewing skills and knowledge of resources may be the most beneficial preparation for engaging a client in this situation.

The relationship between the client and social worker begins as soon as they meet. First impressions are made as you venture forward. During those awkward first few minutes the client and social worker are taking stock. Introduce yourself, share information about your educational background and experiences, and provide a short description of your role and function within the agency setting. It is your responsibility to share with the client information about confidentiality, the helping process, the type of treatment or services offered, and what they can expect as a result of entering services. In addition, let clients know that your intention is to be helpful, favorable outcomes are possible (with a commitment on the part of the client as well), and their needs will be addressed.

Favorable environmental conditions include a private office or space with comfortable seating. A chair facing each other, placed within a comfortable spatial distance for you and the client is preferred. Obviously, few agencies have budgets for office decorating, but think about what you can include in the space to convey who you are as a helper. You can also express a sense of who you are and how you perform as a social worker based on the appearance of your office. A neat and well-ordered office can communicate to the client that you are organized, systematic, prepared, and focused. A messy, cluttered office can send the message that the worker is not prepared, incompetent, scattered, and unfocused. As you set up your office space, consider what types of artwork, pictures, plants, certificates/diplomas, and furnishings can help the client to see you as human and approachable. Displaying artwork and having magazines that represent the client populations you work with can be an effective way of communicating interest and acceptance.

In preparation for the first meeting, the social worker (or designated office personnel) may call to confirm the appointment a few days prior to the scheduled appointment. This call can serve as a reminder as well as conveying that you are looking forward to meeting the client. Of course, some clients can not be reached by phone. In that case you may want to send a short note or an e-mail reminder of the appointment. It is a good idea to leave a number where you can be reached, as well as the exact location of your office to facilitate the client in making the appointment on time.

Keep in mind that you will not 'click' with every client you meet. Clearly the social work adage, *goodness of fit* applies here. It is sometimes difficult to admit when the fit between the client and social worker is not good, and the time may come when you have to refer the client to another person, in part because your interactions may cause the client frustration at best and harm at worst. For example, you may have very strong feelings against abortion and your 23-year-old client is considering this intervention for resolving her unwanted pregnancy. You realize that you cannot be objective in your work with her because your personal beliefs are in conflict with her right to self-determination. Rather than convey a sense of disapproval or disgust, either consciously or unconsciously, refer her to an agency/worker that can provide this service in a more accepting way. To do otherwise would be in violation of the NASW Code of Ethics, specifically, the ethical principle that social workers respect the inherent dignity and worth of the person:

> "Social workers treat each person in a caring and respectful fashion, mindful of individual differences and cultural and ethnic diversity. Social workers promote clients' socially responsible self-determination. Social workers seek to enhance clients' capacity and opportunity to change and to address their own needs. Social workers are cognizant of their dual responsibility to clients and to the broader society. They seek to resolve conflicts between clients' interests and the broader society's interests in a socially responsible manner consistent with the values, [and] ethical standards of the profession" (NASW Code of Ethics).

Regardless of how unprepared you may feel, your clients have a set of expectations that you may be unaware of. It is up to you to come across as a caring person who is interested in learning about them and helping them. The responsibility for this initially rests with you. To accomplish a favorable outcome, you as the social worker must know what you are doing, communicate with the client that you are prepared to help, and plant the seed for change and hope (Kottler, 2000).

Although most BSW-level social workers are trained in the generalist practice mode, you may have developed a specialization along the way. For example, you may be a child welfare worker, but your area of practice is within the foster care arena. The expectation would be that you have a unique perspective, expertise, experience, and understanding of the issues facing the children, biological parents, and the foster parents. Additionally, first-year MSW education focuses on generalist versus specialization of practice. Regardless of your level or area of practice, social work skills must be applied within the values and ethics of the profession in your first meeting with the client and throughout the helping relationship. First meetings set the climate and tone within which the relationship will develop.

The First Face-to-Face Meeting with the Client

Assuming you have some basic information about the client and the presenting problem (what the client described as the reason they are there), you may already have some knowledge about their particular issues or concerns. Smiling at clients and welcoming them with a caring tone of voice and a handshake are ways to help put clients at ease (review session one of each of the four case studies on the accompanying CD-ROM for examples of these attending behaviors). Ask the client how she or he would like to be addressed, as this begins the process of self-determination (Ragg, 2001). If the client is in a waiting area, you may have to walk a long hall together or ride up in an elevator together. Small talk about traffic, the weather may help you both to feel more at ease. Once in the office, motioning or asking the client where they would like to sit is a good way to get started. As much as possible, given the many configurations of offices, be sure that your space is private as possible.

You may share with the client your role and how you became involved in their case. This is also a good place for client introduction. The social worker's opening statements should affirm the client's experience, as they relate to the helping situation. Social worker also needs to normalize the client's feelings by acknowledging that this can be a difficult and uncomfortable process. Finally, it is important for clients to feel a sense of hope that through the helping relationship change is possible. Once you have covered the introductory topics, it is helpful to ask if the client has any questions (Ragg, 2001). As mentioned above, discussing the parameters of client confidentiality and informed consent should also be included in the introductory segment of the session.

An open-ended question, such as, "Can you tell me what brought you in?" or "I have read the reports, can you tell me how you see the situation?" or "What do you see as the problem?" can help begin the first session. These open ended questions invite the client to tell you their story. Of course, not all clients are willing or interested in jumping right into the problem, so be patient. You may need to ask a series of related questions, trying each one out, until one finally hits a note for the clients. But be careful not to come across as an interrogator, as the client will likely feel defensive and frustrated. During this early stage of the relationship building trust and developing an atmosphere of care and concern is essential if the helping relationship is to move forward. Sometimes a statement as simple as "How can I help you today?" can give the client hope that help is here, and prompt her to tell her story.

Home Visits

Social workers have been making home visits since the days of "friendly visitors." Given our commitment to the "person in environment" perspective, a social worker can best understand a client's life situation by viewing, participating, and joining in it (see chapter 3). Many helping professionals only see clients in their office and never have the opportunity to witness what day-to-day life is like for our clients. The benefits of a home visit often outweigh the limitations. You cannot truly visualize the client's life without stepping into it. I once visited a teenage client's home and noted that there was not a single picture of her anywhere. Her sense of lack of place and belonging was confirmed by what I saw, no markers of her presence in the house. Although she had talked about her feeling of isolation and being unwanted, observing how the family interacted with her and each other spoke volumes about her day-to-day life. I had a new appreciation for her sadness and her desperation to leave home.

Clients come from a wide range of socioeconomic backgrounds. For example, you may make a home visit to a very wealthy family with poor parenting skills or a family in which drugs and alcohol are pervasive and the home situation is chaotic. Given that social workers are committed to working with the disenfranchised populations, you will visit families living in housing projects, trailer parks, rooming houses, group homes, and so on. In fact, you can never fully anticipate what you will see on the other side of the door. It is important to understand that many of your clients may live in ways or circumstances that do not meet your standards of hygiene. Be careful not to communicate your displeasure or discomfort. This is your client's home. For better or worse, this is how they live. With time and commitment, you may eventually be able to assist in helping your client to develop better housekeeping skills, but unless the situation is deemed a public health hazard, try to relax. Take time to observe the surroundings, learn about how your client lives. What are some of the obstacles and barriers that contribute to their life difficulties?

In reality, most clients you will see on a home visit are not dangerous and are often glad to see the social worker. For instance, in the CD-ROM, Mrs. Anderson is relieved to see her social worker, Nicole. Because Mrs. Anderson has Multiple Sclerosis (MS) her mobility is limited. Having a social worker come to her home is more convenient for the client and Nicole also has the opportunity to see how Mrs. Anderson is managing now that her granddaughter Maria is living with her. In the CD-ROM, Mrs. Anderson also refers to case aides that visit as well as a homemaker who assists her with some of her more physically challenging chores. Because several people a week are visiting Mrs. Anderson, she feels supported (and maybe a bit intruded upon), but the workers are able to keep a pulse on how she is managing given her medical condition. Any changes or limitations in her ability to manage independently because of her MS, age, energy level, ability to get up and down stairs, driving, and caring for Maria's daily needs can be assessed during the visits. In the CD-ROM, Nicole the social worker makes two visits to Mrs. Anderson's home. In the first clip, you are introduced to the neighborhood and the interior and exterior of her home. During the first visit, Nicole rings the doorbell and waits for Mrs. Anderson to invite her in. Mrs. Anderson's kitchen is a quiet and private place for them to talk. Also note that Nicole thanks Mrs. Anderson for welcoming her into her home. On Nicole's second visit they are seated in the living room, again in a quiet and private space.

When making a home visit always let your supervisor/coworkers know your schedule and destination points. Some agencies now require that social workers make home visits in pairs, for an added measure of safety. If you have a concern about your safety, talk with your supervisor, take advantage of self-defense classes, and always pay attention to environmental cues such as poor street lighting, large groups of people congregating, high bushes and shrubbery, loose animals, or an individual carrying a weapon. Never put yourself in a dangerous situation. Carry a cell phone (or pager), wear comfortable shoes, and be aware of exits. Wear a name tag, carry a business card, or another form of identification as a way of assuring the client that you are a worker from a social service agency. The reality, however, is that you may be on your own. Generally speaking, don't enter a client's home if you suspect drugs or alcohol are in use. (Of course if you are a child protection worker, you may have to enter potentially dangerous situations. It is a good idea to ask for police escort if you anticipate the threat of violence.) To learn more about safety concerns and strategies in social work practice, visit http://www.ssw.pdx.edu/pgField_SafetyConcerns.

Once in a client's home, remember you are a guest. It is important to attend to the family customs, religious beliefs and folk beliefs, and cultural courtesies, such as acknowledging first the oldest member of the household when visiting an Asian American family. In some cultures such as African American, small talk may be perceived as unprofessional. Don't appear hurried during the visit. You want to convey your full and undivided attention. Ask where to sit; if offered food or drink, it is polite to accept.

It may be helpful to suggest a quiet private space to talk if there are a lot of people around. Sometimes the client puts up barriers, such as loud music, the TV blaring, a dog barking as a way to communicate that "I don't want to be meeting with you." It is important to acknowledge that you are not necessarily a welcomed guest. By acknowledging this reality, you may help to reduce the obstacles and work toward collaboration.

Although home visits can be scary, there is no better way to learn about your clients. You have the opportunity to see them in their environment and observe how they interact with their world. Visits also give you insight into environmental barriers of the neighborhood such as lack of public transportation, wheelchair accessibility, safe parks, hallways, etc. For some clients, just the day-to-day task of getting up and facing the world can be truly overwhelming. Being nonjudgmental and supportive can provide the client with hope.

Box 5.7 LaTonya

LaTonya M. is a 12-year-old female. She is currently living with her mother and father. She has a younger brother, Dion age 8. LaTonya has sickle cell anemia disease, an inherited blood disorder which causes anemia (shortage of blood cells) and periodic pain due to sickle shaped blood cells. LaTonya is more vulnerable to infections and has a hard time fighting them off once they start. Because of this disease, she is considered to have delayed growth and is very slightly built for her age. Her parents are both employed by a local grocery store: her father is the 3:00 PM to 11:00 PM manager and her mother is the head cashier.

Box 5.7 LaTonya, *continued*

The school's outreach social worker, Julia was notified by the 7th grade teacher that LaTonya was tired, lacked energy, and appeared to be pain much of the time. Julia contacted the family and identified herself as the outreach social worker, explained the reason for her call and asked about coming out to meet them. Mrs. M. agreed to meet her in their home the following day. In preparation for the visit, Julie read the school file. There was little information except that LaTonya was diagnosed with Sickle Cell Disease when she was a baby. Julia also read some information about the disease (she downloaded information from the Sickle Cell Disease website, at http://www.sicklecelldisease.org/). Julia also talked to LaTonya's teacher, Mrs. Berry, in order to get a better understanding of how she is managing in her classes, both academically and socially. Finally, Julia consulted with the school nurse who has been involved in LaTonya's medical care since she came to the middle school. The nurse indicated that LaTonya has frequent bouts or flair ups related to her disease. LaTonya has missed 10-plus days of school over the past semester. There was no social history or any other information regarding the family in the school records.

Julie is relatively new to her position. She doesn't know the neighborhood well and asked Mrs. M. for directions. Julie arrived on time. Knowing that Mr. M. was sleeping, she knocked on the door. Latoya's younger brother Dion answered the door. Julie introduced herself and gave Mrs. M. her business card.

Julie: "Hi, Mrs. M., I spoke to you on the phone yesterday. My name is Julie." (She gives Mrs. M. her business card.)

Mrs. M. "Hello, did you have any trouble finding us?"

Julie: "No not at all, you gave me great directions."

Mrs. M.: "Come on in, do you want something to drink?"

Julie: "A glass of water sounds good." (She is aware of the offer and doesn't want tot offend Mrs. M. by saying 'No thank you.) "I am a social work intern at University College. Thanks for meeting with me today."

Mrs. M. "So why are you here?"

Julie: "As I mentioned on the phone, LaTonya's teacher, Mrs. Berry is concerned about her and her health and asked if I would come out to talk with you and Mr. M."

Mrs. M.: "LaTonya is fine, she is fine."

Box 5.7 LaTonya, *continued*

Julie: "Mrs. Berry did mention that LaTonya has missed 10 days of school since the beginning of January. Sometimes when LaTonya is in class she is tired and has trouble staying awake."

Mrs. M.: "Well, she goes to bed on time and I make sure that she gets plenty of rest when she is home, This is the first time the school has contacted me about LaTonya."

Julie: "Sorry if my visit is catching you off guard."

Mrs. M.: "Well, yes it is, but tell me more about what is going on at school."

Julie: "I know that LaTonya has sickle cell anemia disease and the teacher was wondering if LaTonya was having any flair ups which might be the reason she is so tired at school. Mrs. Berry also mentioned that LaTonya is having trouble concentrating during her classes."

Mrs. M.: "Maybe it is the sickle cell causing her these problems, but she hasn't had any flair ups or infections recently. She has been eating okay, and I take her to see the doctor when she is sick. I know she has been missing some school, but I make sure that we catch up on all her work."

Julie: "Okay, if it isn't the sickle cell anemia causing her tiredness in school, what do you think it could be?"

Mrs. M.: "I don't know, I try to keep up with all her appointments, but sometimes it does get so busy around here, that I have to cancel or reschedule appointments. I don't do it very often, but.....Things just get so busy here. I have to find a sitter for Dion and my work schedule is busy too. My husband sleeps during the day, so he doesn't help much.

Julie: "So most of LaTonya's health care falls on you."

Mrs. M.: "Yeah, it does, and normally I can handle everything but I am 4 months pregnant and I have been feeling kinda run down myself."

Julie: "You have a lot going on. You are very concerned about her and do what you can to keep her healthy. Let's talk more about what is going on here."

Mrs. M.: "Well, I have the kids, I work all day, my husband works all night. I don't get any break and if I have to go somewhere, there is no one to help me out. I know that LaTonya wants to play with other girls and have friends, but I am not here, so I say "No". She does watch Dion sometimes, but not that often. "One thing for sure, her daddy and me love her. I really want to protect her, I thought I had."

Box 5.7 LaTonya, *continued*

Julie: Well, there are some ways that the school can help you and LaTonya. There is a Girl Scout troop that meets once a week after school. One of the teacher assistants, Mrs. Chin is the troop leader. She is really nice and the girls do all kinds of fun things."

Mrs. M. "I can't pick her up after Girls Scouts because I have to be here when the bus drops Dion off."

Julie: "I don't know if this is possible, but there is a late bus that takes kids home once all the activities have ended. She may be able to ride that bus. I can check into that for you."

Mrs. M. "Oh, I think she would like that. Do they have a tutor for her after school too? Maybe she could get some help with her homework. I just want her to do well in school, she has so many other things to get her down."

Julie: "When you say get her down, what do you mean?"

Mrs. M.: "You know, it is hard for her to feel like everyone else. We try to keep up with everything. Now I am pregnant again. Dion is fine, but......"

Julie: "Are you are worried that this baby will have sickle cell too?"

Mrs. M.: "They tell me it's 50-50. I want them to tell me everything will be fine."

Julie: (Silence)

Mrs. M.: There is nothing I can do, but wait.

Julie: Well, the school nurse was telling me about a parent support group for parents who have kids with sickle cell. I know you have a lot going on, but we could find someone to stay with LaTonya and Dion. It might be helpful to talk to other parents.

Mrs. M.: "The other social worker had mentioned that a few years ago. We did go once, Mr. M and me, but I was not comfortable talking. That's what my sister and my church are for.

Box 5.7 LaTonya, *continued*

Julie: I would be happy to get you some information.

Mrs. M.: Well, that might be okay, but I don't think a support group is for me"

Julie: One positive about talking with other parents is they know about resources and specialists.

Mrs. M.: "Okay, I will think about it and talk to Mr. M. I want to meet with LaTonya's teachers too. I will call Dr. Good tomorrow and see if she can see her this week.

Julie: "I would be happy to drive Latonya to Dr. Good's office, if that would help you out."

Mrs. M. "That would be great, her office is on the other side of town. I will call her office and can I get back to you about the appointment time?"

Julie: "Sure. I will check into the Girl Scouts and tutoring and let you know what I find out the next time we meet."

Mrs. M.: Okay.

In this example, Julie expects to discuss LaTonya's disease with Mrs. M. What she had not anticipated is the issue of Mrs. M's pregnancy and how isolated and responsible she feels. She shifted gears and began to assess the additional family stress, rather than focusing strictly on LaTonya's physical health. Julie presents herself as caring and non-judgmental and therefore Mrs. M. appears to be willing to engage in the helping relationship. She sees Julie as a partner and feels hopeful that LaTonya's situation (and her family's situation) may improve.

Signs of Successful Client Engagement

Although the focus of the chapter is on engaging the client in the helping relationship, it is also important to briefly discuss the next step in the process. You have worked hard to connect with your client, and there is now a connectedness and commitment on your client's part to move forward and make some changes. You have covered all the basics and now it is time to get down to work. It can be very difficult to maintain a sense of direction and focus, and without a goal to work toward clients will lose motivation and interest.

It is important to frame the client's concerns or problem for work in terms that are meaningful to the client. Ask the client about what changes they want to make. Social worker-driven goals provide no incentive for the client to change, but a goal that is truly meaningful to the client may spark action. Mutually agreeing upon goals and objectives is the keystone to effective partnering.

Ragg, (2001) identifies a four-step approach to reframing the problem in an effort to move forward. These are summarized in Box 5.8.

Box 5.8 Reframing the Problem

Listen to the client and understand the client's definition of the problem—How does the client explain their situation? How does the client experience it? Does the client feel challenged or thwarted by it?

Identify the elements of the client's current understanding of the problem that may interfere with solving the problem—Often times the client's perspective is clouded by conflicting factors. Clients may experience multiple, conflicting, and shifting feelings about the situation. It is also important to understand how feelings contribute to behavioral actions. Who else is involved in the problem, what are the dynamics of those relationships? Does the client feel hopeful?

Identify the important themes, constructs and language that the client identifies with the problem—Themes of loss, powerlessness, and hopelessness can keep the client from seeing any possible solution. The duration of these feelings and ongoing and repeated patterns and experiences can contribute to the client feeling overwhelmed by the problem.

Create an alternative definition—Clients can see that change is possible if given the opportunity. Asking the question, "How would you like things to be for you 6 months from now?" *or* "If you could make the current situation different (or better), what would it look like?" *or* "You wake up tomorrow and things are better, what has happened while you were sleeping??" These kinds of questions do provide a new way of looking at an old problem, meaning it is fixable, even if only in small, but often times compelling ways (see Chapter 3).

Referring back to the case of LaTonya, her parents, and the outreach social worker Julia, there is an agreement now about how to move forward in defining goals and interventions. Mrs. M. has successfully engaged in the helping process as indicated by her willingness to meet with Julia again and to contact LaTonya's physician about her medical condition. Julia has agreed to locate childcare services for the family, a tutor for LaTonya and exploring options related to age appropriate activities (and fun ones), such as Girl Scouts. Providing specific services, such as providing LaTonya with a ride to the doctor's office, is essential if LaTonya is to receive the medical care and the emotional care she needs. As in this case, once the client (who really is Mrs. M. as well) has begun to reframe the problems into more workable solutions, you can join together, developing a plan of action that feels manageable and provides realistic ways to move forward. Small and incremental steps work best. Start with the big picture, the long-term goals, and work backwards, taking one step at a time.

In the CD-ROM case study of Maria, Crystal, and Mrs. Anderson, the long-term goal may be Maria's reunification with her mother Crystal. However, the reality of Crystal's life circumstances may very well preclude Maria's return home. In this case, it may be more realistic to work on goals to help Maria adjust to life with her grandmother. Concurrently, as Maria's situation becomes more stable, Nicole the social worker can also work with Crystal in an effort to find employment, pursue drug and alcohol treatment, safe housing, and other supports that she will need in order to become an effective parent to Maria. Taking each one of these goals and breaking them into small and manageable pieces will help Crystal feel successful and hopefully help to maintain her motivation to regain custody of Maria. Nicole can also help Mrs. Anderson identify ways to make this transition more manageable. What kinds of resources might be beneficial to her during this stressful time? (See Treatment Plans related to all four cases on the CD-ROM at http://www.ablongman.com/cummins2e for more information about long- and short-term goals.)

Success is a relative term. What is success to you may be quite different from the client's definition. A good way to evaluate success is to continually assess the client's level of motivation and commitment to goal setting and problem solving. In the social worker's role we are the collaborator, advocate, teacher, broker etc., but the client must "do" the work. The social worker can encourage and assist in this process, but ultimately it is the client's self-determination that will shape the outcome of the helping relationship.

CONCLUSION

The overall goal of the helping relationship is to assist in improving the well-being of clients. How each individual social worker meets this lofty goal may vary greatly in style and creativity, however, varying approaches should be grounded in the same knowledge base, skills, and social work values and ethics. As you develop your own professional style and methods, you will also become more confident. Remember, be yourself. Always be open to learning from your clients. Follow the NASW Code of Ethics, seek help, guidance and information when needed, and use your supervisor's expertise and experience to guide you long the way. This can be a bumpy journey at times, but well worth it.

REFERENCES

Compton, B. R. & Galaway, B. (1999). *Social Work Processes* (6th ed.) Pacific Grove, CA: Brooks/Cole.

Egan, G. (2002). *The skilled helper* (7th ed.) Pacific Grove, CA: Brooks/Cole.

Hackney, H.L., & Cormier, L.S. (2001). *The professional counselor*. Boston, MA: Allyn & Bacon.

Hill, C.E., & O'Brien, K.M. (2004). *Helping skills: Facilitating exploration, insight and action* (2nd ed.) Washington, DC: American Psychological Association.

Kottler, J.A. (2000). *Nuts and bolts of helping*. Boston, MA: Allyn & Bacon.

Miley, K.K., O'Melia, M. & DuBois, B. (2001). *Generalist social work practice: An empowering approach.* Boston, MA: Allyn & Bacon.

National Association of Social Workers (1999). *Code of Ethics.* Retrieved Feb. 18, 2005 from http://www.naswdc.org/pubs/code/code.asp.

Paniagua, F.A. (1998) *Assessing and treating culturally diverse clients: A practical guide.* (2nd ed.) Thousand Oaks, CA: Sage Publications.

Ragg, D.M. (2001). *Building effective helping skills: The foundation of generalist practice*. Boston, MA: Allyn & Bacon.

Sue, S. & Sue, D. (1990). *Counseling the culturally different* (2nd ed.). New York: John Wiley & Sons.

CHAPTER SIX

Social Work Skills

For social workers, the key to working effectively with clients is developing expertise in the basic skills of communication. This pursuit involves formal academic education, professional training, supervision, and an overall commitment to social work skills development. During the interview process the social worker connects with the client through the use of empathic responses such as reflection of feeling, paraphrasing, and attending behaviors. Using social work skills effectively requires more than just knowing the skill; the social worker must determine when it is appropriate to use the skill by gauging the client's likely response. This level of expertise takes considerable effort to develop, but it can be learned. Although social workers who are new to the field occasionally struggle to give the best response to clients, with practice, interviewing clients becomes an opportunity to put in to action the values of the social work profession.

Social work interviewing skills involve both the discipline to practice and the faith that you will eventually develop a skill set that enables you to more forward with confidence and certainty. The more prepared you are, the less anxious you will feel and the more you practice the more comfortable you become. This chapter introduces you to basic interviewing skills and attending behaviors that are the first steps toward a career-long pursuit of excellence in the helping relationship.

INTERVIEWING SKILLS

Lead-In Responses

Before we focus on specific interviewing skills, a few words about lead-in responses are in order. A lead-in response is the introductory part of a sentence stem or question that begins the social worker's response to the client. Lead-in responses give the social worker an opportunity to match the client's verbal style (Brems, 2001). It is helpful to develop a wide variety of lead-in responses so that you are not repeating the same ones over and over. See Box 6.1 for examples of lead-in responses organized by sensory categories. Experienced interviewers can adjust their responses to match a client's primary sensory orientation—for example, if a client seems most focused on the physical, then kinesthetic responses are indicated (i.e., (I could feel…"); for clients who seem to think more visually, visual lead-in responses (i.e., saying "I see.") etc are an effective strategy (Brems, 2001).

Box 6.1 Lead-In Responses

Auditory	Kinesthetic	Visual
What I am hearing you say…	Could you feel…	I am observing…
As I hear it…	You feel…	I detect…
You sound…………	I gather…	From where you are watching …
Does this ring a bell…	From where you stand…	I noticed…
From what I am hearing…	Right now, you feel…	From your point of view…
It echoes the sound of…	I sense that…	I imagine…
You are telling me…	I have the feeling…	You are focused on…
It sounds like…	I gather…	Am I perceiving this correctly…
It sounds as if…	From where you are…	As I see it…
Sounds to me…	Am I close…	My sense is that…
I hear you saying….	I am drawing…	It seems like…
If I am hearing you correctly…	You felt…	You are considering…
It sounds as though you are saying…	**General**	You are describing…
	Correct me if I am wrong…	It appears as though…
	Could it be…	It looks like…
	I wonder what else…	Following what you just said…
	I am wondering if…	I see what you mean…
	Go on…	You appear…
	And…	

Paraphrasing

The social worker uses paraphrasing to confirm the meaning the client has attached to the messages conveyed throughout the interview. Paraphrasing focuses on the content of the client's message. The social worker restates what the client has said, in his or her own words (Boyle, Hull, Mather, Smith & Farley, 2006; Hepworth, Rooney & Larsen, 2002). Paraphrasing elicits feedback from the client, confirming that the social worker understands the meaning of the client's message. It is a statement not a question. A paraphrase conveys that the client has been heard and now can move on to another aspect of the topic. The paraphrase points out what the client has said and his or her view of the situation under discussion. It should not reflect the social worker's view. Box 6.2 demonstrates a social worker using the paraphrasing skill and lead-in responses to better comprehend how the client understands her problem.

Box 6.2 Mary

Mary is a 47-year-old female who has been struggling with finances. She spends money excessively and is deeply in debt.

Social Worker: What do you experience when you go to the mall? (open-ended question)

Mary: I go in the evening, especially when I'm feeling stressed. The kids will get me upset and I'll go straight to the mall after dinner.

Social Worker: If I am hearing you correctly, most of the time you go to the mall because of a difficult situation at home. (lead-in response and paraphrase)

Mary: Yeah, I'll feel frustrated and then when I go shopping, I get this intense rush. I mean it really works. I charge up my credit cards on a lot of things I really don't need. It gives me a quick thrill. But by the time I get home I feel like crap because I realize that I've just dug myself deeper into debt.

Social Worker: Your excessive spending is a way to help you feel better. But, you experience guilt once you get home. (reflection of feeling)

Mary: Yeah, I feel awful and then I feel worthless. That's when my husband and I fight—and then I just want to go back to the mall. The whole thing just keeps going round and round.

Social Worker: You are describing this as a pattern or a cycle. You spend money to relieve stress, but then regret your actions. This leads to more stress, and it starts all over. (lead-in/ paraphrase/reflection of feeling)

Mary: That's exactly how I see it.

In this example, the social worker captures the true meaning of Mary's addictive spending pattern. Hearing this "cycle" repeated back to Mary highlights for her the major counseling issue: developing other ways to reduce stress and conflict in her life. Also, in this example, the social worker uses two types of lead in responses, auditory ("If I am hearing you correctly….") and visual ("You are describing….").

Paraphrasing should not be used excessively, so as to avoid conveying the impression that the social worker is simply mimicking what the client is saying (Hepworth et al., 2002). In using a paraphrase, the important words and ideas are conveyed back to the client. Be true to the essence of what the client has said. Paraphrasing should be used in conjunction with other methods of facilitating the client's responses, such as reflection of feelings and interpretation. Paraphrasing helps the client to see clearly what he or she is thinking or experiencing. Hearing the social worker restate ideas gives the client an opportunity to rethink or to see issues from a different perspective (Hepworth et al., 2002). It is always a good idea to check back with the client after delivering a paraphrase by asking "Is that right?? or " Am I following you correctly?"

Reflection of Feeling

Reflection of feeling is one of the most important skills in the social worker's repertoire. It requires the social worker to restate and explore the client's affective (feeling) statements. Frequently, the client is experiencing a wide variety of feelings and has difficulty separating them from each other, and understanding how these feelings are related to one another. Social workers use reflection of feelings to understand how a client responds emotionally to life (Cormier & Cormier, 1998).

The social worker must also be sensitive to nonverbal language, since feelings tend to express themselves nonverbally (i.e., a nervous laugh, a rolling of the eyes, nervous twitching, blushing, or looking down). Additionally, if the client has difficulty expressing a feeling, the social worker may want to present several feeling words, all with similar meanings, so that the client can select the one with the best fit (Kadushin & Kadushin, 1997). For example, "I am observing that things are overwhelming and challenging for you right now, but you also get a thrill out of winning the game and finishing first. Am I correct?" This enables the client to confirm the feeling, but without experiencing the pressure of identifying feeling states. The social worker can also normalize feelings for example, "Many people who lose a parent feel the way you do—very empty and alone." Reflection of feeling is a technique that helps the social worker explore the extent of the client's problems, and how the client views the problem situation. Validating the client's feelings can be good modeling, thus showing the client that his or her feelings matter and have a powerful effect on cognition and behavior.

Social workers must be comfortable in the world of feelings in order to assist clients in the management and understanding of their emotional responses. Clients can express their feelings either explicitly (outward indication of feeling state) or implicitly (the inner emotional response but not necessarily expressed). Client may correct the social worker's attempt to pinpoint the feeling. With that "correction," the social worker can gain valuable insight into how the client describes the experience versus the social worker's perception of it.

It is important to determine the readiness of the client to explore feelings. For some clients, dealing with emotions is a very unnatural and foreign concept. Testing out feeling choices by offering some alternatives can open the client to deeper exploration of feelings. The social worker can sometimes infer what the client is feeling and reflect that understanding back to the client.

Clients often experience conflicting feelings regarding the same situation. For example, being excited about summer camp and at the same time fearful and scared about being away from home for the first time. Exploring these conflicting feelings can be very helpful in assisting the client in understanding the complexity of life. Resolving conflicting feelings can also lead the client to change. Conversely, strong feelings can interfere with a client's ability to make rational life choices.

Stay with feelings in the moment, i.e., "Right now I get the sense that you are uncomfortable talking about your dad. Your tone of voice changed and you are fidgeting in your chair...Let's talk about what is so painful for you in relation to your dad." This gives the client feedback and allows for on the spot, in the moment, discussion and focus. Box 6.3 demonstrates the social worker utilizing the skill of reflection of feeling.

Box 6.3 Eileen

Eileen is a 35-year-old female seeing a social worker because of depression. She has recently remembered episodes of childhood sexual abuse by an adult relative. She has managed to avoid the issue for 20 years, but now feels overwhelmed.

Eileen: I just don't know how to deal with this pain.

Social Worker: It's a lot to digest. Right now you're hurting, and feeling very confused. (reflection of feeling)

Eileen: I just wish I could run away from the world.

Social Worker: I imagine that your memories of the abuse are really having an overwhelming effect on you. (lead-in response/reflection of feeling)

Eileen: I just never really thought about it before. It just makes me so crazy. I'm having a difficult time staying focused at work and at home.

Social Worker: That's understandable. You are trying to make sense of what happened to you. It was a frightening and scary time. (lead-in response/reflection of feeling)

Eileen: Yeah, it was. I know it is important to deal with this. I've hid it from myself for so many years. I never really let myself *feel* anything.

The social worker in this case is validating Eileen's ambivalent emotions. Eileen begins to realize how the experience of abuse has had a significant impact on her life. By helping Eileen identify the layers of feelings and thoughts, she will gain more insight into her problem, which will lead to progress in functioning more effectively and alleviating feelings of distress. Eileen recognizes that she has hidden her feelings for a long time. By acknowledging this, she has gained insight into how sexual abuse as a child affects her current relationships ("I never really let myself feel anything").

As this example illustrates, it is important for the social worker to have a rich vocabulary of feeling words in order to match the affect of the client and to mirror the client's depth and intensity of feeling. For example, a social worker who is working with a depressed client can use words ranging from "down" (weak expression of sadness), "dejected" (moderate expression) or "hopeless" (strong expression) in reflecting feelings back to the client, depending on the intensity of the client's feelings. See the companion website http://www.ablongman.com/cummins2e for a comprehensive list of feeling words.

In conclusion, there are a few additional points to consider regarding the reflection of feeling skill:

- Feelings have two dimensions: the *category* of the affect such as happy, angry, and sad, fearful and the *intensity* of the affect. (Hepworth et al., 2002). To accurately reflect feelings, the social worker must be cognizant of and use both dimensions of this skill.
- Cultures vary in the extent to which emotions are expressed (Hackney and Cormier, 2001). You may have a very expressive client who is Italian-American or a very reserved client whose family comes from China. Sue and Sue (1990) observed that Asian Americans value the restraint of strong feelings. Consider the cultural context of your client's life when using a reflection of feeling during the interview process. Keep in mind that in collectivistic cultures (client's identity emphasis lies within the family and community), such as Asian and Native American cultures, affective expression is likely to be withheld. It means that the client is experiencing the feeling, but is reluctant to express it outright. (See Chapter 4 for more information.)
- Strong feelings can interfere with your client's ability to think clearly about a situation. Giving the client the opportunity to vent and then restating the affective message (in a calmer voice) can help to de-escalate the client and lead to more rational and thoughtful action.
- Feelings can change over time as circumstances change. Be aware that how a client feels at a particular point in time may be quite different from how he or she feels just moments, hours, or days later. Be patient with your client and be patient with yourself.
- Always attend to the nonverbal messages. For instance, "I see a smile on your face. You must feel pleased with the way things have turned out."

Open-Ended Questions

Asking questions comes naturally to the social worker. Sometimes however, the social worker may be uncomfortable asking very personal and intimate questions. It is important to do so, however, if the question is relevant, and can yield new information. Asking relevant, purposeful, and insightful questions requires skill. The social worker can direct the interview by asking relevant questions, thus exploring the issues and situations that concern the client. Using an open-ended question such as "Please tell me, what is it like for you at school?" the social worker can prompt the client to elaborate on a point. This gives the client the opportunity to discuss important aspects of the problem in more depth (Kadushin & Kadushin, 1997). Questions also convey interest in what the client has to say. It is important to pace your questions, giving your client time to respond. Also, using a variety of interviewing skills is preferred, as there are many other techniques and skills for gathering data.

Questions can be asked in a linear fashion. For example, asking for the sequence of events, "What happened first," "And then what happened?" These questions provide insights into the client's thought processes as well. Asking a hypothetical question may also be useful in getting the client to elaborate. In this instance, the client may share some insight about an "imaginary situation" while at the same time giving the social worker some important information about how the client may think, feel, or behave in a similar circumstance. For example, the social worker might ask, "If you were in your daughter's place and had to choose between good grades or spending time with your friends, but you can't do both, how would you have chosen, knowing what you know today?" or "If you were in her shoes, and could make the whole situation better, how would you fix it?"

Asking an open-ended question at the beginning of an interview can be very effective. This gives the client an opportunity to decide what she or he would like to talk about. Open-ended questions tend to be general (i.e., "How are you feeling today?"). Once the social worker has an overview of the situation, asking more specific questions will fill in the picture (i.e., "You said that you are very upset about having to talk to me. Please tell me, what aspects of being here troubles you the most?")

When asking an open-ended question, there are several issues to consider: Is the question relevant, and does it help achieve the purpose of the interview? Questions should be phrased in a way that invites a response, not in a way that demands a response (i.e., "Please tell me," "Can you please elaborate" versus "I must know"). Questions can take the form of who, what, why, where, when, and how (Ivey & Ivey, 2003. See Box 6.4 for some examples.

Box 6.4 Examples of Open-Ended Questions

What--what are the facts/details about situation
What happened after _____?
What are some of the issues about _____ that concern you?
What would you like to talk about today?
What was your reaction?
What have you tried thus far?
What if that doesn't work out?
What do you make of all of this?

Box 6.4 Examples of Open-Ended Questions, *continued*

How--elicits process or sequence about a situation or elicits emotions
How do you feel about _____?
How does this whole situation change your view of _____?
How do you feel about that?
How do you suppose you could find out more about it?
How does this affect you?
How do you suppose this will work out?
How do you explain this to yourself?
How does it look right now?
How do you view the situation?
How did you feel when that happened?
How can I be of help?

Why--reasons or rational
Why are you so angry at _____?
Why do you feel such anger toward _____?
Why is this so important to you?
Why do you think that you feel the way you do?

Where--details about location/place
Where does the great source of pain for you come from?
Where would you like to see your relationship with _____ a year from now?"
Where do we go from here?
Where do you plan on being in the future?

When--various time frames
When you think about this whole situation how do you feel?
When in your life did you realize he wasn't coming home?
When is it most difficult for you to talk to him?
When do you think this all started taking place?
When do you feel that like this all started taking place?
When are you going to be able to move on?

Who--types of details about the people involved
Who else in your life has experienced the kind of pain you have surrounding _____?
Who do you count on for support in your life?
Who else have you talked to about this?
Who are your social supports?

Could—a request for information or clarification
Could you fill me in on the background?
Could you give me an example?
Could you tell me a little more about that?
Could you help me understand?

The best questions are short, focused on the client, and to the point. Ask yourself, what exactly do I need to know in order to fully understand the issue at hand? Also, does my question focus on the client's strengths? You want to ask questions that help the client begin to explore issues and go deeper into the issue, situation etc. You have begun to probe for deeper meaning, which can lead to new insights, which in turn can lead to change.

Social workers must be careful in using "why" questions. Frequently, clients don't know why they do something a certain way. Asking them to explain themselves may cause them to become defensive and feel judged, closing down communication (Boyle, Hull, Mather, Smith & Farley, 2006). The client can feel criticized or blamed. Sometimes clients may not understand their own motives and why they do what they do. Therefore, "why" questions should be asked infrequently and with discretion (Sheafor & Horejsi, 2003). If the client becomes angry, use a paraphrase or reflection of feeling response, and then ask the question another way (i.e., instead of "Why are you so sure you can't do it on your own?" ask "Please tell me, what makes being on your own so hard?"). Box 6.5 demonstrates the social worker asking an open-ended question.

Box 6.5 Latisha

Latisha is a 30-year-old female client who is struggling with her role as a stepparent. She and her husband Frank are separated. They are attending counseling sessions under court order as part of the divorce decree

Latisha: I never expected that I would have such a hard time parenting a five year old and an eight year old.

Social Worker: Latisha, how do you see your role as a stepmother? (Open-ended question)

In this example the question focuses the interview, while still allowing the client to respond in any way she chooses.

If the client responds to an open-ended question with a "yes" or a "no," the social worker can try rephrasing the question. If, after several attempts, the client still does not fully respond, the topic of conversation should be changed (i.e., "I can tell that you don't want to talk about Andre. Let's spend some time discussing your housing situation. I know the landlord has decided to refurbish the building. How does this affect you?").

In closing, as with all social work interviewing skills, remember that asking questions in some cultures can be seen as intrusive and rude. One way to address this issue is to ask the question, "Can you tell me about…." This question allows for client self-determination about sensitive or difficult issues as clients consider whether they would like to discuss this aspect of the problem.

Closed-Ended Questions

A closed-ended question (i.e., "How many times has your daughter run away?") enables the social worker to check details of the client's narrative for accuracy. They also can help gather small, but useful, pieces of information such as date of birth, number of siblings, and number of previous arrests (Cormier & Cormier, 1998). Closed ended questions can also be used to scale the severity, intensity and/or frequency of a problem. For example, asking your client to rate her level of martial satisfaction (level of depression, motivation etc.) on a scale from 1-10 is a good way to quickly assess the situation from the client's point of view.

Closed-ended questions can also bring into focus a particular issue and, depending on the answer, the social worker can then follow up with related questions. Box 6.6 demonstrates the social worker asking a series of closed-ended question.

Box 6.6 Mario

Mario is a 14-year-old male student who has been referred to the social worker due to severe conflicts at home. His parents are threatening to send him to his aunt's home in another city.

Social Worker: Tell me about things at home between you and your parents. (open-ended question)

Mario: It's okay. I don't really want to talk about this with you.

Social Worker: I know, it's hard to talk to a stranger about your family. (paraphrasing)

Mario: It's not me, it's my parents. They order me around all the time. I can't stand all the yelling.

Social Worker: How often do you get yelled at? (closed-ended question)

Mario: Probably 15 times a day.

Social Worker: As you see it, what seems to start the arguments? (lead-in response/open-ended question)

In this example, Mario is initially reluctant to talk. Because the social worker has conveyed her understanding of his situation, he starts communicating. By answering the simple closed-ended question, the client has given the social worker an opening to pursue a deeper understanding of his conflicts with his parents.

Beginning social workers can overuse closed-ended questions. Be careful not to rely heavily on this skill because the interview can feel more like an interrogation, which may cause the client to feel frustrated with the interview process. The interview can become social-worker focused. You are doing all the work, trying to come up with questions and simultaneously the client can sit back and simply answer "yes" or "no." While closed-ended questions are very useful in pinpointing the details of a situation, asking too many in close succession can make for a superficial interview (or interrogation) that fails to get at underlying issues (Hepworth et al., 2002).

When working with non-talkative clients, asking a series of closed-ended questions can get the interview moving. Pay attention to the client's nonverbal communication and if you see some form of interest develop, switch to an open-ended question as a follow up. You may have sparked enough interest to get the client talking more expressively.

Clarification

Clarification is a skill that allows the social worker to identify what a client is thinking, feeling, and experiencing. When the client's messages are too abstract or hazy, the social worker may ask for the client to be more specific about the meaning of words, or the frequency and duration of problems. Clients may assume that the social worker understands their messages and therefore may not fully explain their meaning unless the social worker asks for clarification. For example, an adolescent gang member may state that he "hangs out" with his buddies. The social worker may want to clarify what, precisely, "hanging out" constitutes by asking for details. Be sure to clarify what a client means when referring to "they", "them", "us", "my friends," etc. It is important to know all the important players. A client may use qualifiers such as "always," "sometimes," or "kinda." The astute social worker will want to determine exactly what these qualifiers mean (Cormier & Cormier, 1998).

To further clarify, the social worker can check with the client their understanding of what the client just said. For example, "You are saying that nothing is going well in your life right now. Am I hearing you correctly?" This gives the client an opportunity to confirm, disagree, or clear up any misunderstanding the social worker might have.

In addition, many clients have a "pop culture" understanding of psychological jargon and circumstances. Watching TV, reading self-help books and magazines have exposed clients to a wide range of issues, many of which may be misunderstood by the client. For example, your client states, "I was watching Oprah on TV last week and this doctor talked about this thing called bipolar disorder. I think that is what my wife has, she is up one day and down the other." Given this information, it is the social worker's responsibility to make clear or decode what the client has learned from the "TV expert" and help to educate or clarify further.

Clarification should be used when a client is discussing a situation that the social worker does not fully understand. In turn, the social worker must make responses as clear as possible, so the client understands the true meaning of the social worker's words. Clarification thus becomes a reciprocal process between the social worker and the client (Hepworth, Rooney & Larsen, 2002). The social worker may misinterpret the client's messages and develop incorrect perceptions or assumptions about the client's situation. Therefore, it is essential that the social worker clarify when she or he is uncertain about the client's message, asking, for example, "Is this what you mean?" or "Is this what you're saying?" Additionally, the social worker may want the client to elaborate on a particular topic or to give specific examples regarding the situation, behavior, or feeling (Cormier & Cormier, 1998). Box 6.7 provides an example of the social worker using clarification to better understand the client's point of view.

Box 6.7 Ralph

Ralph is a 16-year-old male attending sessions with a social worker because of his repeated fighting with other students. He has a history of behavioral disruptions at school and is in danger of being expelled.

Ralph: It's not fair. The teachers are always busting me for fighting. They have it in for me.

Social Worker: You think that's the reason you're here, because of all the fighting? (lead-in response/clarification)

Ralph: Yeah, I was sent to your office because the teachers are definitely out to get me.

Social Worker: When you say the teachers are out to get you, what does that mean, exactly? (clarification)

In this example the social worker attempts to gain an understanding of Ralph's point of view on his troubles at school. The social worker wants to be certain that they are "speaking the same language" (i.e., "What does that mean, exactly?"). If Ralph is given the opportunity to present and clarify his position without feeling blamed or accused, he is likely to contribute more to the session.

Summarization

When using summarization, the social worker pulls together relevant pieces of information from the interview into a composite response. Both the feeling(s) and content of the client's message are incorporated in the social worker's summary. Summarization is used throughout the interview to focus the discussion on relevant issues as well as to make transitions from one topic to another. Summarizations are delivered as a statement, not a question. Summarizations are helpful in beginning and ending sessions. Generally, a good way to begin a session is to summarize what was discussed in the last session(s).

This technique ensures continuity across sessions. Summarization can also be useful at the end of a session to highlight relevant topics from the session, and to set the agenda for the next visit (Hepworth et al., 2002). This skill is also useful as a tool to curb clients who have a tendency toward longwinded storytelling. The social worker can recap what was said and then attempt to refocus the interview to more relevant parts of the problem. For some clients, this sprawling explanation is a good way to divert and deflect the interview process, by focusing on tangential issue (Hepworth et al., 2002).

Summarizations are also used to review progress over time. It allows the social worker to reflect back on past sessions and to bring to the fore themes and patterns that have emerged throughout the therapeutic relationship. This is a good technique to use when the social worker is trying to organize thoughts and concerns about the issue under discussion. Clients can also work toward organization of content, as they too attempt to review what was said either in the session or across sessions. Box 6.8 demonstrates the skill of summarization being utilized by the social worker.

Box 6.8 Kate

Kate is an 18-year-old female who has been living with a foster family since age 8. She is discussing recent events in her life with her social worker, focusing particularly on her relationship with her biological mother.

Kate: Dennis and Julia [foster parents] have taken good care of me. I know that they're proud of my accomplishments, especially me getting accepted at the university.

Social Worker: You've done so well and proven that you can make it. (paraphrasing)

Kate: Yeah! I want to make something of myself. I want to do better than my Mom did for me. You know, she didn't even show up for my graduation. Dennis and Julia were there, cheering me on.

Social Worker: You sound very hurt and let down that your Mom didn't come and celebrate your special day. (lead-in response/reflection of feeling)

Kate: I know I should have prepared myself—she's not going to show, but I always hope she will.

> **Box 6.8 Kate,** *continued*
>
> Social Worker: You're feeling really frustrated with her right now. (lead-in response/reflection of feeling) Can you tell me more about your relationship with you Mom? (open-ended question)
>
> Kate: I don't know. I wish that she wanted to be a part of my life. Sometimes I think she's jealous of Dennis and Julia. Maybe she feels bad about everything that has happened, especially the stuff with her husband. He never wanted me around and maybe that's part of why she stays away too.
>
> Social Worker: Although you love Dennis and Julia, you wish things had turned out differently with your Mom. You understand her circumstances, but it doesn't change the fact that you feel hurt and disappointed by her time after time. Does that capture how you feel? (summarization and clarification)

In this example, Kate talks about several important issues: 1) her relationship with her foster parents; 2) graduating from high school and going to college; 3) disappointment with her mother, yet understanding her situation; and 4) wanting to do things differently in her own life. The social worker pulls together several issues presented by Kate and develops a concise statement reviewing the important points.

Summarization provides focus throughout the interview, highlights important points and helps identify themes, patterns, and insights. A summarization is not merely a "list"; rather, it is a composite of the most significant parts of the interview. It can be beneficial to ask the client to summarize at various points throughout the interview. It gives both the social worker and client an appreciation for the client's point of view and can serve as a way to confirm the accuracy and the understanding of the message by both parties. The social worker can also clarify or ask an open-ended question to be certain a full understanding of the situation has been achieved. It is always a good idea to ask the client to confirm the accuracy of your understanding. For example, "You are still feeling hopeful, even after all these disappointments, that you will be able to one day get out of your wheelchair. Do I understand what you just said?" Finally, when providing a summarization, be sure to recap what the client said, not your opinions, values and judgments.

Information Giving

The social worker uses information giving when the client is in need of useful knowledge. Information may include knowledge about available resources in the community such as a local food pantry or a homeless shelter (Murphy & Dillon, 2003), or, it might be factual information relevant to the client's presenting problem (i.e., informing a client with a substance abuse problem about the progressive nature of an addiction). You can use this skill to convey details and an explanation about the helping process, the role of the social worker, and interventions to be used. Sharing specifics about developmental norms, life transitions and consequences of behaviors is important, as this information can help the social worker and client sort out what is a fact, a falsehood, or myth (Gambrill, 1997).

Information should always be presented in a way that is sensitive to the client's culture. For example, in talking to an African American client about mental illness, it is important to understand that within this minority group, sources (or the cause) of mental illnesses are often thought of as organic or inherited. Talking about medication as the first treatment choice may convey that the social worker does not want to work with the client (Paniagua, 1998). Some clients assume that social workers can't be trusted because they are members of the dominant group. In this case, understand the trepidation a client might experience when asking for more traditional social services. It is your responsibility to convey understanding, interest and provide services that are relevant to their needs.

In terms of potential language barriers, if you have clients who do not understand English, having written materials available in their native language is important. Providing the client with concrete recommendations or services early on in the helping process is also beneficial (Paniagua, 1998). If you don't speak Spanish, for example, a translator may be required to assist with the interview. Be aware that a translator, whether a family member or a professional, can be seen as intrusive. Certainly, training bilingual social workers to provide services to members of their ethnic or racial group can be an effective way to convey consideration and sensitivity. It is essential that as a helper, you understand that external sociopolitical forces have influence and shape the worldview of our clients. (See Chapter 4 for more information related to the cultural context of interviewing.). Box 6.9 demonstrates this skill.

Box 6.9 Mandy

Mandy is a 19-year-old female who discloses in the middle of a session that she is very anxious. She recently attended a party where she had unprotected sex with a man she only knows casually. She is concerned about STI (sexually transmitted infections) and being pregnant.

Mandy: I can't believe I did this. I mean, it was really stupid.

Social Worker: Having unprotected sex could have serious consequences, one of which is getting infected with a sexually transmitted infection (information giving) and of course pregnancy.

Mandy: I get the pregnant part, but do you mean like AIDS?

Social Worker: Yes. (information giving)

Box 6.9 Mandy, *continued*

Mandy: But I feel OK. I don't think I have a diseases and I sure hope that I'm not pregnant.

Social Worker: The only way you'll know whether you're infected will be to get an HIV antibody test in three to six months. (information giving) I know you must be scared about all this. (reflection of feeling), including the possibility of getting pregnant.

Mandy: My parents are going to kill me. We are Catholic and no matter what the circumstances, sex is a sin.

Social Worker: So to make a difficult situation even worse, you are scared and anxious about your parent's reaction. (reflection of feeling)

Mandy: Yep. If I'm pregnant, an abortion is out of the question. In my family, it would be better to die from AIDS than to be a single mom or a baby killer.

Social Worker: You feel like there are no good choices, but let's talk about one thing at a time. There is no reason right now to panic about the "what if's". Let's take it slowly. Where do you want to start?"

In this example, Mandy is expressing concern about her health status, possible pregnancy, as well as her lack of judgment in having unprotected sex. The social worker provides relevant information to Mandy and then refocuses the interview on her emotional state. In addition, the social worker empowers Mandy by suggesting that she decide what she wants to discuss first. Also note that the social worker does not interject an opinion here. The worker is referring to the facts only. No judgment is attached to the information imparted.

Social workers present information to educate clients about options and help them to make changes, not to dictate choices in a judgmental way. We provide information as a way to teach or instruct. For instance, showing a client how to use the public bus system or develop a budget are examples of information giving. Keeping within the social work ethic of self-determination, information should always be presented in a way that allows the client to accept or reject the information being offered. Specifically, it is important to distinguish between advice and information. Giving "advice" is telling clients what you believe to be in their best interest; while providing information allows clients to make choices based on all the available alternatives (Sheafor& Horejsi, 2003).

If the social worker doesn't have the necessary information, he or she should be honest and amenable to gathering the information for the next session. It is important to remember that social workers don't know all the answers and reaching out to others for resources, information, and referrals on behalf of our clients is a necessary part of our work. Providing a reading list, a brochure, or pamphlet about a service or agency can be very empowering to the client. Be sure your information is up to date. It is a good idea to review and critique any articles, brochures, or informational sheets before giving them to a client. Always consider the reading level of your client. Sometimes you may need to present or adapt the information in a way that addresses the client's cognitive level or limitations. If your client has access to the Internet, providing addresses of reputable websites is another way to get up-to-date information regarding any subject matter.

Before giving information determine what the client already knows. For instance, you wouldn't want to repeat the steps involved in applying for medical assistance if the client has already completed the application. Check back with clients to ascertain if they understand all the information. This way you can clear up any misunderstandings or gaps in the information shared. Pay attention to the client's verbal and nonverbal reaction to the information and use either a paraphrase, reflection of feeling or clarification to make sure you understand their point of view. ("You look surprised that there are so many steps to enroll your child in school. It does require lots of paper work, but I do this with parents all the time.")

A word of caution about giving information: be careful not to use information as a way of sounding like the expert. Overwhelming your client with the breath and depth of your knowledge may impress you, but at the same time intimidate the client. The timing of information, in small, understandable, and relevant doses, works best for both you and the client.

Information is power and the more our clients are equipped with resources, data and facts, the more empowered they are to make changes in their lives. Decision making and self-advocacy are outgrowths of information, at both the case (micro practice) and class (macro) levels of intervention.

Confrontation

Confrontation is a skill that a social worker uses to address a discrepancy in the client's message (Hepworth et al., 2002). This discrepancy can take two forms: 1) the client's behavior in contradiction to his or her statement or 2) the client's statements in contradiction to one another. An example of the first type of discrepancy, when the client states one thing yet behaves differently, would be the following scenario: A client says, "I want Claudia back—the agency is keeping her from me. You want to give her to that foster family." The social worker responds by saying, "I know you want Claudia to be with you, but as we have talked about before, if you continue to miss visits with her it will delay her coming home." It is important to note that the social worker may be confused by this apparent disconnect between the client's verbal and nonverbal messages and may need to explore this further. An example of the second type of discrepancy, when two or more of the client's messages or statements contradict each other, would be a client denying that she is experiencing stress in her relationship with her husband while also reporting in the same session that she hates talking to him. The social worker points out this discrepancy in hopes of providing some insight that could possibly lead to client change. It is best to offer a series of recent examples rather than a distant event the client might not remember as a way of reinforcing the message (Hill and O'Brien, 2004). A confrontation should be offered in a nonjudgmental and nonthreatening and nonadversarial way. Regardless of the way a confrontation is delivered, it may be difficult for the client to accept or acknowledge identified discrepancies. There may be a tendency to save face.

Hill and O'Brien (2004) suggest the social worker use the following two-part format when confronting clients:

- On one hand you... but on the other hand...
- You say... but you also say...
- You say... but nonverbally you seem...
- I am hearing... but I am also hearing...

For confrontation to be used effectively in the helping relationship, the social worker must first establish a trusting and safe environment with the client. This will lower the client's defensiveness and reduce the client's anxiety and feelings of being "attacked." Therefore, it is important that the social worker has developed a strong therapeutic relationship with the client before using confrontation. Confrontation is a skill that should be used sparingly and with a great deal of support from the social worker. This skill helps clients address issues that they may have been avoiding. A confrontation is also helpful in identifying the reality of a situation, versus the client's perception (Hepworth, et al., 2002).

As the social worker, always remember that your life experiences can affect your reaction to clients and their circumstances (Hill & O'Brien, 2004). Be sure to keep your values, personal standards, and beliefs out of the helping relationship. Monitor your reactions to clients. If you find yourself getting angry (or abrasive) with the client, it is important to process this response, and what it might mean, with your supervisor.

Small confrontations over a period of time may work best with some clients. These individuals may need more time to absorb the reality of what the confrontation may mean in the long term. Think of these lesser confrontations as chipping away at the client's protective shell, bit by bit. Often a client may be scared or ambivalent about confronting issues that have contributed to long-standing patterns or ways of doing something. Understanding a client's reluctance to immediately change, and to do or think about something in a different way is unrealistic. Change takes time and occurs over a period of time. For many clients this is the decision point, "Do I use these new insights to make changes or remain stuck with the status quo?"

Box 6.10 Diane

Diane is a 45-year-old married female who is the mother of three teenage sons. Recently, her 75-year-old father, who has been diagnosed with Alzheimer's Disease, has come to live with the family following his wife's death.

Diane: Dad can be so demanding of my time and energy. I know this is related to the Alzheimer's, but...

Social Worker: You can end up feeling very overwhelmed. (reflection of feeling)

Diane: Yeah, especially when I get so little help from my husband and kids. They all head off to their activities, leaving me alone with Dad. Then Dad starts to wander out of the house while I'm getting dinner ready. I can't just let him wander off, so I have to lock him in his room.

Social Worker: I hear the frustration you're experiencing. (reflection of feeling) However, locking your father in his room is not okay. It's illegal, and it could be very dangerous. (confrontation)

Diane: I know you're right, but I don't know any other way to keep him safe.

Social Worker: I understand the dilemma—caring for your dad, your husband, and your children leaves you feeling exhausted and depleted. (summarization)

In this example, the social worker confronts Elaine about the treatment of her father. She points out the problems related to leaving him locked in his room. She also conveys understanding of the frustrations associated with caring for an elderly disoriented parent. Because Elaine feels understood, she is more likely to acknowledge the dangers involved in her choice. The next step in the helping process will involve discussions between the social worker and Elaine on how to improve her father's care and maintain a balance in her life.

Confrontation should be used with professional discretion and always with the best interest of the client in mind. Consider asking for the client's reaction to the confrontation. Remember to attend to the client's reaction (both the verbal and nonverbal) to the confrontation by offering a paraphrasing, reflection of feeling, or summarization response.

Leave enough time after offering a confrontation for the client to talk about it and learn from it. When clients come to a new insight, awareness, or realization, using the skill of interpretation (see next section) may be helpful in beginning to explore the rationale behind the action, thought, behavior, or belief. (Hill & O'Brien, 2004). See Box 6.11 for an example of confrontation.

Box 6.11 Melvin

Melvin is a 55-year-old male. He has been married three times. He has two children from his first marriage but has very little contact with them.

Social Worker: You have talked about how much you love your children. I can see in your face and hear in your voice, your pride in them. (reflection of feeling)

Melvin: I do love them, but it is too late to try and get things back on track. Too much time has passed. They are teenagers now and don't need me for anything but money. Those are the only calls I get these days.

Social Worker: I hear what you are saying, but do you want to give up? You seem to be very disappointed and hurt by the way things have worked out. You are blaming yourself and you certainly are a part of this relationship too. (lead-in/closed ended question/reflection of feeling/paraphrase)

Melvin: Yeah, my ex-wife is on me a lot. She wants me to call the kids, send cards, you know that kind of stuff, but after so many years of not really seeing them, it feels forced.

Social Worker: Can you continue to let things go as are or maybe try a new way of approaching them? (closed-ended question)

Melvin: I don't think I can handle their rejection—what if they really want nothing to do with me?

Social Worker: Melvin, they really may want nothing to do with you, but you are the parent. You make it seems as if it *their* responsibility to make things better. If you don't take some responsibility for contacting them and keeping in touch, it is possible that too much distance will develop between you and the girls. If that happens, you may find yourself cut out of their lives completely. . (summarization/confrontation/information giving)

Melvin: How do I do it? It is so hard to admit that I have screwed up, but I know I have. Plus, their mom doesn't help much…she tells them I am a bad parent and not to count on me for anything.

Social Worker: This is a very difficult for you. I can see the sadness in your face. Let's talk about how you see yourself as their father and what you want to do to make things better. (reflection of feeling/open-ended question)

In this example, the social worker is helpful in moving Melvin toward a possible reconciliation with his children. She points out some of the conflicts he is experiencing. By attending to his feeling of despair and sadness, she slowly moves toward assisting him in possibly reaching out to his children

Always consider the individuality of your client. Although not specifically related to the skill confrontation, be cautious with clients who have a long history of disorderly conduct and aggressive behavior. These clients may need to be confronted in a more careful way, sometimes direct and forceful, other times providing reassurance and speaking in a gentle and soothing manner. Demonstrate empathy and understanding of their frustration and anger. Be sure to pay attention to the client's nonverbal behaviors and reactions as well. Intervening with a potentially violent or aggressive client will require that the social worker be alert to indicators of escalating behaviors such as the presence of firearms, being under the influence of alcohol, or membership in a violent peer group. In a dangerous situation, your safety comes first. Trust your gut feeling. Be aware of escape routes and office procedures that outline emergency responses to volatile situations. When making home visits always inform your agency of your whereabouts. (Sheafor, & Horejsi, 2003).

In the examples presented in the CD-ROM, three different types of confrontations were delivered by the social worker. See Box 6.12.

Box 6.12 Case Examples

James the social worker, confronts Anthony very firmly, by commenting on his 'yes, but' approach to life. He challenges Anthony to consider his attitude about his future. Through this confrontation, Anthony may be more willing to confront himself and make better choices regarding his gang activities.

Karen, the social worker challenges Mike a in a very straightforward and direct manner. She presses him firmly to acknowledge his behaviors (drinking, being hung over, missing work) and how they conflict with his statement, "I haven't missed a day in six years." She doesn't let him 'off the hook,' and reluctantly, he does acknowledge the discrepancy.

Nicole the social worker very gently confronts Mrs. Anderson. She addresses the issue of unsupervised and unauthorized visits between Maria and Crystal and the possible consequences. Nicole is clear in her confrontation, but does so in a soft and quiet way.

As with every interaction, be mindful of the cultural context of the client's life. See Chapter 4 for more information on this topic.

Interpretation

Interpretation is a skill that the social worker employs to go beyond the client's stated problem to find deeper meaning. This is a process of getting to underlying issues associated with the problem. (Cormier & Cormier, 1998). By definition, this skill can call upon both the social worker and client to be introspective. Given the level of discomfort or vulnerability a client might experience as you begin to "peel away the layers of the onion," be sure there is a well-established relationship of trust and good will. Otherwise, the client may become self-protective and annoyed. Remember, not all clients have the capacity to, or interest in, interpreting their behaviors, actions, and intentions. Some clients are more interested in behavioral changes, where the results are more immediate. However, it is often the case that behavioral change is dependent on the client developing a deeper understanding of the situation.

Interpretations can point out the causal connection between repeated behaviors, feelings, and thoughts. In this case, the light goes on and clients may see their way clear to change long-standing patterns. These insights may be enough to motivate the client toward significant change as they reevaluate their goals. Focusing on the client's strengths and potential is also an important part of using this skill. For example, what does the client see as personal and professional assets? How can those characteristics be used to make changes?

Frequently, clients are emotionally attached to a problem, and their judgment is clouded. Consequently, they have difficulty seeing a way out of the situation. Interpretation allows clients to see the problem in a new light, which can give them hope that change is indeed possible; however clients may need time to absorb new ways of looking at the issue or situation. Timing is critical—always consider whether the client is ready for a deeper understanding. If not, the client will most likely reject the interpretation. When offering an interpretation, it should relate closely to the client's experiences and reality. For example, your client has a long history of being passive and submissive in her marital relationship. She reports that her husband wants a divorce. She states that she will need to talk to her teenage children about this, as she doesn't want to make any decisions on her own. You see the connection between her passiveness as a spouse and in her role as a parent. Given the current crisis, consider whether the timing is right to identify this pattern and process its meaning and impact on her life or to wait until the crisis has been resolved and then explore these issues in retrospect. As with any social work interviewing skill, consider both the impact of using a particular skill in the moment and over the long term.

Good interpretations are based on data. A lofty interpretation may make the social worker sound like an intelligent and gifted professional, but at the same time, the interpretation may make the client feel "psychoanalyzed." Be sure to offer an interpretation that is fairly short so as to not lecture the client (Hepworth et al., 2002).

Box 6.13 demonstrates the social worker interpreting the probable underlying message of a client.

Box 6.13 Pamela

Pamela is a 45-year-old female who is experiencing multiple problems. Today she is discussing her boss. This is her third session with the Employee Assistance Program (EAP) social worker.

Pamela: I hate this guy. He's always looking over my shoulder on the assembly line. So what I do is show up late, I take a few minutes more for lunch. That really gets to him. (said with a smile)

Social Worker: So, you do things that you know will irritate your boss. (paraphrasing)

Pamela: Yeah, I mean he never has a kind word to say, he's never given me a raise, he finds fault with everything I do.

Social Worker: You seem to have figured out how to make things uncomfortable for yourself at work. (paraphrasing)

Pamela: Yeah, but it is kinda fun to piss him off. Once he is mad, he loses his train of thought and gets all red in the face. I kinda like seeing him pissed.

Social Worker: I wonder what causes you to find ways to make people mad at you in your life. For instance, you said that you and your husband fight a lot too. Could it be that you find it hard to be close to people? Given the way your dad treated you, being criticized and yelled at is what you are used to. Setting up a conflict between you and others in your life is something you know how to do very well. (lead-in response/interpretation-said very softly and carefully)

Pamela: Yeah, I hadn't really thought about it that way before. I have been getting into fights with people my whole life. That is pretty much how I am with everyone. Pretty messed up, huh?

Pamela reports that she purposefully behaves in ways that make her boss angry. The social worker focuses on the underlying issue—not feeling valued as a child growing up, as an employee, and as a spouse. This new insight can help Pamela address her own responsibility and hopefully bring about change in her work and home situation.

Offering an interpretation is a delicate process. The social worker offers a tentative statement and then gauges the client's reaction to find out whether the interpretation was helpful: for example, "I wonder if it could be...," or "Could it possibly relate to...." (Cormier & Cormier, 1998). It is important to note that the client may accept or reject the social worker's interpretation. Also, by responding to the actual client message, the social worker is less likely to impose a personal bias. The client may offer his or her own interpretation if the one offered by the social worker doesn't fit. Success in using this skill is very dependent on the length, timing, and quality of the social worker-client relationship. Interpretation is most beneficial when the social worker and the client have a good rapport, and the client appears ready to explore underlying issues related to the problem (Kadushin & Kadushin, 1997). Asking the client for their interpretation of "why they do what they do" may be a good way to assist them in coming to their own conclusions. This approach also is consistent with empowerment and self-efficacy. Conversely, the client may want your interpretation and ask, "Why do I do what I do?"

As the social worker offers an interpretation, he or she should be alert to the client's verbal and nonverbal responses. Interpretation can stimulate a variety of feelings in the client. If the social worker feels that the client needs additional support to deal with the new insight, then interpretation should be paired with paraphrase, reflection of feeling or summarization (Hepworth, Rooney & Larsen, 2002). Box 6.14 provides some examples of possible social worker responses to a client's reaction of the interpretation.

Box 6.14 Possible Social Worker Responses Following an Interpretation

"I can tell that you are uncomfortable with what I just asked…"

"It makes sense that you had a strong reaction to what I just said, let's talk about that…."

"You seem to understand the consequences of the situation. Your tears say it all. Let's focus on your sadness….."

"What caused you to response so strongly to that?"

"Your feeling are very understandable, it is hard to face this alone…"

"There is a lot of stress and pressure on you right now, I can see the tension in your face, what is your reaction….?"

ATTENDING BEHAVIORS

Social workers must be verbally and nonverbally responsive to clients. One way that a social worker conveys interest is through the use of words and another way is through nonverbal communication. It is important for the client to feel listened to and valued. If clients sense a genuine interest on the social worker's part, they will be more open (Kadushin & Kadushin, 1997). As a social worker is it your responsibility to become sensitive to cultural variations and patterns of communication and in doing so acknowledge and respect your client's uniqueness (Hackney and Cormier, 2001). (See Chapter 4 for more information regarding cross cultural counseling.) The social presence, being fully there and available, is instrumental in the establishment and further development of the relationship. Another way for a client to feel attended to is for the social worker to be on time for sessions, remembering details from previous meetings, and following through on promises made. These actions on the part of the social worker convey interest and concern and become valuable assets to the relationship (Shebib, 2003).

When considering the location of an interview, whether it is in your office, in the client's kitchen or at the park, minimizing environmental distractions is also a part of attending. Be sure that your space is private to ensure client confidentiality. For example, in a client's home, it may be appropriate to sit away from the television (if it is on), in a corner of a room or in a room where you can have some privacy. In your office, having the telephone calls diverted to voice messages or the receptionist can provide uninterrupted time with your client. If you share an office, a Do Not Disturb sign can indicate that you are in session with a client. In a public place, find a remote spot for a private conversation.

There are several ways that the social worker can communicate concern, caring, and involvement with the client nonverbally. Tone of voice, eye contact, body positioning, head movements, a warm smile, furthering responses, and mirroring the client's emotional/facial responses are all components of this skill known as 'attending behavior' (Cormier & Cormier, 1998). Body positioning, what we communicate through hand gestures, leaning in and facing our clients, and maintaining a relaxed and approachable stance are all important ways of conveying "I'm here with you, you have my undivided attention." You are conveying, "I am following your pace or lead and I am listening."

Seating arrangements will be dependent on the setting of the interview. If visiting a client's home, wait for the client to indicate where to sit. In an office, it is best to place the chairs about three to four feet apart. This distance appears to be the least anxiety-provoking for the client (Cormier & Cormier, 1998). Always be aware of the client's need for personal space and be respectful of this need by allowing the client to determine the most comfortable distance. Should three to four feet not be enough or too much, allow the client to adjust accordingly. This is of particular concern when working with clients from different cultural backgrounds. For example, if the client pulls the chair too close, invading your personal space, either subtly move back your chair or tactfully ask the client to move back a bit. Most importantly, find yourself a comfortable sitting position and relax!

Touch is also a part of how a social worker uses his or her body to convey interest. Touch can be perceived as positive or negative, depending on the type of touch and the context in which it occurs (Cormier & Cormier, 1998). Always be aware of the client's cultural background and past experiences (i.e., having been sexually abused as a child), and gender-related issues (i.e., could the touch be interpreted by the client as a sexual overture?). Used correctly, touch can be a very potent, nonverbal way of communicating "I care, I'm listening, and I'm concerned." A nonthreatening way to attend to a client who is crying is to offer a tissue, thus attending to the need without actual touch. You can also ask the client if it is all right to touch them.

Maintaining eye contact with the client conveys understanding and responsiveness (Kadushin & Kadushin, 1997). This is not the same as staring or glaring at a client, which can cause extreme discomfort. Eye contact on the part of the client and/or social worker can demonstrate a readiness to get down to "business" and delve into the problem situation.

Tone of voice is another aspect of attending behavior. It is not just the spoken words, but also the way the words are delivered (Cormier & Cormier, 1998). Tone of voice adds color and richness to the message. Being verbally expressive, the social worker can mirror or match the client's feelings. Box 6.15 provides an example:

Box 6.15 Tone of Voice

Social Worker: You sound really sad (said in a quiet, soft tone).

Client: I am very depressed, I've never felt worse in my life.

Social Worker: It's understandable; you are still in mourning over your son's death (said with an intonation of sadness).

Here the social worker matches the tone of voice to the words chosen. The client thus experiences the social worker's concern at many levels. Be sure to speak clearly, not too loudly (or softly) and vary your tone and pitch. Pace your speech, questions and responses in a way that conveys interest not boredom.

Using silence appropriately in the social work interview can be a very effective way to communicate. There may be some anxieties about silence in an interview. For instance as the social worker, you assume you are not doing an adequate job; therefore we might jump in too quickly and try to fill in the gaps or "rescue" the client. For example, a client might be very quiet and withdrawn. In order to keep the conversation flowing, the social worker continues to ask a series of questions or moves to a topic that might be less emotionally challenging for the client. In this case, the social worker jumps in and directs the interview, which is what the client may have wanted all along. Resist the urge to fill every silence with a question or response. Conversely, if the silence continues and the client is becoming uncomfortable (squirming in their seat, looking to you directly for assistance), interrupting the silence can be useful. In this instance, the social worker may comment on the possible meaning of the silence: "You seem to be struggling with this issue, I am sensing you need to slow down the pace," or by asking an appropriate question: "You are so quiet, I wonder if part of your silence relates to all the struggles you feel inside?"

According to Shebib, 2003, there are six types of silence.

- Thinking—client needs time to process information and respond
- Confused and unsure about what to say or do—client doesn't know what is expected and therefore may become anxious. Here the social worker may need to interrupt the silence and clarify the question, expectation or direction.
- Encountering painful feelings—client needs space to feel and experience pain and anxiety
- Dealing with issues of trust—client is reluctant and self-protective, may be involuntary
- Quiet by nature—client is quiet by nature and prefers other ways of communicating for example through art or a journal
- Reached closure on a particular point—client has nothing more to say on the topic or idea.

In each of these instances the social worker will respond differently to the meaning of the client's silence. For example, the involuntary client who is dealing with issues of trust uses silence as a way to control the interview and demonstrate hostility (Shebib, 2003). The client who is quiet by nature and is not used to giving lengthy explanation, may be more comfortable sitting with thoughts rather than giving a spontaneous response.

Generally speaking, the best approach to silence is not to be intimidated by it or intolerant of it, but to understand and embrace the silence as an appropriate attending behavior. Wait with patience, take a deep breath, drink a sip of water, but remain relaxed and attentive. As you develop your ability to use this skill, you will find that silence is an asset to the relationship. Being able to sit quietly, waiting to see what happens next, what new revelation will emerge is worth the wait.

Furthering responses offered by the social worker are another way of conveying understanding. Furthering responses can be used to highlight a particular word (e.g., Client: I doubt he'll ever forgive me! Social worker: Forgive you?). Hand gestures or nodding of the head are other ways of nonverbally communicating that the social worker is listening and for the client to continue.

Single word utterances, such as "hmmm" "uh-huh," "um," and "go on" also convey an interest in the client and serve as inducements for the client to proceed. Furthering responses provide noninvasive support and a way to monitor the flow of the interview (Hill & O'Brien, 2004).

The following example illustrates the use of this attending behavior.

Box 6.16 Franny

Franny is in her mid-70s. She is living on a very limited budget. She is concerned about her daughter's financial demands.

Client: My daughter refuses to discuss her finances with me, but she insists she has no money and needs a loan.

Social Worker: A loan? (clarification)

Client: A loan, for something, but she won't tell me what. That leaves me thinking the worst, like she owes money to some bad guys.

Social Worker: And... (furthering response)

Client: It scares me to death. I don't want anyone coming after her or me.

Social Worker: That is unsettling. (paraphrasing) What do you think is going on with her? (open-ended question)

Client: I don't know, but she always ends up in some kind of trouble, with me bailing her out.

Social Worker: hmmmm (furthering response)

Client: I know she counts on me to help her and I usually do, but I won't lend her money unless she tells me what it is for. I can't keep doing this. It's tearing me up inside.

Social Worker: silence (10-15 seconds—a furthering response strategy)

Client: You know I really feel angry about this whole thing. She uses me and doesn't give it a second thought. She feels justified and entitled to anything I have. I think I am doing something wrong...so many people in my life treat me this way. She is my daughter so I make excuses for her. But as much as I hate to admit it, it isn't just her. (self-confrontation on the client's part)

Social Worker: You see a pattern; people take advantage of your good nature and you end up feeling used. (summarization) Can you describe some other situations when you have felt this way? (open-ended question)

Through reflection of feeling statements, paraphrasing, summarization and furthering responses social workers convey to clients an understanding of their experiences.

Social workers can also do this nonverbally by using facial expressions to mirror back to the client awareness of the client's emotional state. If a client is talking about the great time she had at the high school dance and excitedly describes this new experience, it is appropriate for the social worker to smile with pleasure. Conversely, if a client is discussing how lonely and out of place she felt at the school dance, the social worker's face should mirror back a sense of sadness and disappointment (but not pity). The social worker's facial expressions should reinforce the verbal communication (i.e., saying, "I'm interested in hearing your side of the story" and looking interested in the client, not looking bored or distracted). This nonverbal display of interest can speak volumes to the client and serve as a reinforcement to continue.

In addition, it is also imperative for the social worker to attend to the incongruence of the client's words and facial expressions (i.e., the client saying, "I feel great" as tears stream down her face). Using this example, the social worker can respond to "the tears versus the words" by saying "Although you say you feel great, your tears tell me something different. I'd like to talk about the sadness you're experiencing right now."

The social worker's head movements can also offer nonverbal feedback to the client as a way of encouraging or discouraging the client from further discussion. Head nodding up and down offers a sense that the social worker is listening and agreeing. Because the client feels understood, the communication is likely to continue. Shaking of the head from left to right may convey that the social worker disagrees or disapproves, causing the communication to stop or be severely limited. Be careful not to over nod your head, as it may be a distraction for your client.

INTEGRATING SOCIAL WORK SKILLS AND ATTENDING BEHAVIOR

Interviewing skills work best when used in combination with one another. The social work interview becomes richer and deeper in meaning when skills are used in tandem. The following example illustrates the use of several skills used together.

Box 6.17 Lois

Lois is a 57-year-old female. Her daughter Mary ran away several months ago. There has been no word from Mary since she left home.

Social Worker: You said the days just drag on and on as you waited for a phone call about your daughter Mary. (paraphrase) How do you manage to get through the day? (open-ended question)

Lois: I try to keep myself busy. Since she ran away I haven't been able to sleep much. I wake up because I have these terrible nightmares. My husband acts as if none of this is happening.

Social Worker: That must make it seem even more painful for you, like you're in this alone. (reflection of feeling; the social worker leans toward the client, pauses and maintains eye contact) What is your relationship with him like right now? (open-ended question)

Lois: Very distant. I can't talk to him; he doesn't want to hear it now. I think it is too painful for him, but as usual, he says it is all me. I want her to come home. I can't stop thinking about her. He is no support at all. I wish he had left, not Mary.

Social Worker: You are very concerned about your daughter and what is going on with her and at the same time you feel regret. Do you think you are responsible for her running away? (Summarization and closed-ended question?)

Lois: Yes, she left home because of all the yelling and screaming. Mary was into drugs. Getting high all the time, skipping school, basically ruining her life. She refused to listen to me, her dad just tuned us both out. He was not home much, but when he was, it did get ugly.

Social Worker: What do you mean by ugly? (clarification)

Lois: He yelled all the time. He came home drunk almost every night. He is in no position to judge her behavior, he is a lousy drunk.

Social Worker: You sound really angry at him. I am wondering, do you blame him for Mary leaving? (reflection of feeling and interpretation)

Box 6.17 Lois, *continued*

Lois: I mostly blame myself. I saw this coming. I didn't want to leave him, but now I think I should have. Here I am without my daughter, not knowing if she is dead or alive. (Client is crying)

Social Worker: (The social worker remains silent for approximately one minute, then says "This is so painful for you." (more silence, leaning in, handing the client a tissue)

Lois: (The client is still crying) "I haven't cried about this in a long time"

Social Worker: I am here, it is okay (direct eye contact, offering assurance and information giving and more silence)

CONCLUSION

Establishing and maintaining a helping relationship is critical to planned change. It involves putting your client's needs and interests at the forefront. It means fully listening, comprehending and incorporating their life situation and experiences into your frame of reference. It means not being preoccupied by your own biases, values, internal voice or distractions. This "tuning in" (or attending to) is an essential ingredient to the helping relationship. Without this level of commitment, focus, and concentration the helping relationship cannot evolve and move forward.

Remember, when social work skills are first used by the beginning social worker, they can seem mechanical. With time and practice, they will become almost second nature. Keep in mind, though, that even the most experienced social workers benefit from an ongoing commitment to improve their interviewing skills. Through contact with other social workers, membership in professional organizations such as NASW, and most importantly, the development of the habit of self-evaluation, you are well on your way to becoming a skilled professional.

REFERENCES

Boyle, S., Hull, G., Mather, J., Smith, L., Farley, O. W. (2006). *Direct practice in social work.* Boston, MA: Allyn & Bacon.

Brems, C. (2001). *Basic skills in psychotherapy and counseling.* Pacific Grove, CA: Brooks/Cole.

Cormier, W. & Cormier, S. (1998). *Interviewing strategies for helpers* (4th ed.) Pacific Grove, CA: Brooks/Cole.

Egan, G. (2002). *The skilled helper* (7th ed.) Pacific Grove, CA: Brooks/Cole.

Gambrill, E. (1997). *Social work practice: A critical thinker's guide.* New York: Oxford.

Hackney, H.L., & Cormier, L.S. (2001). *The professional counselor.* Boston, MA: Allyn & Bacon.

Hepworth, D., Rooney, R., & Larsen, J. (2002). *Direct social work practice: Theory and skills* (6th ed.) Pacific Grove, CA: Brooks/Cole.

Hill, C.E., & O'Brien, K.M. (2004). *Helping skills: Facilitating exploration, insight and action* (2nd ed.) Washington, DC: American Psychological Association.

Ivey, A.E. & Ivey, M.B. (2002). *Intentional interviewing and counseling.* Pacific Grove, CA: Brooks/Cole.

Kadushin, A. & Kadushin, G. (1997). *The social work interview* (4th ed.) New York: Columbia University Press.

Kottler, J.A. (2000). *Nuts and bolts of helping.* Boston, MA: Allyn & Bacon.

Murphy, B.C. & Dillon, C. (2003). *Interviewing in action: Process and practice.* Pacific Grove, CA: Brook/Cole.

Paniagua, F.A. (1998) *Assessing and treating culturally diverse clients: A practical guide.* (2nd ed.) Thousand Oaks, CA: Sage Publications.

Ragg, D.M. (2001). *Building effective helping skills: The foundation of generalist practice.* Boston, MA: Allyn & Bacon.

Sheafor, B.W. & Horejsi, C.R. (2003). *Techniques and guidelines for social work practice* (5th ed.) Boston, MA: Allyn & Bacon

Shebib, B. (2003). *Choices: Counseling skills for social workers and other professionals.* Boston, MA: Allyn & Bacon.

Sue, S. & Sue, D. (1990). *Counseling the culturally different* (2nd ed.). New York: John Wiley & Sons.

CHAPTER SEVEN

Pitfalls

DETECTING MISTAKES

Knowing how and when to correctly use social work interviewing skills provides the foundation for the helping relationship. Developing the competence to utilize the skills is a learned process. Skills are not used in isolation, but in conjunction with each other as a way to further deepen and expand the relationship. Social workers strive to ask the "perfect" open-ended question, or deliver the "perfect" paraphrase. Even the most skilled professionals make mistakes. The goal of this chapter is to provide an explanation of common mistakes, or pitfalls, made by beginning social workers and the negative consequences that may result. Being aware of the pitfalls, or "what not to do," can help the social worker avoid potential problems that could damage or abruptly end the helping relationship. When a client reacts (verbally or nonverbally) with embarrassment, anger, or silence, the social worker may have fallen into one of the common interviewing pitfalls.

If you find yourself making a mistake by inadvertently stumbling into a pitfall, you can recover and continue with the interview. For example, if you ask an inappropriate question and realize that you have done so, refocus the interview by posing a question that relates more to the topic at hand. You may want to acknowledge that the question was "off-base" before trying again. Should you respond judgmentally, you will probably be able to tell by the client's verbal and nonverbal reaction. In that case, use an empathy statement such as, "I can tell from your reaction that I have said something that has caused you to feel judged or evaluated—that was not my intent and I am sorry. What I meant to say was…"

In Box 7.1, the social worker uses the pitfall of false assurance and then recovers from the mistake by acknowledging her error and moving forward with the interview.

Mrs. Betsy Kern is a 70-year-old female. She was in a car accident several months ago. She suffers from constant pain as a result of the accident. She was driving at the time and her good friend Hazel was injured too.

Social Worker: You look tired today Mrs. Kern. (social worker is attending to her nonverbal cues)

Mrs. Kern: I can't sleep. I keep having flashbacks from the accident. I don't think I will ever be able to drive again.

Social Worker Pitfall: Oh I am sure once your injuries have healed you will be ready to get out there and drive again. (false assurance)

Mrs. Kern: Oh honey, just the thought of getting behind the wheel makes me sick. I get so nervous even riding in a car now. I worry that I won't ever feel like myself again. (said with tears in her eyes)

Social Worker Recovery Response: Mrs. Kern, I didn't mean to suggest that it would be easy for you, just to say that maybe things will feel better for you eventually. I am sorry if I made it sound like no big deal. You have been through a lot. What has been going on since the accident? (corrected response and open-ended question)

Mrs. Kern: It has been so hard for me. I am in a lot of pain too. I can't ever get comfortable and if I see anything moving fast towards me, I get panicky. In fact the other day......

In this example, the social worker quickly realizes that Mrs. Kern is having more difficulty with the situation than she had initially understood. In the social worker's effort to provide a sense of hope, she inadvertently minimized Mrs. Kern's feelings and experiences related to the accident. Once she attends to Mrs. Kern's response, she corrects the mistake and in a more appropriate and sensitive way continues with the interview.

THE PITFALLS

Advice Giving

Social workers should not tell the client what to do to solve the problem. It is vital to the helping process that the client be an active participant in the therapeutic relationship. The ethic of self-determination is critical because the purpose of the social work relationship is to empower the client to make decisions that will improve his or her own life (Kadushin & Kadushin, 1997). The client will ultimately live with the consequences of decisions, weighing the costs and benefits of each decision that is made. If a social worker does offer advice, it should focus on the means or ways toward problem resolution. Social workers should not give advice regarding the ends or major life decisions that clients have to make for themselves. Once a client has made a decision that involves the end point or goal, giving advice about how to reach the goal can be very helpful and instructive. Box 7.2 illustrates this distinction.

Box 7.2 Example 1 of Pitfall 'Advice Giving'

Mr. Tim Randall is a 63-year-old high-school English teacher. He is considering retiring within the next few years. One of his concerns is a sense of being a "has been." He worries that he will have too much idle time on his hands and will miss interacting with students and fellow teachers.

Mr. Randall: I have taught for over 30 years. Same subject, basically the same students, year after year. I guess that I am bored with teaching.

Social Worker: What do you see yourself doing if you do retire? (open-ended question)

Mr. Randall: I don't know. I don't know what I want to do with my life; I just know that teaching is not as interesting or challenging to me anymore. I have a hard time getting myself to work everyday. My best teaching years are behind me.

Social Worker Pitfall: I would retire. You've put in a lot of good years. Use your pension money to travel (advice giving)

Correct Social Worker Response: What does seem to interest you? (open-ended question)

Mr. Randall: I like to travel, but I am alone.

Social Worker: So as you see it, retiring means lots of quiet and unoccupied time, but it doesn't have to be that way. If you decide to retire, there are ways to fill some of the voids. (paraphrase and information giving)

In this example the social worker is telling the client what she thinks he should do, which is counter to client self-determination. Should the client decide to retire, the social worker can then provide information about retirement options. This type of advice can help to broaden Mr. Randall's life choices, many of which he may not even know exist.

If the social worker is too quick to give advice, the client may never learn the art of problem solving, self-responsibility and making well-informed decisions. Developing a sense of independence and autonomy is very important because the social worker's involvement is time limited. The lifelong skill of problem solving will always serve clients well.

It is the social worker's role to help clients discover options for probable solutions and together agree on a realistic direction. The social worker helps clients evaluate past decisions and how they have affected their life circumstances in positive or negative ways. The focus is on helping the client examine the current situation from a clear perspective. The social worker can usurp this right by jumping in and advising because of self-imposed pressure to fix the problem (Hill, & O'Brien, 2004). Social workers who are new to the field may have an inclination to give the client advice within the helping relationship, with the potential of establishing an unhealthy client dependence on the social worker (Hepworth, Rooney & Larsen, 2002). A "quick fix" to a problem that may stem from deep-rooted patterns of dysfunctional behavior will eventually reemerge if the origins of these behaviors are not thoroughly explored and resolved. For example, a gay client continues to meet men via the Internet. The social worker's advice to him might be, "Stop using the Internet to meet men, crazy people search the web looking to prey on vulnerable people." The underlying concern for this client may be lack of self-esteem, feeling unattractive and unlovable as well as a lack of opportunity to meet gay men. He may see Internet dating as a safe, accessible and less threatening way to meet people. By quickly dispensing advice, the social worker may have cut off any discussion about issues related to his choice and the meaning he attaches to it. In addition, the social worker may be conveying a possible judgment about his sexual orientation.

In another example, Alicia is a divorced female who has been involved in a string of unhealthy relationships. She asks the social worker about her current relationship, wondering why her boyfriend is so verbally abusive and what she should do to remedy the problem. The social worker should refrain from offering her a prescription. Instead, the social worker should explore the nature of the relationship and the dynamics that are perpetuated not only by the boyfriend but also by Alicia. Once Alicia has developed some insight into this repeated pattern of unhealthy relationships, with the assistance of the social worker, she may be willing to commit energy into developing strategies to assess and determine what she wants and needs in a relationship.

In Box 7.3 the social worker is exhibiting the pitfall of advice giving.

Box 7.3 Example 2 of the Pitfall 'Advice Giving'

Amanda is a 25-year-old female who recently gave birth to twins. She also recently learned that her mother has cancer. She is talking to the social worker about her current stresses.

Amanda: I have six-month-old twins, a boy and a girl. They are as wonderful as can be, but I am tired all the time. I try to take good care of them, take care of the house and my husband. I am scheduled to go back to work full time next month. I really enjoy my job, but I don't know how I am going to manage. My mom, who had originally agreed to take care of them one or two days a week, was just diagnosed with cancer. So I have that to worry about too.

Social Worker: You do have a lot going on right now. What about waiting to go back to work until the twins are older and your mom is hopefully better? (advice giving)

Amanda: I can't do that, we need the money.

Social Worker Pitfall: But you will burn yourself out trying to take care of the twins and working a full time job. I think you should wait. You have managed on one income for six months; why not continue doing what you have been already doing? (advice giving)

Correct Social Worker Response: Amanda, it sounds like you are trying to take care of everything and everybody. Right now there is a lot to handle. What part of your situation do you want to tackle first? (paraphrase and open-ended question)

In the example in Box 7.3, the social worker is advising the client rather than helping her to explore options regarding her life stressors. Telling the client what she should do takes away any opportunity for the client to tap in to her internal and external resources.

Inappropriate Use of Humor

When a social worker uses humor inappropriately, the client can feel belittled, criticized or mocked. Humor or sarcasm should never be used at the client's expense (Hill & O'Brien, 2004). Clients may believe that you are minimizing the problem and not taking them seriously (Kadushin & Kadushin, 1997). Additionally, sarcasm may be misunderstood as rudeness or insensitivity by the client, creating a climate of mistrust in the social worker-client relationship. If the social worker makes an inappropriate comment it could deeply anger the client. The social worker may find humor in the client's situation, but the client may not have the same subjective perspective.

Inappropriate humor can also convey that the social worker is not empathic or sensitive to the client's point of view (Kadushin & Kadushin, 1997). For example, Maurice is a 45-year-old client who is frustrated because he has been unable to find a job. Cracking a joke about becoming homeless or begging on the streets is ill timed and insensitive. Maurice will assume that you are not taking his unemployment situation seriously and will feel foolish for coming to you in the first place.

The client may use humor to mask a problem. The social worker should be aware of this possibility and search for deeper meaning in the client's message (Hepworth, Rooney & Larsen 2002). Certainly humor has its place in any human relationship, and it can lighten the tension. Sometimes the best thing to do in a crisis is to diffuse some of the seriousness with lightness, to allow the sadness to be lifted with hope (Brems, 2001). Laughing and humor can also help the client see a situation in a different light. In a counseling relationship there may be humorous moments; however, it should never detract from the professional helping process. It is very common that the general gravity of what clients discuss in social service settings is quite serious and emotionally charged. Thus humor should be used with great discretion (Kadushin & Kadushin, 1997). Box 7.4 illustrates the social worker using the pitfall of inappropriate humor.

Box 7.4 Example of the Pitfall 'Inappropriate Humor'

Nick is a 19-year-old male discussing his disappointment in not getting a music scholarship. He has spent years of his life devoted to music and has great expectations for a musical career. Nick just learned that he did not get the scholarship he was counting on:

Nick: I am so upset about the way things turned out. I wanted to get that music scholarship to the university. Everyone kept reassuring me that I would get the scholarship and could finally leave home. I have always wanted to be a musician; even before I could walk I was banging on pots and pans in the kitchen. Drumming is my passion, my life. I am obsessed with percussion. Now what do I do???

Social Worker Pitfall: Well don't hit me on the head with those drum sticks!!!! (inappropriate humor)

Correct Social Worker Response: What a huge let down. You were really counting on the scholarship to the university. (reflection of feeling)

Nick: Yeah, I was. I'm sick of working for minimum wage at the bookstore. This is not how I see my life turning out.

Correct Social Worker Response, continued: Is your only option the music scholarship to the university? (closed ended question)

In the example in Box 7.4, the social worker makes fun of and belittles her client when she makes light of the client's disappointment by joking about her own safety! In the corrected response, the social worker appropriately acknowledges Nick's disappointment and then asks a closed ended question, are there other options?

Interrupting the Client and Abrupt Transitions

In the course of an interview, social workers ask many questions. The social worker who is attuned to the client is an active listener and aware of the verbal and nonverbal cues signifying that the client has not finished speaking. Too many interruptions may cause the client to lose his or her train of thought, or to feel that the social worker does not care about the problem. As a consequence, the focus of the interview tends to be more on the social worker than on the client's concerns. Inappropriate interruptions can be annoying and disruptive to the client, and may divert the client from exploring important areas and feelings (Hepworth et al., 2002). For example, Jamie is a 25-year-old drug addict. She begins to give the social worker details related to her drug history and usage. Before she is able to complete her statement, the social worker interrupts Jamie with a question about where she slept last night. In this case, the focus shifts from the client to the social worker. Jamie is likely to feel cut off and frustrated. It's possible that Jamie might have revealed important information about her situation, but the opportunity has been lost.

A well-paced interview includes taking turns speaking (Cormier & Cormier, 1998). Both the client and the social worker may need sufficient time to put together what it is they want to say, to ask, how to respond, etc. There may be some silences. However, unfilled space is preferred to cutting the client off. Silence can be an effective tool the social worker uses in helping the client realize what is being discussed (Kadushin & Kadushin, 1997). It also allows the social worker to make nonverbal observations of the client. (For more information about using silence in an interview, see Chapter 6)

Abrupt transitions or moving to a new topic very suddenly can leave the client feeling annoyed. Sometimes, the social worker may be uncomfortable with topics such as sex, death, religion, ethnicity and politics or disinterested with the subject matter and therefore steers the interview to another (possibly safer) topic. If the social worker disagrees with the client's views or opinions, rather than get involved in an uncomfortable exchange, the social worker might change the topic to something more compatible with his or her views. It is imperative that the social worker reflects on why he or she is moving away from these areas and to identify ways to increase the comfort level with such issues. For example, a client is discussing the recent death of his child. Because the social worker is uncertain how to proceed with such a difficult issue, he moves the client away from feelings about the child's death to how other family members are reacting. The topic is still relevant, but the focus has changed significantly. In this case, the abrupt transition is social worker driven, not client driven. Box 7.5 illustrates the social worker using the pitfalls, interruption and abrupt transition.

Box 7.5 Example of the Pitfalls 'Interrupting the client' and 'Abrupt transitions'

Linda is a 35-year-old female, talking about her desire to start a job-training program at the community college. She is seeking the social worker's help in locating possible child-care options (and funding) so that she can further her education and eventually secure a job.

Linda: My case manager told me to come and talk to you.

Social Worker Pitfall: About what? (interrupting the client)

Linda: Well…I want to start a job-training program, but I need child…

Social Worker Pitfall: How many children do you have? (interrupting the client)

Linda: Child care for my daughter, who is mentally…

Social Worker Pitfall: Yes, I see on this intake form you indicated that your daughter is mentally retarded. (interrupting the client)

Linda: Yes, she is.

Social Worker Pitfall: Oh…..well, let's talk about what it is like to be her parent, before we discuss childcare. (abrupt transition)

Correct Social Worker Response: So you need to think about a program that provides appropriate services and education for her too. (paraphrase)

In the example in Box 7.5, the client has come to the social worker for specific reasons, childcare and financial resources. The social worker is not listening to the client and interrupts as she shares her reason for coming. The social worker then abruptly shifts direction, away from the childcare issue to her daughter's mental retardation. This fits the social worker's agenda, but clearly avoids what the client has in mind. In the corrected response, the social worker acknowledges Linda's concerns.

Inappropriate and Irrelevant Questions

As social workers we are curious about our client's lives. We are interested in asking them questions about what makes them tick. However, be careful not to over question the client. Asking too many questions may make the interview seem more like an interrogation than a helping session (Egan, 2002). Use questions to get only needed information. While the social worker may be curious about the client's "back story," only questions that pertain to the helping process should be asked. Irrelevant questions do not produce new and helpful information. The social worker doesn't have the inherent right to all information about the client, only the information that is essential to the helping process.   Seeking information about the client that is not relevant to the presenting problem may feed the social worker's curiosity and interest, but is not in the client's best interest.   This is a misuse of the client/social worker relationship. In this instance, the social worker's "entertainment" or voyeuristic needs supersede the needs of the client. Asking questions unrelated to the problem can also cause a lack of focus in the session, leading the client to feel distracted and misunderstood.

Brems (2001) identifies several types of problematic questions:

- Leading/Suggestive—gives hidden (or not so hidden) advice disguised as a question.
  EXAMPLE:
  CL: "I want to be more independent and not count on men to rescue me."
  SW: "Given your interest in becoming more self sufficient, have you ever been to the home shows at the convention center?"
  In reality, the social worker is expecting the client to go to home shows.

- Assuming—gives the impression that the social worker is expecting a particular answer.
  EXAMPLE:
  CL: "I work day and night, I never having enough time with my family. And, if I am with them, I fall asleep."
  SW: "You really don't mean that you fall asleep, do you?"
  In reality, the social worker is telling the client how she thinks he should respond…this may cause the client to 'pretend' to agree

- Controlling or intrusive questions—Ignores the client's agenda and needs and instead focuses on the social worker's interests (or need to avoid), usually for some personal reason.
  EXAMPLE:
  SW: "I don't want to focus on your marital finances right now, please tell me more about your sexual practices."
  In reality, the social worker is meeting her own needs, her curiosity about the client's sex life versus the financial difficulties within the marriage. Or conversely, the social worker maybe comfortable talking about finances and steers clear of more intimate material.

- Tangential—stems from a lack of empathy, questions are off the mark and fail to get to the heart of the issue.
  EXAMPLE:
  CL: I wish everyone would leave me alone, I am tired of all this crap. I can't wait to get out of here. Life is miserable."
  SW: And where do you plan to go??"
  In reality, the social worker misses the most relevant issues, the client's feelings of frustration and hopelessness. Instead she focuses on tangential information that may be important at some point, but not at this time.

- **Pseudo questions**—disguised commands or directives when there is no choice.
  EXAMPLE:
  SW: "Do you want to begin now?"
  In reality, the social worker is not asking the client his or her preference, but is directing the client to begin.

- **Judgmental**—"why" questions may suggest disapproval and lead to the client feeling defensive.
  EXAMPLE:
  CL: "Yesterday the check-out lady at the drug store yelled at me again. This time in front of everyone in line. Like she thought I was shoplifting or something. I go there all the time and this is probably the 20ᵗʰ time she has done this to me. I was so embarrassed."
  SW: Why do you shop there then?"
  In reality, the social worker is judging the client's choices and excusing the inappropriate behavior on the clerk's part. The client likely feels as if she needs to explain or defend her reasons for shopping there. This type of question will not move the therapeutic relationship along.

- **Attacking**—these questions are demeaning and embarrassing and serve to shame the client.
  EXAMPLE:
  CL: "I left the party last night feeling really mad about the whole thing. My boyfriend wants me to get high with him, I just don't want to though. I think he's gonna break up with me if I don't start doing what he wants."
  SW: "Do you want to be a doormat for the rest of your life?"
  In reality, the social worker is degrading the client and causing her to feel ashamed. The social worker may be on to an issue that is important to address, but not in this mean-spirited way.

- **Stacking**—asking several questions at one time, leading the client to be confused about which question to respond to first. Stacking questions also convey uncertainty about the direction of the interview.
  EXAMPLE:
  CL: I want to go back to college next semester, but my grades are so bad, I doubt I will be readmitted. I really blew it and I am paying a high price. Everyone is giving me a hard time, but no one is harder on me than I am on myself."
  SW: What happened that caused you to flunk out of school? And what have you been doing this past semester? What are you doing to get your life together?"
  In reality, these questions are suitable to ask, given the situation, but the social worker's questions are confusing to the client. Stacked questions can also diffuse the significance of each question, as the client is considering one question only to be distracted by another (Hepworth et al., 2002).

- ***Shotgun***—a long series of closed ended questions that covers nothing in depth or breadth, leaving the client to feel bombarded.

  EXAMPLE:

  CL: *I stopped taking my medication about a month or so ago. It wasn't helping any more."*

  SW: *"Do you think that was such a good idea?"*

  CL: *"Well, I am not sure, but since I wasn't feeling too bad, I didn't see any reason to   keep taking it. Plus, it is very expensive and my insurance only covers about 50% of the cost."*

  SW: *"When exactly did you stop taking it?"*

  CL: *" My prescription ran out May 15. I feel fine."*

  SW: *"Do you know how serious the side effects can be when you abruptly stop taking your medicine?"*

  CL: *"But I feel fine, better than I did when I was taking my medication."*

  SW: *"What insurance do you have??"*

  CL: *"The state program."*

  SW: *"How long had you been on the medication before you stopped taking it??"*

  CL: *"I think 8 months or so."*

  <u>In reality,</u> the social worker is overwhelming the client with questions, none of which produce very helpful information. This exchange is an interrogation, and not productive at all.

Box 7.5 Example of the Pitfalls 'Irrelevant' and 'Inappropriate Questions'

Mrs. Frieda Goldberg is an elderly widow talking about her living situation. She discloses to the social worker that she has some fears about living alone, now that her husband has recently died:

Mrs. Goldberg: I am living alone now. My husband died two months ago. I like my apartment, but I don't care for my neighbors. They are very loud and have lots of late night parties. In fact I told the landlord about all the noise and she has talked to them a few times. I hate to cause problems, but I don't feel safe anymore in my apartment.

Social Worker Pitfall: How old are your neighbors? (irrelevant question)

Mrs. Goldberg: I don't know, they look pretty young, but these days everyone looks young to me.

Box 7.5 Example of the Pitfalls 'Irrelevant' and 'Inappropriate Questions', *continued*

Social Worker Pitfall: How old are you? (irrelevant question)

Mrs. Goldberg: 83, but what does that matter?

Correct Social Worker Response: I am sorry to hear about your husband's death. (Long pause) Now that you are living alone, you don't feel as safe as you did before. (lead in response/paraphrase)

Mrs. Goldberg: No I don't. The landlord keeps telling me to calm down, that the noise isn't all that loud.

Correct Social Worker Response continued: But that doesn't help when you are trying to sleep or get some rest. Being alone now is hard enough; it is even more difficult because you don't feel as if she is listening to your concerns. (Lead in response/reflection of feeling)

In the example in Box 7.5 the social worker misses some very important pieces of information by focusing on irrelevant questions. The client's loneliness, vulnerability and fears are ignored by the social worker. He is too busy asking questions that don't produce new information or attend to the client's concerns.

Judgmental Response

The client is coming to the social worker for help, not to be judged. Part of the social worker's role is to understand the client's problems. With that understanding, the social worker helps the client to find solution(s) to the problem. If the client perceives that he or she is being labeled or judged, a defensive response may occur that can delay or impede the development of trust between the client and the social worker. This could create further difficulties in the helping relationship because the client will not feel comfortable discussing personal information and may view the relationship as an adversarial one (Hepworth et al., 2002).

As a social worker, it is sometimes difficult to separate our personal feelings, values and beliefs from our professional values and obligations. Part of a social worker's professional development includes accepting clients who may have very different values, perspectives, and life styles. Respecting differences and not expecting clients to see the world in the same way as the social worker is a core social work value (NASW Code of Ethics, 1999). For example, Lisa is a 30-year-old female who recently came out to friends and family about her relationship with her partner Melody. Today, Lisa discloses that she is exploring the possibility of becoming pregnant through artificial insemination. The social worker responds negatively to her plan, stating, "It's one thing to be a lesbian, it's another to bring a child into this. Have you thought about how your child will be affected by your decision?" Lisa will likely react with disbelief, in part because up to this point the social worker has appeared supportive of her lifestyle. Now that the social worker's true feelings (judgments) have surfaced, Lisa is likely to respond defensively and with anger and therefore withdraw from the helping relationship.

Judgmental responses made by the social worker clearly violate the social work ethic of a nonjudgmental attitude and acceptance (Hepworth et al., 2002, NASW Code of Ethics, 1999). Judgmental responses carry with them the social worker's ethical, moral, personal, or political standards. The client may take into account the social worker's judgmental remarks when thinking of his or her own self-concept. Such remarks are detrimental to the entire helping process. Our job is to help our clients learn how to make and use good judgments about their life choices, but not to make judgments about the client.

Box 7.6 Example of the Pitfall 'Judgmental Response'

Marta is a 22-year-old single African American mother talking with a child welfare worker. She is struggling to manage the care of her three children, all under the age of five.

Marta: I have three kids, ages 2, 4 and 5. They are good kids, but sometimes I just lose it with them. My sister says I am a bad mom, but I think she is in my business. She is the one that called you about me. I told her to keep away, that I am okay, the kids are okay, but she thinks she is all high and mighty.

Social Worker: What do you see as the problems? (open-ended question)

Marta: Well, I am tired a lot; I have three kids running around all day. I try to calm my nerves, but I can't sometimes. Everybody is in my business. If she thinks I am such a bad mom, why doesn't she come and help me out?

Social Worker: Have you asked her for help? (closed-ended question)

Marta: No way, if I ask for help she will have all the reasons she needs to keep in my business.

Social Worker Pitfall: So, someone is offering help and you are too stubborn to accept it. Just because of your pride. What about the kids? I thought *you* people are supposed to care about helping each other. (judgmental response)

Correct Social Worker Response: I get the impression that it is hard for you to accept help and that you are worried she will be more involved in your life than you want her to be. Can you tell me what it is like here with your kids all day? (lead-in response/reflection of feeling/open-ended question)

In the example in Box 7.6, the social worker is conveying criticism and frustration with the client and her circumstances. The client will be reluctant to share any other information with the social worker, given her condescending attitude. The appropriate social worker response invites the client to elaborate on her life and the struggles she is experiencing.

Inappropriate Social Worker Self-Disclosure

Although the social worker and client may have much in common, the focus of the session should be on the client's concerns. When the social worker shares too much personal information, the client may assume that the social worker is a friend, not a professional (Murphy & Dillon, 2003). It is safe to say the client will be curious about you, what you think and believe. It is common for clients to ask personal questions (in part to relieve their own anxiety) in an effort to get to know the social worker better. This is a common response, as the client is sharing very personal information with the social worker. Should the situation arise, ask what motivates their interest and then decide if the information requested is something you want to share. When sharing personal information, be sure to gauge the client's verbal and nonverbal reactions.

Using self-disclosure appropriately takes time to learn, in part because there are *some* instances where self-disclosure is necessary and helpful. For example, sharing with a client that you too are a recovering alcoholic may help move the relationship forward as rapport is established. That sense of camaraderie, intimacy, trust, and shared understanding can be therapeutic. It is a good idea to tell the client upfront that there may be some times when you feel it is appropriate to share something about yourself, but do it only if it is useful to the client, and not to meet your own needs (Egan, 2002). Double-check your intentions by asking yourself, "Why am I sharing this information?" and "What do I hope to accomplish by disclosing this about myself?"

Box 7.7 offers some examples of appropriate kinds of information to disclose and modeled social worker responses.

Box 7.7 Appropriate Information to Disclose

Education and work (specialized training) related credentials:

Examples:
1. Social Worker Response: "I am an undergraduate student at the University. I am doing my internship at the Office on Aging. I have been here a few months and really like what I am doing."

2. Social Worker Response: "I have an undergraduate degree in social work from the University, and three years of work experience with the state child welfare agency. Most of my clients are kids who are living in foster care right now."

3. Social Worker Response: I am an intern in the social work program at the university. I don't have a lot of experience yet, but I am here to help and also learn from you. Do you have any questions for me?

Disclosure of feelings about a particular issue in an effort to model feelings for clients:

Examples:
1. Social Worker Response: "I feel passionate about kids and what happens to them. I take my responsibilities very seriously. I am not here to judge you, I am here to try and help make things better for everyone involved."

2. Social Worker Response: "I am married and I have two children. I can relate to how hard it is to find the balance between taking care of them and their needs and trying to find time for my marriage too. I would like to know more about your family and the issues that are of most concern for you."

Disclosure of feelings in an effort to normalize the experiences:

Examples:
1. Social Worker Response: "Many people struggle with depression and sadness, particularly after experiencing a traumatic event. What you are feeling is normal."

2. Social Worker Response: "In my life there have been times when it has been difficult for me to go with the flow too. But, I think it is unrealistic to expect everyone around you to pick up the pieces, especially after such an unexpected event. It makes sense that people are being cautious and careful."

Source: Hill & O'Brien (2004)

As you share information about yourself, you are modeling what is appropriate to talk about and ways to do it (Egan, 2002). The client has the opportunity to learn by your example. This type of self-disclosure communicates commonalities and shared perspectives. If you do share something personal about yourself, be sure your disclosure is short and to the point, and that you immediately return the focus to the client. For example, Daniel is a 50-year-old Jewish scholar who has been in counseling for three months. His presenting problems focus on his relationship with his wife, Marian. In an effort to convey commonalities, the social worker discloses that she converted from Judaism to Catholicism in order to marry her husband. This self-disclosure has the potential to harm the helping relationship. Given Daniel's strong faith and religious background, he may have a difficult time separating his feelings related to her conversion. He now has information that may change his view of the social worker, causing him to be distracted from the problems related to *his* marriage.

This Box 7.8 offers a few points to consider as you think about the benefits and risks associated with social worker self-disclosure.

Box 7.8 Cautions about Self-Disclosure

With too much or inappropriate self-disclosure from the social worker, the client can:
- Perceive the social worker as a friend and expect mutuality in the relationship
- Feel compelled to "help" the social worker
- Feel as if the social worker can't help, because the social worker's own life issues are so distracting.
- Use the information shared by the social worker in a self-serving or manipulative way
- React negatively and feel cheated out of their opportunity to disclose

---

Going into details and reminiscing about the social worker's life experience is distracting. The client may feel uncomfortable and put on the spot to respond to the social worker's message (Kadushin & Kadushin, 1997). However, providing general information can help to establish and maintain a relationship (i.e., saying "I have children, too. They can be a handful," instead of "Let me tell you about my daughter, Susan. She is such a handful. Last night...").

Social worker self-disclosure must be relevant to the client's problem (Kadushin & Kadushin, 1997). Never reveal any information that might be detrimental to the helping process (i.e., I sometimes drive drunk, but so far I haven't been caught).

The social worker needs to be careful not to disclose feelings of disapproval or shock. The client may interpret this as judgment or disbelief. "I'm disgusted by what you just told me, how you could hurt your wife like that!"

Box 7.9 Example of 'Inappropriate Social Worker Self-Disclosure'

Laura is 17-year-old female talking about the possible changes in her life. She is in jeopardy of being evicted from her apartment. She has a long history of conflicts with her parents. Laura is trying to maintain her independence and distance herself from her parents.

Laura: My life is a mess. I'm just about to get evicted from my apartment and my probation officer told me if I don't find another place, I may end up having to move back with my parents. That would be a disaster. I have worked really hard to get away from them. They are crazy. You know what I mean, you've met them.

Social Worker Pitfall: Your parents seem nice. They are concerned about you. My parents haven't spoken to me in three years, so in my eyes, you are lucky! I wish they cared about me like your parents do. I don't know if I should reach out to them, or let things just be. (inappropriate social worker self-disclosure)

Correct Social Worker Response: Laura, you have managed to get through some very miserable times with your parents. But, you have shown us that you are resourceful and strong. For the time being, there is a shelter on Main Street where you can stay for the next few nights if necessary. We can also start looking at other places for you to live. I am really glad that you came to see me before making any decisions. (summarization/information giving/self-disclosure)

In the example in Box 7.9, the client and social worker have some things in common. However, in this case, the social worker moves too far toward inappropriate self-disclosure. The focus has shifted from the client to the social worker as she reminisces about her losses. The corrected social worker response stays focused on Laura's problems and offers support and information.

Premature Confrontation

The social worker must approach the client with respect and concern. Challenging the client too early in the relationship can hinder the development of trust and confidence (Kadushin & Kadushin, 1997). At the early stage of the relationship, the client may not believe that a confrontation is in his or her best interest (Egan, 2002). Before confronting a client about inconsistencies between stated goals and behavior, the social worker should be able to answer "yes" to the following question: Have I demonstrated my ability to help the client concerning less volatile issues? Pace your confrontation according to the development of the relationship (Brems, 2001).

Sometimes a social worker may be incorrect in his or her perceptions about a client's situation because of the social worker's own issues or because there is not enough information about the client. Make sure that the confrontation is not to meet your own needs, such as appearing insightful, to retaliate, or to elevate yourself in relation to the client (Hill & O'Brien, 2004).

The skill of confrontation should be used sparingly and should not be a style of interviewing. It is not about forcing the client: "Oh, I caught you!" or "Do this or else," but about helping the client develop new insights and awareness. A confrontation is a therapeutic intervention, not a social interaction (such as with a family member or friend) (Brems, 2001) For example, Jacob is a 30-year-old single parent. His wife abandoned the family five months earlier, leaving him to care for their sons, ages 8 and 4. Jacob is currently unemployed and reports that he is looking for a job, but has been unsuccessful in his efforts. The social worker believes that Jacob has a drinking problem and that he was fired because of his sporadic attendance and poor job performance. The social worker confronts him with suspicions, stating, "I think that you have a problem with alcohol, and that's why your wife left and you are out of a job." Jacob feels attacked by the social worker and refuses to continue in treatment, stating, "How dare you accuse me of having an alcohol problem? I'm out of here." Box 7.10 is an example of the social worker using the pitfall premature confrontation.

Box 7.10 Example of Premature Confrontation

Max is a 25-year-old male. He recently graduated from college and started working part time as a computer programmer. He is talking to a social worker about his mother.

Max: My Mom has a gambling problem. She used my two credit cards and maxed them out at $5,000 each. I am trying not to let this bother me.

Social Worker Pitfall: What do you mean, you don't mind? If you don't stop her, *your* credit will suffer. I realize that she's your mother, but come on... (premature confrontation)

Max: I can't say anything. My Dad would kill her if he knew what was going on.

Social Worker Pitfall: Don't you see, if you don't stop her she'll end up ruining both your credit and your life? (advice giving and premature confrontation)

Max: Well, what am I supposed to do? She can't help herself; I'm the only person she can count on. I know it's not the answer, but she is my Mom.

Box 7.10 Example of Premature Confrontation, *continued*

Social Worker Pitfall: You have a problem then.... it is not your responsibility to keep her out of trouble. What do you think is going to happen down the road? Have you thought of that? (judgmental response and premature confrontation)

Correct Social Worker Response: You are feeling responsible for your mom and determined to take care of her and her gambling problem. Max, what do you think about this predicament you are in now? (lead-in response/reflection of feeling/open-ended question)

As Box 7.10 illustrates, the social worker may have some good points to share; however the timing and tone are too confrontational. There is no relationship established and the social worker is being critical of the client's choices. This confrontation feels hurtful and will likely push the client away. The corrected response illustrates the social worker challenging the client, but in a thoughtful and nonthreatening manner.

Overwhelming the Client with Too Much or Irrelevant Information

Giving the client too much information makes it difficult to identify what is the most important part of the social worker's message. Excessive information can overwhelm the client and confuse critical issues that the client must take time to consider (Egan, 2002). Presenting information in small doses, from most to least significant, can assist the client in taking necessary action (i.e., "Let's talk about finding a safe place for you tonight. Tomorrow you can contact the State's Attorney about an Order of Protection against your husband.").

Sherry is a 40-year-old stay-at-home mother with three children, ages 12, 7, and 5. She has expressed an interest in going back to school and getting an undergraduate degree in education. She has some concerns regarding admission procedures, financial aid requirements, and her ability to do college-level coursework. The social worker states, "There are so many details to getting into the university. First you have to get a copy of your high school transcript to send in with the application. Then you will fill out the application and send a $50.00 check to cover the cost of processing your application. Financial aid and loans are available too, especially because you are a returning student." Because Sherry has been given too much important information at once, it is difficult for her to sort out her priorities. She is left feeling confused and overwhelmed with details. It is possible that she may not act on her plan because it feels so daunting.

Providing too much information may undermine the client's self-efficacy. Be careful not to sound like the expert and "know it all." You may be impressed with the vast amount of information you have, but it can come across as condescending. Provide information sparingly, as it should not be your primary mode of interacting. Information should be up to date, accurate, understandable and relevant to this situation or problem.   Also, remember, if you share your opinion with a client, it is important to identify it as opinion, not fact.

Far from empowering the client with new knowledge, giving too much information may also cause the client to become confused about all of the options thus leading to inaction. The timing of information is critical. Ask yourself, Is the client ready to hear what I'm sharing? Preparing the client for emotionally potent information is best done in small doses (Egan, 2002).

Box 7.11 Example of the Pitfall 'Overwhelming the Client with Too Much Information'

Tony is a 48-year-old male, talking about his recent job loss with a case worker.

Tony: I just lost my job. I want to find out if I qualify for any financial help.

Social Worker Pitfall: Depending on your circumstances, you may be eligible for unemployment. The office hours are from 9 to 5, Monday-Friday. They tend to be very busy in the morning, so I'd suggest going at around 3:30. The person you want to speak to is Rose--she's the most helpful. I'd call before going down there, just to be on the safe side. The phone number is … (overwhelming the client with too much information)

Tony: Do you think I will qualify for benefits? I don't want to go all the way over there if they are just gonna say, too bad.

Social Worker Pitfall: You will never know until you get yourself down there. The eligibility requirements vary depending on how long you have been employed and the circumstances surrounding your job loss.. It is very important that you look for a job at the same time you are collecting benefits, because you have to document that you have completed so many job-finding tasks per week. (overwhelming the client with too much information)

Tony: What do I do first?

Correct Social Worker Response: The Employment Security Administration is a good place to start. Here is some information about who qualifies for unemployment benefits, regulations,   office hours, and the address. Before you head over there, how are you and your family managing? (information giving and open-ended question)

Tony: Okay, I guess, this came out of the blue……..

The illustration in Box 7.11 points out the problem with overwhelming the client with too much information. In this case, the client is trying to keep up, but falls behind. The social worker sounds like the expert who can't wait to share all her knowledge and expertise. In the appropriate social worker response, she offers written information that the client can take with him, as well as concern for Tony and his family..

Premature Problem Solving

Social workers are skilled at problem solving; however this does not mean that the social worker is there to solve the problem for the client. A full understanding of the problem is necessary in order to help the client choose the next step in problem resolution (Hepworth et al., 2002). If the social worker problem solves too quickly, important information may be overlooked. It is also a missed opportunity for the client to be involved in the process. In order for problem solving to be effective, the client has to be invested in moving and reaching toward his or her goals. If problem solving occurs too early in the process, the opportunity to capitalize on the client's strengths is lost (Kottler, 2000).

Clients explore problems and develop an understanding of their problems at varying speeds. What may be the apparent problem may be a symptom of another layer of dysfunction or the result of associated patterns of behavior. If the social worker moves too quickly to problem solving, the methodical process of problem exploration, assessment, and intervention is circumvented, thus leading to a limited understanding of the risks and benefits associated with the goal. The client and social worker need time to explore all facets of the problem. By moving too rapidly toward problem resolution, the social worker's agenda may be met (i.e., "I have three home visits to make this afternoon," or "I get this situation, I have heard it 100 times before") but the pacing needs of the client are ignored (Kottler, 2000). For example, David is a 40-year-old homeless veteran. He has been living in shelters off and on for the past four years. He is eligible, but is not receiving Veterans Administration or Social Security benefits. David has come to the shelter for the night. He informs the social worker that he is a veteran and hasn't received a check for one year. He appears somewhat disheveled and disoriented during the intake interview. The social worker says, "The first thing we have to do is get your benefits reinstated." The social worker completely overlooks his current situation and begins to focus on financial resources. Although this is a viable avenue to explore with David, his immediate need of food and shelter was completely ignored.

Remember, what the client presents as "the problem" may not be the "real problem." Therefore, if the social worker jumps to problem solving, the social worker may miss essential information that could help resolve the problem. Even a good solution can create new problems. Change occurs both internally and externally and we develop goals with our clients to address both facets. Meaningful and lasting change takes time and commitment, and can't be done in a hurried or directive fashion.

Finally, there are some situations that require very quick information gathering, assessment and planning. For instance, a client who will be without shelter by sundown or a client who will not have enough medication to get through the next day will require immediate intervention. These types of crises require the social worker to take on a more active role in order to ensure client safety (Egan, 2002).

Box 7.12 Example of the Pitfall 'Premature Problem Solving'

Gina is a 10-year-old student talking to the school social worker about being bullied. She is scared to provide any details about the bullying incidents for fear of retaliation.

Gina: The kids pick on me at school. I don't tell the teachers because if I do it will make things worse.

Social Worker Pitfall: Who are these kids? (irrelevant question)

Gina: I am not giving names, you know what will happen to me if I do.

Social Worker: Okay, so then what seems to cause the problems at school? (open-ended question)

Gina: They pick on me because of the way I look and my clothes.

Social Worker Pitfall: Oh. That's easy to take care of. Let's find some fashionable outfits for you to wear. (premature problem solving)

Correct Social Worker Response: Gina, from what you are sharing with me, it sounds like other kids are bullying you. This is a serious problem. I know you don't want to give me anyone's name. Let's talk about what we can do to better protect you. (paraphrase and information giving)

In Box 7.12 the social worker rapidly jumps to problem solving with Gina. She misses some very important messages the client was attempting to share...her fear, the impact of bullying, and the personal circumstances that may have caused her to be so vulnerable. By rushing to solving the "outfitting problem," she ignored more relevant issues.

Offering False Assurance/Minimizing the Problem

Although a social worker should always look for strength and hope in a client's situation, being realistic and honest is an imperative (Hepworth et al., 2002). When the social worker provides false assurance, the client's problem is minimized. False assurance can lead the client to feel discouraged and resentful toward the social worker when things don't work out as hoped (Hepworth et al., 2002) False assurances can also cause the client to overlook possible roadblocks, thereby making a problem worse. Clients must come to terms with their difficulties and possible consequences of the situation. These realizations help prepare the client to take action. Additionally, meaningless clichés such as, "That's the way it goes," or "Things will be better in the morning," gloss over a client's pain. These responses are hollow and have no therapeutic value. For example, Rose is a 70-year-old resident of a nursing home. She has been there for two weeks and is eagerly waiting to be discharged into her daughter's care. Today, her daughter Eve called stating, "Mom can't move in with us. My husband refuses to let her stay here, even for a few weeks." The social worker says, "I'm sure that you can convince him to reconsider. Really, your mom is doing much better and I'm certain she would not get in his way at all." The social worker ignores Eve's concerns and jumps directly into offering assurances. Clearly, the social worker wants to gloss over the problems and focus on *her* task--discharge planning. This approach serves the needs of the social worker, not the client. Eve isn't heard or understood, causing her to feel even more confused and guilty.

False assurances may overlook the client's feelings of discomfort, hopelessness, or despair. However, it is also important for the social worker not to be *overly* sympathetic toward the client's situation. The social worker should strive to convey understanding, not pity (Hepworth et al., 2002).

If the client senses an implicit message of "it's no big deal, why are you bothering me" from the social worker, the client is likely to withdraw from the relationship. The client may also feel that he or she is overreacting, based on the social worker's minimal reaction. Remember that the client may also attempt to minimize the impact of the problem situation. The social worker uses problem identification and assessment skills to analyze underlying issues (perhaps unexpressed or downplayed by the client) that determine the severity of the problem.

For the client to feel understood, the social worker must be able to communicate a full understanding of the significance of the situation (Cormier & Cormier, 1998). The client may be feeling overwhelmed by circumstances. To offer support, the social worker should use words that capture the intensity of the problem. If the social worker misses the intensity (i.e., CL: "I am so angry I could just strangle him." SW: "You sound sort of upset right now."), the client may wonder whether the social worker is truly listening.

Coming across to a client as being artificial, insincere, or rude can cause the client to become suspicious of the social worker's intentions. A straightforward and honest manner communicates authenticity (Sheafor & Horejsi, 2003; Kadushin & Kadushin, 1997). Clients can detect a social worker pretending to care, or to listen, very easily. Simply going through the motions, responding with little interest or concern, detracts from the helping relationship. For example, Irving is an 80-year-old male, currently a patient in a rehabilitation hospital. He suffered from a stroke one month ago and his recovery process has been slow and painful. He wants to regain all of his capacities, and he is currently expressing frustration with himself and others. Having heard this at every session, the social worker uses a very harsh and angry tone of voice to say, "Irving, you will get better, just be patient." Although the words are reassuring, the tone of the social worker's voice conveys a lack of care or concern. Irving is likely to feel even more frustrated and isolated by his circumstances and withdraw from the relationship.

In Box 7.13, the social worker uses the pitfall false assurance.

Box 7.13 Example of the pitfall 'False Assurance'

Mr. Quinton is a 57-year-old male, who recently lost his business during a tornado. He is talking to a social worker employed by the Red Cross.

Mr. Quinton: My business was destroyed in the last tornado. There is nothing left of the building, just piles of rubble. The insurance company guy came to talk to me last week about rebuilding and getting the business going again. I just don't see how I can start all over. I am old and I don't have the energy.

Social Worker Pitfall: So many people count on you for jobs around here. I have no doubt that folks will help in every way they can. This community pulls together, you know that. I am sure it will work out. (false assurance)

Correct Social Worker Response: You have lost so much and are still in shock. It is too soon to decide anything. (reflection of feeling and information giving)

In the Box 7.13 illustration, the social worker is trying to reassure the client that all will be well, just 'hang in there.' He points out strengths and reasons to move ahead, but ignores and minimizes the client's significant losses. In the corrected response, the social worker acknowledges the client's loss and also provides useful information.

Box 7.14 Example of the Pitfall 'Minimizing the Problem'

Theresa is a 12-year-old 7th grader. Her parents recently informed her that because of her mother's job change, they will be moving to a new community. Theresa doesn't want to leave her friends and her school. She is afraid of moving, in part because it has always been difficult for her to make friends. She is very shy and introverted.

Theresa: I don't want to move—my friends are here. My parents said I have to and now I am so scared that I can't eat or sleep.

Social Worker Pitfall: Moving can be fun and exciting, and you'll be able to start off with a clean slate." (minimizing the problem)

Theresa: Yeah, but I'm in junior high. It's hard to meet people, especially when everyone already has their friends.

Social Worker Pitfall: But you'll be the new kid, people will be curious about you. (minimizing the problem)

Theresa: Yeah, right. I'm ugly and I don't like meeting new people.

Social Worker Pitfall: You are not ugly, you are a lovely young lady! (minimizing the problem)

Correct Social Worker Response: Moving can be scary. There is no way to make this easy but talking to your parents and keeping in touch with your friends here at school might help a little bit. (paraphrase and information giving)

Theresa: I can't talk to my parents. They are already packing boxes. They don't understand me at all.

Correct Social Worker Response, continued: They don't get how hard this is for you because right now they are so involved in their own excitement. (paraphrase)

Theresa: Yeah, they figure since they are happy, I should be happy. But I am NOT happy.

Correct Social Worker Response continued: I can tell that you are very upset about this. Let's talk about some ways you can get ready for the move. (reflection of feeling and open-ended question)

Although the social worker's response may be true, Theresa's concerns are not addressed. The social worker attempts to reduce the complexity of the issue to a few statements. Theresa is likely to feel unheard, causing her to retreat even further. In the corrected version, the social worker acknowledges Theresa's feelings of despair and begins to focus on how she might manage this upcoming change in her life.

LEARNING FROM MISTAKES

When mistakes are made during an interview, the social worker's goal should be to learn from the experience, so that when presented with a similar situation, he or she can respond with a new level of professionalism. Sometimes, social workers fail to recognize pitfalls. However, clients often react in ways that highlight mistakes (i.e., saying "That's not what I said," or using nonverbal cues such as avoiding eye contact or not showing up/canceling the next appointment) when the social worker has said something that has hurt, angered, or offended them.

For example, a social worker who has just responded to a client in a judgmental manner should apologize and start over (i.e., "I can tell my comment has made you very upset. I'm sorry, that was not my intent. Let me rephrase what I was trying to say"). This is a face-saving measure for both the social worker and the client. Hopefully, the relationship has not been permanently damaged, and the client and the social worker can move on in the problem-solving process. Being able to admit a mistake also models another important life skill, acknowledging an error and attempting to repair the damage. .

Box 7.15 Social Worker Recovery Statements (Fill in the Blanks)

- I can tell my comment about _____ upset you, that was not my intent
- You look upset by what I just said about your _____, let me try to say it another way
- Sorry, that came out wrong about your _____, what I meant to say was....
- That was rude, I can tell I hurt your feelings when I said _____.What I should have said was ....
- That came out all wrong; I sometimes put my foot in my mouth. I will try again...
- Ooops, that was out of line.
- You are right to be confused by what I said....
- I will rephrase that....
- It doesn't sound the way I had intended, I apologize.
- I regret the way that sounded. You are right to feel angry.

Box 7.16 Example of Pitfalls and Social Worker Recovery Statements

Molly is a 21-year-old female who was recently discharged from the mental health unit and is speaking to the caseworker in the outpatient unit. Molly had attempted suicide and suffers from a long history of depression.

Molly: I think I am doing okay. I have been taking my medication, but my parents don't believe me, so they watch my every move.

Social Worker Pitfall: What makes them doubt that you are taking your medicine? Is it something you are doing? (premature confrontation and stacked questions)

Molly: I don't think so, I am following the directions on the bottle. My doctor said that I should be responsible for taking my pills, not my parents. I am 21, you know.

Social Worker Pitfall: I know that you're old enough, but in the past you haven't followed through with taking your medication. I am sure that's why your parents are so concerned. (premature confrontation and false assurance)

Molly: Yeah, but I haven't given them any reason to doubt me this time

Social Worker Pitfall: Have you tried to talk to your parents? (premature problem solving)

Molly: I have, but they treat me like a child, just like you are.

Social Worker recovery statement: You are right. I *am* sounding like your parent too. Sorry about that, let's get back on track. You were saying that you take your medication independently and have been doing this for the past two weeks.

Molly: My parents do care about me, I know that, but I feel like a five year old, needing a parent's hand to cross the street.

Social Worker recovery statement continued: There is a part of you that is really scared. You have been through a lot in the past few years. You want to be more independent and take charge of your own life. Right now, that seems like a far away dream. Is that how you feel? (summarization and clarification)

Molly: I do feel that way. My parents always step in and bail me out. I want get better on my own. I just need them to have faith in me.

Social Worker recovery statement continued: Well, let's talk about some things you can do to convince them that this time you want to do things differently. Any ideas? (open-ended question)

Through practicing social work skills and maintaining an awareness of common pitfalls social workers can achieve a positive, helping relationship with clients. Remember, even as seasoned professionals, we all make mistakes. There is no such thing as a perfect response or question. It is up to you to learn from your mistakes and to reflect on ways you can improve. Take time to learn and challenge yourself when you do make a mistake.

CONCLUSION

Throughout this text, you have been presented with information that is relevant and essential in your development as a competent social work professional. You have been exposed to the meaning and breadth of social work, the roles we fulfill in an effort to provide the best service possible, and to the ethics, values and theories that guide our practice. You have also had the opportunity to learn about developing cultural competence in your practice with clients. All of these components of knowledge come together as a complete practice ensemble when you fully engage your clients in the helping process.

The accompanying workbook will give you the opportunity to practice the essential interviewing skills and attending behaviors that are the foundation to practice and expose you to common pitfalls in practice, providing you with techniques for recovery when errors are made in the interviewing process. Individual and small group exercises are designed to increase your self-awareness and cultural competency in practice.

The CD-ROM and companion website complete this package. Use the CD-ROM and virtual client interviews to observe how a session is conducted. There are many opportunities for you to test yourself and assess your own skill development using the "Try It" and "Quiz" features. Be patient (and positive) as you continue to review the interviewing and attending skills. As you watch the case examples, put yourself in the social worker's place i.e., how might you respond, given all you have learned. What might you do differently from the social workers on the CD-ROM? Continue to assess your skill development as you move through this learning process.

The website also provides you with many additional learning tools such as examples of treatment plans, contracts and case notes. All scripts, including the video clips, narration and sessions are available for your review. You can access many additional websites though companion website at http://www.ablongman.com/cummins2e.

Finally, we learn in incremental steps (as do our clients). It takes time and practice to achieve a level of comfort and competence as a professional. Even the most skilled and seasoned professionals are learning and fine-tuning their skill sets. It is a lifelong journey and well worth the time and effort. Gook luck as you move forward in your education and social work career.

REFERENCES

Brems, C. (2001). *Basic skills in psychotherapy and counseling.* Pacific Grove, CA: Brooks/Cole.

Cormier, W. & Cormier, S. (1998). *Interviewing strategies for helpers* (4th ed.) Pacific Grove, CA: Brooks/Cole.

Egan, G. (2002). *The skilled helper* (7th ed.) Pacific Grove, CA: Brooks/Cole.

Hepworth, D., Rooney, R., & Larsen, J. (2002). *Direct social work practice: Theory and skills* (6th ed.) Pacific Grove, CA: Brooks/Cole.

Gambrill, E. (1997). *Social work practice: A critical thinker's guide.* New York: Oxford.

Hill, C., & O'Brien, K. (2004). *Helping Skills: Facilitating exploration, insight and action* (2nd ed.) Washington, DC: American Psychological Association.

Ivey, A.E. & Ivey, M.B. (2002). *Intentional interviewing and counseling.* Pacific Grove, CA: Brooks/Cole.

Kadushin, A. & Kadushin, G. (1997). *The social work interview* (4th ed.) New York: Columbia University Press.

Kottler, J.A. (2000). *Nuts and bolts of helping.* Boston, MA: Allyn & Bacon.

Murphy, B.C. & Dillon, C. (2003). *Interviewing in action: Process and practice.* Pacific Grove, CA: Brook/Cole.

National Association of Social Workers (1999). *Code of Ethics.* Retrieved Feb. 18, 2005 from http://www.naswdc.org/pubs/code/code.asp.

Ragg, D.M. (2001). *Building effective helping skills: The foundation of generalist practice.* Boston, MA: Allyn & Bacon.

Sheafor, B.W. & Horejsi, C.R. (2003). *Techniques and guidelines for social work practice* (6th ed.) Boston, MA: Allyn & Bacon

Shebib, B. (2003). *Choices: Counseling skills for social workers and other professionals.* Boston, MA: Allyn & Bacon.

WORKBOOK:
SKILLS

This workbook is designed to teach social work interviewing skills and uses a two-pronged approach to do so: skill development and practice exercises. Under each skill you will find two sections. Part I focuses on interviewing skill development. Part II provides relevant exercises that will enhance your overall development as a professional. Part II exercises are to be done primarily in small groups, referred to "practice partner(s)". These exercises encourage the interaction and integration of theory and skill.

PARAPHRASING

Read the following items and identify

a)   The key points in the client's messages (at least 2); and
b)   In your own words, restate what the client has said. <u>Use different lead-in responses for each of your entries.</u>

Example:

"I love to play hockey. I love coaching. My kids don't play any more, but the other kids need me. My wife thinks I should spend more time at home. I don't agree with her. I'm home plenty."

a) Key points in the client's message:

i.   <u>**hockey comes first**</u>
ii.   <u>**disrupting marriage**</u>
iii.   <u>**husband and wife have different expectations**</u>

b) Your paraphrasing response:

<u>**I hear you saying that hockey is a really important part of your life, but you and your wife see this issue differently, which is causing trouble at home.**</u>

1. *A 40-year-old African-American male, talking to the community mental health clinic case worker.*

   "I really need to talk to my doctor. It's been two weeks since I had my medication. I have to have it now. You don't understand. without the doctor's okay, I can't get my medicine. The pharmacy closes at five o'clock tonight. It's the only one in town that accepts my medical card. If I don't get my medicine soon, who knows what will happen to me—I need it for my nerves."

a) Key points in the client's message:

i)

ii)

iii)

b) Your paraphrasing response:

2. *A Latina mother talking to the school social worker about her 8-year-old son.*

"My son, Juanito, has a learning disability. He has a hard time in school. I know his teachers are frustrated with him, but I don't think they are doing enough to help him. We've only been in this country for three years; there have been a lot of changes in his life. It's hard for me too, but I try not to think about that too much."

a) Key points in the client's message:

i)

ii)

iii)

b) Your paraphrasing response:

3. *A father talking to the home interventionist about his children.*

"I want to get my life back in order. I know I messed up in the past, but I want my kids back. They have been away from me for too long—it's been almost a year. Imagine, strangers raising my kids. I know the foster care system is supposed to help us. Frankly, I think things are much worse since that social worker got involved."

a) Key points in the client's message:

i)

ii)

iii)

b) Your paraphrasing response:

4. *A 22-year-old female talking to the intake worker at an out-patient treatment program.*

   "No, I'm not an alcoholic. Sure I drink, everyone I know drinks. It's part of being a college student. The DUI I got last month was no big deal, it was just a stupid mistake. I won't drive after drinking again, that's for sure. Everyone makes my drinking into a major catastrophe. I wish people would back off."

   a) Key points in the client's message:

   i)

   ii)

   iii)

   b) Your paraphrasing response:

5. *An 18-year-old male, talking with an adoption specialist about his desire to locate his birth mother.*

   "My adoptive parents are great. I know that they love me a lot, and I love them too. But there is this feeling inside of me. I want to know who gave birth to me. I want her to tell me why she gave me up. Five years ago, the other social worker told me that I could look for her when I was older. Now I'm ready."

   a) Key points in the client's message:

i)

ii)

iii)

b) Your paraphrasing response:

6. *A 35-year-old male, talking about his relationships with friends.*

"*My friends seem to get bored and tired of me. They go out a lot without me. I find out later, like maybe they've gone to a movie. I call them. I hardly ever get calls back. It's weird. I always end up chasing people down.*"

a) Key points in the client's message:

i)

ii)

iii)

b) Your paraphrasing response:

7. *A 17-year-old high school senior talking to his guidance counselor.*

"*Physics is really hard for me, but I want to be an engineer. My dad and grandfather are both engineers. They love their work. I've always dreamed of being part of their firm. Now, I'm flunking physics and will probably end up with a low grade point average. My teacher asked me if I have a learning disability. I don't know...I don't want to think I have a problem with my brain.*"

a) Key points in the client's message:

i)

ii)

iii)

b) Your paraphrasing response:

8. *A 30-year-old male, talking about the impact of prejudice on his life.*

   "I was born in Mexico and came to the United States when I was three. People sometimes look at me as if I have no right to be here. I'm an American citizen. I work hard to take care of my family. I'm a part of the community. I just don't understand why people question me all the time!"

   a) Key points in the client's message:

      i)

      ii)

      iii)

   b) Your paraphrasing response:

9. *A 15-year-old female, talking with the school social worker.*

   "My relationship with my step-dad has always been awkward. I have never felt comfortable around him. He definitely treats his own kids better than he treats me. I'm not saying I'm jealous or anything. In some ways it's easier when he treats me like an acquaintance. Just saying hello and goodbye, and then going our separate ways. But sometimes I wish he'd be proud of me too."

   a) Key points in the client's message:

      i)

      ii)

iii)

b) Your paraphrasing response:

10. *A 40-year-old female, talking to the intake worker at an eating disorder clinic.*

   "I've gained 25 pounds in the last 16 months. I try to control my eating habits, but it's hard. I always end up stuffing myself when I feel stressed. I've tried all the weight loss programs, nothing seems to help. I just keep getting bigger and bigger."

   a) Key points in the client's message:

   i)

   ii)

   iii)

   b) Your paraphrasing response:

PART II

With your practice partners, complete the following role play exercise. Three students are necessary to complete the exercise: 1) client; 2) social worker; and 3) observer.

Identify and discuss ways in which you can communicate your understanding of your client's cognitive/thinking processes.

Using the Paraphrasing case # 3, in which a father is talking about his children, and role play this scenario for five minutes.
Client: Be sure to elaborate or enhance the situation so you can continue the role play for approximately 5 minutes.
Social worker: Listen to the client and use the skill paraphrase when appropriate.

PART II, *continued*

Observer: Identify the key components of the client's messages. What issues are most significant to the client? How did the social worker convey care, concern and sensitivity to the client's life experiences? What cultural consideration should the social worker attend to?

After five minutes of role play, discuss the observer's feedback within the practice group. What might the social worker have done differently? What were the strengths of the interview?

REFLECTION OF FEELING

After reading each item,

a) List four appropriate feeling words;
b) Write your reflection of feeling response, using a different feeling word than one of the four listed below.
c) Combine a reflection of feeling statement with a paraphrase. Be sure to use different lead-in responses for each of your entries.

Example: "My Dad and I always fight. He doesn't care about my feelings. He just keeps on accusing me falsely. No matter what I do, he refuses to listen. I just can't win."

a) **Feeling words:**

1. **frustrated**
2. **hurt**
3. **angry**
4. **confused**

b) **Your feeling response:**
   You sound very hurt by your Dad.

c) **Combined response:**
You want things to be better between the two of you. You sound hurt and disappointed.

1. *An 80-year-old male, talking to the nursing home case worker.*

   "This nursing home is not working out. My family is too far away, and I don't know anyone here. I just suffer here alone. The folks here are nice, they are just not family. My daughter and son were planning to come and visit me last month, but something came up. I hope that they get here soon—who knows how long I'll last"

   a)   Feeling words:

   1.
   2.
   3.
   4.

   b) Your feeling response:

   c) Your combined response:

2. *A 17-year-old female, talking to the school social worker.*

   "I really want to make the volleyball team. All my friends are varsity players. My grades are too low, even though I've tried really hard to bring them up. The coach wants me to talk to you. He thinks I'm not working hard enough. My parents have put a lot of pressure on me too. I feel really bad about myself. I can't seem to do anything right."

   a)   Feeling words:

   1.
   2.
   3.
   4.

   b)   Your feeling response:

   c)   Your combined response:

3. *A 12-year-old male, talking to a hotline worker.*

   "My Mom and Dad always fight. Sometimes they scream so loud that they wake me up at night. I wish they'd stop it. I lie awake waiting for them to stop. They just keep on and on and on. May be if they didn't live together they'd stop fighting. Is there any hope things will get better?"

a)   Feeling words:

1.
2.
3.
4.

b)   Your feeling response:

c)   Your combined response:

4. *A 23-year-old male, talking to his social worker.*

   "It's not enough that I went to college. I doubt I'll get a job when I graduate. Who would want to hire a person with cerebral palsy! People are uncomfortable around someone like me, stuck in a wheelchair. They don't understand that I'm a very capable worker."

a)   Feeling words:

1.
2.
3.
4.

b)   Your feeling response:

c)   Your combined response:

5. *A 40-year-old male, talking to a grief counselor.*

    "My youngest brother was killed in a plane crash. [very angry tone] He was the greatest guy in the world. Where was God? How could God let this happen? My faith has been shaken. It's just not fair. I've gone to church to pray, but it doesn't help. Nothing does."

a)   Feeling words:

1.
2.
3.
4.

b)   Your feeling response:

c)   Your combined response:

6. *A 44-year-old lesbian female, talking to a Child Protective Services case worker.*

    "You are absolutely wrong about me. I don't want to talk to you any more about this. You social workers are all the same. I can't believe you. You must have made a lot of enemies in this business. I would appreciate you leaving me alone. I can manage just fine. I always have, and I always will. Now, if you'd excuse me…"

a)   Feeling words:

1.
2.
3.
4.

b)   Your feeling response:

c)   Your combined response:

7. *A 68-year-old male, talking to the senior citizen case manager.*

    "Things really are great. My kids are coming here from Alaska for the holidays, and this new relationship I'm in has my head spinning. I'm so happy and so thankful things have worked out. Five months ago I was considering killing myself. Today I feel great. You have no idea how helpful talking to you has been. Thank you."

a)   Feeling words:

1.
2.
3.
4.

b)   Your feeling response:

c)   Your combined response:

8. *A 50-year-old female talking to a domestic violence shelter worker.*

    "I'm relieved to be out of that violent situation. I was scared for so many years. I hardly know how to act now. I still find myself looking over my shoulder, just waiting for him to find me. But mostly I'm thankful to still be alive."

a)   Feeling words:

1.
2.
3.

4.

b)   Your feeling response:

c)   Your combined response:

9. *A 24-year-old Mexican-American female, talking to a sexual assault counselor about a sexual assault that occurred eight years ago.*

"I was raped when I was in high school. I knew the guy, but we weren't friends. He pretended as if he liked me. I have never told any one because I always felt like somehow I had encouraged him. It wasn't until recently that I've even started to think about what happened. I felt guilty then, but I blocked it out. Now I'm so angry. I feel so violated. It's very difficult to discuss this with my family."

a)   Feeling words:

1.
2.
3.
4.

b)   Your feeling response:

d)   Your combined response:

10.   *A 25-year-old female, talking to an intake worker at an alcohol treatment center.*

"I want to get married to Tom. My parents hate him—because he drinks. I know that he drinks; he's never denied it. So what if he gets out of control occasionally? I grew up in an alcoholic family. It is second nature to me. I know how to handle him. I know how to handle me"

a)   Feeling words:

1.

2.

3.

4.

b)   Your feeling response:

c)   Your combined response:

PART II

Discuss ways in which conveying understanding of a client's feelings can enhance the relationship.   Under what circumstances might the discussion of emotions be problematic?

Think back to a time when you were very emotional (the type of emotion is not relevant for this exercise). Discuss how you felt and ways that you did or did not attempted to express your feelings. How did others respond to you at the time? Did they know that you were experiencing extreme emotions? How do you read other people's emotions, what signs do you look for?

Given the diversity of the client's we work with, what are some important issue to keep in mind regarding the expression of emotions?

PART II, *continued*

> With your practice partner(s), role play the reflection of feeling case # 5, a grief-stricken man who is mourning the loss of his brother.
> <u>Client:</u> Do NOT convey any emotions, just speak the words. Continue this role play for 5 minutes. Discuss what the role play experience was like for both the client and the social worker.
>
> Now repeat the exercise again, using the same example, but this time as the client use your voice, gestures, facial expressions to reinforce the emotional message.
> Discuss how these two role plays were different.

OPEN-ENDED QUESTIONS

> After reading each item, identify
>
> a) At least two specific pieces of information that would further your understanding of the problem; and
> b) An open-ended question that would prompt the client to provide additional information.*
>
> *In completing Part b, start by either reflecting the client's feelings or by paraphrasing the content of the client's message, and then ask the open-ended question.
>
> **Example:**
>
> **Client:"I took my medication last night. I didn't want to, but I did. Now I am thinking about whether this is a good idea. I know I am depressed, but I should be able to get through this without drugs."**
>
> a) **Additional information needed:**
>
> i.   <u>**How is the client managing on the medication**</u>
> ii.   <u>**Type of medication**</u>
> iii.   <u>**Reservations about medication**</u>
>
> b) **Your open-ended question:**
>
> <u>**You are not sure about whether you want to continue taking the medication.**</u>
> **(paraphrase)**
> <u>**What concerns do you have about taking the medication?**</u> **(open-ended question)**

1. *A 50-year-old fundamentalist Christian female, talking with the social worker about her relationship with her daughter.*

   "My daughter is living with her boyfriend. We have talked about it a lot. She knows how I feel about her living situation. My religion means everything to me and she knows that too. She is throwing all of her sins in my face. We've never been close, but this felt like the last straw. She is hurting me and hurting God."

   a)   Additional information needed:

   i.
   ii.
   iii.

   b)   Paraphrase/reflection of feeling and your open-ended question:

2. *A 30-year-old male, talking to the social worker about his reactions to a car accident 6 months ago.*

   "Since my car accident, I'm really afraid to drive again. I get into the car and I feel my heart start to pound and my hands get really sweaty. I don't want to end up behind the wheel and start to panic, but that is what is happening right now. I panic. I've tried to make myself do it, but...I can't. I have flashbacks from the accident; the car turned upside down and I'm trapped inside"

   a)   Additional information needed:

   i.
   ii.
   iii.

   b)   Paraphrase/reflection of feeling and your open-ended question:

3. *An 80-year-old female, talking to the home interventionist.*

   "Like I told the other social worker, my children mean the world to me. Really, I'd do anything for them. But I have to draw the line. I can't lend them the money, it would leave me with nothing if I did. I thought once they were adults I wouldn't have to take care of them. Don't they understand that? I'm broke. I can barely make ends meet. This is too much."

   a)   Additional information needed:

   i.
   ii.
   iii.

   b)   Paraphrase/reflection of feeling and your open-ended question:

4. *A 30-year-old Indian male discussing his relationship with his parents.*

   "I told my parents that I am gay. They are very traditional, and it's hard talking to them about this. I knew it would freak them out, but I wanted them to meet Michael. We've been together for two years. He's a great person, and I'm finally happy. I just wish they could be happy for me."

   a)   Additional information needed:

   i.
   ii.
   iii.

   b)   Paraphrase/reflection of feeling and your open-ended question:

5. *A 35-year-old female, talking to the respite care worker about her 5-month-old daughter.*

"I have always wanted to be a parent. But how can I be a mom to a child who is mentally retarded? The doctors are of no help to me. This is not the way it's supposed to be. I just feel like I'll never be able to love her the way that I should. Last week, another social worker from the Children's Home came to interview me. She suggested that I meet with you. I know I need the extra help--can't do this alone."

a)   Additional information needed:

i.
ii.
iii.

b)   Paraphrase/reflection of feeling and your open-ended question:

6. *A 17-year-old female, talking to the case manager at the Public Assistance office.*

"I'm really excited about having this baby. My boyfriend Dion is giving me a hard time though. He doesn't want the baby. Well...too bad, because I want this baby. I don't need him. We'll be just fine. I've got $400 saved up and a car to get us around. Plus I'm sure that you can help me too."

a)   Additional information needed:

i.
ii.
iii.

b)   Paraphrase/reflection of feeling and your open-ended question:

7. *An 18-year-old female, talking to the school social worker.*

   "I am the youngest of seven children. Sometimes I feel invisible. Sometimes I feel smothered. My oldest sister has always acted like she's my mom. I guess that makes me really mad. Plus, mom shows up when she feels like it, and that makes me angry too. I want to have a normal family when I get married. But, I look around and everyone I know is pretty messed up.

   a)　　　Additional information needed:

   i.
   ii.
   iii.

   b)　　　Paraphrase/reflection of feeling and your open-ended question:

8. *A 50-year-old male, discussing his home situation with the Employee Assistance Program social worker.*

   "I love watching movies. It's the best way for me to relax. I can get away from the craziness of my day. My wife gets mad, though. She expects me to be more involved with the kids. I can't be with them when I feel so torn up inside. There's so much pressure. I'm supporting the family, helping out with my parents, and trying to keep my job."

   a)　　　Additional information needed:

   i.
   ii.
   iii.

   b)　　　Paraphrase/reflection of feeling and your open-ended question:

9. *A 30-year-old female, discussing her reactions to the sexual assault survivors group.*

"This support group is not working for me. People in the group just come here to complain about their terrible lives. I want to move on with my life and not stay stuck in my misery. I feel like if I continue to come here, it will wear me down completely."

a)   Additional information needed:

i.
ii.
iii.

b)   Paraphrase/reflection of feeling and your open-ended question:

10. *A 15-year-old Native American female, talking to an outreach worker.*

"I've never had much to do with my Mom, and now my Grandmother is very sick. She is the most important person in my life. I couldn't bear it if something happened to her. I know I'm only 15, but I'd rather be on my own than have to stay with my Mom. I doubt she'd want me to live with her anyway."

a)   Additional information needed:

i.
ii.
iii.

b) Paraphrase/reflection of feeling and your open-ended question:

PART II

Refer to the Box 5.1 in Chapter 5, the BSW student's field log entry. Discuss with your practice partner(s) issues surrounding the ethical dilemma of this student. What are some of the possible consequences for this student should she continue advocating for Mrs. W to return home? Discuss in detail how you would proceed with this case. Provide a rationale for your decision.

List 5 open-ended questions you would ask to Mrs. W; her daughter and the physician assigned to her medical care. What questions would you anticipate being asked by them? Have your response ready to share.

CLOSED-ENDED QUESTIONS

Read the items listed below and identify

a) At least two specific pieces of information that would further your understanding of the problem; and
b) A closed-ended question that would prompt the client to provide additional information.

Example:

A 29-year-old male, talking to the outreach caseworker.

"I moved to this country from Argentina. I like it here, but I miss my family."

a) Specific information needed:

i.   **How long has the client lived here?**
ii.   **Who is still in Argentina?**
iii.   **Who is here with the client?**

b) Closed-ended question:

   How long have you been in the United States?

1. *A 14-year-old male, talking to the school social worker about his suspension from school.*

    "I've never gotten into trouble at school. I wish the teachers would all drop dead. This one time I messed up and now I'm busted. Here I am talking to you. My parents are going to freak. They are not going to understand. They yell at me even when there is nothing to be upset about. This will just add more to my problems.

    a)   Specific information needed:

    i.
    ii.
    iii.

    b)   Your closed-ended question:

2. *A 10-year-old White female, talking to her outreach worker.*

    "My mom yells at me a lot. Sometimes she's nice, sometimes she's mean. I never know which way she's going to be. I try to do things right, so she doesn't get mad at me. I hope she'll be nice to me after my meeting with you is over. She didn't like it when that social worker from Child Welfare came to our house."

    a)   Specific information needed:

    i.
    ii.
    iii.

    b)   Your closed-ended question:

3. *A 16-year-old African-American female, talking to the group home social worker.*

    "Everyone gets to go to the concert but me. The staffers here at the group home are so strict. They never let me go out with my friends. They practically keep me locked up in my room. I hate being here, jail would be better."

    a)   Specific information needed:

i.
ii.
iii.

b)   Your closed-ended question:

4. *A 65-year-old female, talking to the caseworker at the senior citizens center.*

"We've been together for a long time. You would think by now my children would accept our marriage. They pretend like my husband doesn't exist. I want them to get along. Is that too much to ask? Sometimes I feel like they treat me as a child. They think he is going to take all my money. Is that crazy or what?"

a)   Specific information needed:

i.
ii.
iii.

b)   Your closed-ended question:

5. *A 35-year-old Hispanic female, talking to the community organization representative about her living situation.*

"My landlord has great plans for this building. Those plans include kicking us out so he can fix the place up and charge a higher rent. We would never be able to afford it. I don't have an extra dime at the end of the month. I've always kept the place nice and paid my rent on time. I have no where else to go. It is so unfair. I hope that you will be able to help me."

a) Specific information needed:

i.

ii.

iii.

b)   Your closed-ended question:

6. *A 47-year-old female, talking to the Red Cross crisis intervention counselor.*

   "My house was destroyed by the last hurricane. I have spent five days here in the Red Cross shelter. You people have been nice, but now it is time for me to leave. I don't know where to start. The city is trying to get things up and running again, but all of this is just too much for me to bear.

a)   Specific information needed:

i.

ii.

iii.

b)   Your closed-ended question:

7. *A 20-year-old African-American male, talking to his social worker.*

   "I got a full scholarship for the next year. I worked so hard. I gave up everything in my life, my friends, my job, to win it. Now I feel let down—it's like nothing will ever satisfy me. I go for the top achievement, but once I get there it's never enough for me to be happy. I want to feel a sense of accomplishment. All I feel right now is a giant hole. Sometimes I feel selfish because my parents never had the opportunity to go to college."

a)   Specific information needed:

i.

ii.

iii.

b)   Your closed-ended question:

8. *A 25-year-old White female, talking to the social worker in the eating disorder clinic.*

    "Of course I eat properly. My parents and boyfriend are the ones who have a problem with my weight. They are completely obsessed with how I look and what I eat. It's really none of their business. I feel fine; I don't see any reason to talk about this with you or them."

a)   Specific information needed:

i.
ii.
iii.

b)   Your closed-ended question:

9. *A 55-year-old HIV-positive male, talking to a home interventionist social worker about his medical problems.*

    "I take anti-viral medication on a regular basis. When my T-cell count is stable, I feel much better. I just wish I didn't have HIV. It's awful."

a)   Specific information needed:

i.
ii.
iii.

b)   Your closed-ended question:

10. *A 75-year-old Puerto Rican male, talking about faith with the hospice social worker.*

"My religion has always been a comfort to me. No matter what, I've always turned to prayer during the rough times. You people might think I'm crazy, but I'm leaving my fate up to God. No more medicine, no more doctors. I have had it. It is my time to go. I have faith."

a)   Specific information needed:

i.
ii.
iii.

b)   Your closed-ended question:

PART II

Using the closed-ended question case # 10, a Puerto Rican male talking about his faith, list three different questions you want to ask.

Role play the example with your practice partner(s), integrating into the role play your questions. Continue the role play for 5-7 minutes. Then, answer the following:

How did the client respond to the questions?
Were the questions asked in a culturally sensitive way?
What issues are of importance when working with a client who is dying?
What issues are of importance when working with a client who has such a strong faith?

CLARIFICATION

Read the following items and identify

a) Information that needs to be made clearer (at least two); and
b) A clarifying response.

Example:

"No matter how hard I try, they always yell at me."

a) **What needs to be clearer:**

i.   <u>Who are they?</u>
ii.   <u>How often is always?</u>

b) **Clarifying response:**

<u>When you say "they," whom do you mean?</u>

---

1.   *A 40-year-old Puerto-Rican female, talking to an outreach case worker.*

> *"We're going to be evicted, I just know it. We have no money and I don't know what to do next. My parents said we couldn't live with them. I've got my kids to worry about too. I came here from Puerto Rico for a better life, but I'm still in the same situation."*

What information needs to be clearer?

i.
ii.

a)   Your clarifying response:

2.   *A 34-year-old White female, talking to the home interventionist caseworker.*

> *"I admit that the kids are fighting all the time. My husband wants me to settle it, but I don't see that as my job. I end up sticking up for them, which really makes him mad. I can't seem to win. I hate that I can't handle this on my own, that I have to meet with you. Here I am in the middle again."*

a) What information needs to be clearer?

i.

ii.

b) Your clarifying response:

3. *A 16-year-old White male, talking to the caseworker from the Child Protection Agency.*

> *"So what if it's illegal! We got really high last night. It was a great time. I love being high. I can forget all my worries. You social workers are all alike, trying to tell me what to do."*

a) What information needs to be clearer?

i.

ii.

b) Your clarifying response:

4. *A 25-year-old White female, talking to the Employee Assistance Program social worker about frustrations related to her job.*

> *"I've been working at this job for five years and the crap I have to put up with! My boss always singles me out and criticizes me in front of my coworkers. Can you believe that? Five years! Five long years!"*

a) What information needs to be clearer?

i.

ii.

b) Your clarifying response:

5.   *A 35-year-old White male, talking to his unemployment counselor about making the transition back to school.*

   "I'm trying hard to understand these chemistry problems. I was never a very good student, especially in science. Now here I am, 35 years old and back in college. I'll never get through this. Some of my family is behind me, and I don't want to let them down."

   a)   What information needs to be clearer?

   i.
   ii.

   b)   Your clarifying response:

6.   *A 38-year-old White female, talking to a sexual abuse counselor.*

   "My grandfather did awful and disgusting things to me when I was young. He made me promise not to tell my parents which I never did. Now I'm a mom myself, and I can't stop thinking about him and what happened."

   a)   What information needs to be clearer?

   i.
   ii.

   b)   Your clarifying response:

7.   *A 15-year-old African-American male, talking to his foster care caseworker.*

   "I've never liked living with this foster family. They just seem to "put up" with me. My foster brother, Jimmy, is picking on me all the time, and he makes fun of me, especially at school. Could you please find me a new family? I don't think I can take it any more."

   a)   What information needs to be clearer:

i.

ii.

b) Your clarifying response:

8. *A 25-year-old male, talking to a caseworker about his social relationships.*

    "I have a lot of trouble saying no. People always ask me to do them favors I don't want to do, but I wind up doing them anyway. I've always been this way. I always end up with a sick feeling in my stomach."

    a) What information needs to be clearer:

    i.
    ii.

    b) Your clarifying response:

9. *A 40-year-old White male talking to a community-based social worker about his father.*

    "I grew up in a troubled family. My Dad has been in and out of mental institutions and prisons most of his life. I never really had a chance to get to know him. Now he's being released, and he'll be living in a halfway house. Someone is supposed to meet with me next week to help me figure out what other resources he'll need. I don't know what to do, and I don't know how I feel about all of this coming down on me."

    a) What information needs to be clearer?

    i.
    ii.

    b) Your clarifying response:

10. *A 35-year-old female, talking to the shelter case worker.*

> *"We've been living on the streets for a couple of months. My kids and I eat here at the shelter; sometimes we sleep there. Summer is almost over, which means that life gets even harder. I know they have to go to school too and that worries me a lot."*

a) What information needs to be clearer?

i.

ii.

b) Your clarifying response:

PART II

As you reflect on the skills you have learned, what information, techniques, attending behaviors, etc. need to be clarified? Ask your practice partner(s) 4 clarifying questions.

You will need a minimum of 4 people for this exercise: one client and three social workers. Think back to the game you may have played as a child, **20 Questions.** This exercise will follow the same format, but will focus on a client situation that the social workers will need to tease out through asking **20 Questions** (or less!!)

Client: Think of a situation but give out no information unless the Social Worker asks you a clarifying question.
Social Worker: Take turns asking only clarifying questions and wait for the client's response before proceeding to the next person. You, as a collective group, may ask no more than 20 Questions. See if you can figure out the situation the client had in mind.

SUMMARIZATION

Read the following vignettes and

a) Identify the key aspects of the client's statement; and
b) Provide a summarization response to the client's statement. Be sure to use appropriate lead-in responses.

Example:

A 40-year-old White male talking with a caseworker at the domestic violence prevention center.

Social worker: So, tell me more about your experience in the support group. I know you've been attending the sessions for the past 12 weeks.

Client: Well, it's okay. Most of the guys are a lot like me. We want our wives to stay home with the kids. Things would be better if my wife listened to me and stopped hassling me so much.

Social worker: You want Leslie to back off and give you some breathing room.

Client: Definitely. She does things that aggravate me. Sometimes it feels as if she purposefully pisses me off. Like she's just waiting to see what I'll do next.

Social worker: What happens at those times?

Client: It depends. Sometimes I yell. Most of the time I leave now. I know that if I stick around, I'm likely to do something that I'll regret, maybe hit her.

a) Most important aspects of the client's statement:

    i. <u>He attends a batterers support group.</u>
    ii. <u>He feels as if his wife is purposefully testing him.</u>
    iii. <u>He has seen some change in his behavior since attending the group.</u>

b) Your summarization response based on the entire dialogue:

<u>Now you are able to identify certain situations that could lead to hitting Leslie. Through the help of the support group, you're learning other ways of dealing with your wife.</u>

Case 1:

A 40-year-old overweight female talks with an intake social worker about her failures and loneliness.

SW   Jeanne, let's talk for a minute about some of the things that are bothering you.

CL: My weight. I guess it's all cyclical. I mean being overweight, not a lot of people want to be your friend. I feel lonely. I've always felt rejected since I was little.

SW: It's hard for you to remember a time when you felt as though you belonged?

CL: Yeah. I feel crappy about myself. Lonely. I don't make any friends. I hurt the people who actually do love me. I let down my family all the time.

SW: Tell me about that. How do you let your family down?

CL: Well, they always try to build me up. They support me. When I quit school, I knew it hurt them. I work at a laundromat, I'm sure they want more for me than that. I guess I was never motivated enough to learn another trade. So I work in a laundromat, and I guess I do okay there. I don't know.

a)   Most important aspects of the client's statement:

     i.
     ii.
     iii.

b)   Your summarization response:

Case 2:

A 60-year-old female talking with the hospital social worker. She is considering suicide after recently learning that she has terminal cancer.

CL: The news is terminal cancer, so I am not going to live like this! I don't want to feel myself dying every day. I think I'm just going to take care of it on my own.

SW: What do you mean, "take care of it"?

CL: I think I'm just going to go off on my own, and whatever happens, happens. I don't want to live. I don't want to end up incapable of taking care of myself. I'm going to die anyway. I'll say my goodbyes while I'm okay.

SW: You feel hopeless about what the future holds.

CL: Yeah, I do. I've always had a full life. Lots of friends. My family is the best. How can I put them through my slow and painful death? I don't want to burden anyone with caring for me. It would be so unfair.

a) Most important aspects of the client's statement:

i.
ii.
iii.

b) Your summarization response:

Case 3:

A 75-year-old African-American female who is living in a nursing home. She wants to go back home, but her children feel strongly that this is her only option.

SW: Eleanor, you've been at the nursing home for the past six months. I know at times you've been very unhappy here. How have you been doing recently?

CL: Well, I just hate it here. I absolutely hate it here. My roommate, Emma, cries all the time. There's not a moment's peace. I get hungry, and I can't eat. I can't eat until they come get us for breakfast, lunch and supper. My kids haven't been here to see me in three months. I'm really lonely. I am miserable,.

SW: As time wears on, it's even harder for you to make peace with being here?

CL: Yes, it is just getting worse. I don't see it ever getting better. I hate being here. It's really depressing and I was happier before I came. I had the fall and broke my hip and, next thing you know, here I am. I have my wits about me. I know who I am and I feel like I can take care of myself. I just don't feel like I belong here.

SW: I know it's been very hard for you, but from talking with your son and daughter, they feel it's not possible for you to go home. There's just no help available.

CL: Well, I just don't think they give me enough credit. I think that I could take care of myself and that I would not need somebody with me 24 hours a day. I don't know why they think that. I just feel like they're throwing me away.

SW: They don't see your strength? That you are capable of managing with some assistance?

CL: I realize that when I first broke my hip, I was incapacitated and was not able to do for myself. But I'm better, and I'm getting around with my walker. And there are many things I can do by myself now.

a)   Most important aspects of the client's statement:

     i.
     ii.
     iii.

b)   Your summarization response:

Case 4:

A 17-year-old White male, talking to the school social worker. He is considering dropping out of school.

SW: I know this is a really big decision for you, whether or not to stay in school.

CL: It's just those teachers, the homework, and the tests. It's just everything. I've pretty much come to a conclusion that school's got nothing to do with the real world. I'm sitting here learning about geography, snow glaciers, and what does this have to do with life, with the outside world? I think I've had enough. It's the conformity, and the structure, and all the rules. I'm thinking about quitting. A friend of mine quit. He's not employed right now; but he's doing okay. Not that I want to be a brain surgeon or anything. I just want to get a good job, and pay my bills, and to live on my own.

SW: What would you do if you quit school?

CL: I'd get a job. I don't know. Maybe just hang out for awhile. I could use a breather.

SW: What else is going on in your life right now that you need a break ?

CL: The regular stuff, my parents ragging on me, my failing grades, you know that kind of stuff.

a)   Most important aspects of the client's statement:

    i.
    ii.
    iii.

b)   Your summarization response:

Case 5:

A 40-year-old male, talking to a hotline worker. He is a single parent with two teenage daughters, and is feeling overwhelmed.

CL: Being a single parent and having two teenage daughters isn't the easiest thing in the world, I tell you. They are rebellious. They use the phone a lot. They're coming home later and later. I want to give them their space, they're individuals. But I'm worried about them too.

SW: You sound like you're concerned about your girls and also realistic, knowing that part of being a teenager is having some freedom.

CL: Recently, I gave them a curfew and they are furious with me. They say, "Dad, you're not being fair. You're being too strict with us." Well, I don't want them out at all hours of the night. I want them to respect the rules of the house. They respect me, and I respect them.

SW: That's very reasonable. You are the parent.

CL: It's not reasonable in their eyes, and we have been getting into fights. And it's just chaos. And I really wish my wife was still alive, because it's a lot for one parent. I guess dads and daughters are a struggle. It's a struggle.

a)   Most important aspects of the client's statement:

    i.
    ii.
    iii.

b)   Your summarization response:

Case 6:

A 22-year-old African-American female who won't be graduating with her class. Her mother is supporting her financially. She is talking to her college counselor.

SW: Kamaria, the last time we met, we spent time talking about your frustration at not graduating on time. We agreed that we would talk more about that today. Where do you want to start?

CL: Well, I'm still feeling like I'm letting my Mom down and that I should be graduating this May. And that upsets me, and it makes me feel like I'm not doing what I should. My Mom tells me, "Don't worry about it, everybody does things in their own time." I know that when she was in school, she finished...she went to a two-year college, and then came here. Plus, she had me. She graduated from here and she finished on time. I don't have any children, I don't have anything to set me back. It's just me. And it's gonna take me longer than it took her. I don't have those obstacles standing in my way and I'm still not where I think I'm supposed to be. I feel bad about that.

SW: Sounds like you feel guilty.

CL: I do. I don't have any of the complications that she did. The only responsibilities I have are credit card bills. So I work part time. I should be graduating in May. She says I haven't let her down, but I still feel like I have. She tells me that I don't have to live up to anybody's standards, but I feel like I'm letting myself down too.

a) Most important aspects of the client's statement:

    i.
    ii.
    iii.

b) Your summarization response:

Case 7:

A 23-year-old male who recently ended a relationship with his girlfriend. She has attempted suicide and he feels responsible.

CL: I thought things were over. Then she called me again on Monday.

SW: Just two days ago?

CL: Right. Well, yeah. It's been OVER for me. I thought it was over for her too.

W: These last three months have been up and down, things change from minute to minute.

CL: Yeah.

SW: David, what's your take on her suicide attempt?

CL: Well, a couple days before the suicide attempt, we had a party at my house. I was running around trying to keep the house organized. And she kept yelling at me, "David, why don't you hang out with me?" Well, she got really upset with me, and trashed my room. We got into an argument out in the parking lot. She grabbed me tightly. I still have some marks on my arms from a fight two months ago. I said, "Stop, you're getting violent." She said, "I'll show you what violent is." I walked away, and she got down on her knees and banged her head on the concrete.

SW: That must have been very frightening for you.

CL: It was. I don't know but I think she needs help, and I can't help her. I have too much going on in my life. I care for her, but I've done my part. I called the Crisis Hotline and her parents.

a)   Most important aspects of the client's statement:

       i.
       ii.
       iii.

b)   Your summarization response:

Case 7: Continued with David- Session #2

SW: David, we spent our last session talking about Lisa, your ex-girlfriend who was very abusive to you. When we ended, we talked about exploring other relationships that you've been in and how you tend to get into relationships with females that are not necessarily good for you.

CL: Well, I think it started with my first girlfriend, my freshman year in high school. I was nice to her. When I broke up with her, she tried to kill herself. I felt like it was my fault. Then, I dated a couple of people off and on. I had a really great relationship my senior year in high school. It lasted for a year or so. It was really good until we went away to college. And after that, I really haven't met any girls who have been very stable.

SW: It seems as if you are questioning for yourself...What is it that attracts these women to me or me to them? How can I make better choices in a relationship?

CL: Yeah! The thing I keep finding out about myself is that I'm too nice. I don't want people to be mad at me. I'll do anything for anyone.

SW: What do you mean when you say "I'm too nice"?

CL: Just that I'll do whatever anybody wants me to. I want people, especially girls, to like me. Even if it means I get hurt. I know it sounds crazy.

a) Most important aspects of the client's statement:

    i.
    ii.
    iii.

b) Your summarization response:

Case 8:

A 33-year-old White male, talking to his caseworker at the day treatment program. He is chronically depressed and is not taking his medication.

SW: You know, Tony, we've been talking a lot about your medication, and you said that you would take your medication every day.

CL: Right. I know if I don't take my medication, I get very depressed. And I've been depressed all week. I've been slipping, taking my medication. So I think that I need to be on a very strict regimen.

SW: When do you take your medication?

CL: Well, I'm supposed to take it three times a day: in the morning; at noon, and right after dinner. You know, if I'm out with my friends, it's a struggle for me to take it. I get lazy. I understand the importance. I just need, I guess, to be more structured. I know that when I come in here, I always promise you that I am going to do everything on the treatment plan, and I screw up. I don't want to do that anymore. I didn't like myself this week. I scared myself. I was really, really depressed.

a) Most important aspects of the client's statement:

    i.
    ii.
    iii.

b)   Your summarization response:

Case 9:

An 18-year-old female, talking to a probation officer. She was recently arrested on drug charges. She denies that she's addicted to drugs, but acknowledges that she's afraid of the legal consequences.

SW: What happened after you were arrested for possession of illegal drugs?

CL: Well, my Mom and Step-dad came and bailed me out of jail. I've got a public defender and I go to court in a couple of months. I got caught with cocaine. It wasn't very much; it was less than a gram. But it seems that cocaine, any possession of any of it, is a felony offense. So I'm concerned about that. And my parents are really pissed off. They didn't really know that I was involved in drugs. They're real freaked out and they want me to go into treatment. I don't think that's necessary because I don't have a drug problem.

SW: You're not concerned about your drug usage, just the possible legal consequences.

CL: I suppose, yeah. I don't want to end up spending time in prison. I couldn't hack that. Plus my parents are threatening me, too. It just seems like they're always surprised. Each time they find out about something new, something "bad," they're shocked.

a)   Most important aspects of the client's statement:

        i.
        ii.
        iii.

b)   Your summarization response:

Case 10:

A 45-year-old female talking to a social worker about her struggles since her daughter was deployed by the military.

CL: Things haven't been going very well since the war started. My daughter is in the military and I worry constantly about her safety.

SW: That is understandable. It must be hard to have her so far away and not see her to be sure that she is okay.

CL: It is. And to make matters worse, I have her two sons living with me right now. They miss her terribly. They have bad nightmares. Both boys call out for her in the middle of the night. I don't know how to comfort them.

SW: It must be very difficult to take care of them when you are also in so much pain. How do you manage day to day??

CL: I am numb most of the time……just trying to get them off to school. The boys are involved in lots of activities, which is good, but it keeps me on the go too much. I am old now.

   a)   Most important aspects of the client's statement:
           i.
           ii.
           iii

   b)   Your summarization response:

PART II

Using the summarization in case #4, a student considering dropping out of school, list three aspects of the problem situation. Next write down summary/transition statements, moving from one component to the next. Once you have completed the first two steps, role-play the situation using the transitional statements you developed as a group.

Client: Put yourself in the client's place. Use your empathy skills to understand the client's perspective and experiences. Remember being in the client role is a very useful learning experience, as you have the opportunity to think and feel as the client might.

Social worker: Use the written summary/transition statements in the role play that were developed by your group. Remember to use all the interviewing skills you have learned so far. Role play for 10-15 minutes.

INFORMATION GIVING

After reading each item, complete the following:

a) Generalize the problem (in universal or global terms);
b) Identify the most important piece of information in the client's statement; and
c) Provide an information-giving response. <u>Use a paraphrase or refection of feeling response either before or after giving the client information.</u>

Example:

Client: "I'm devastated. I want to have a family. My husband and I tried every medical procedure possible. We've spent all our savings; plus, it seems like we've talked to every specialist in the state. We have reached the end. We agreed if I wasn't pregnant by the time I turned 40, we would give up."

a)   Generalize the problem:

There are significant constraints related to getting pregnant at age 40. Anger and disappointment are normal feelings.

b)   Most important pieces of information:

i.   They have spent all their savings in an effort to have a baby
ii.   Time is also running out
iii.   Feelings (disappointed, frustrated, anxious)

c)   Your information-giving response:

It's understandable that you feel angry, frustrated and disappointed, after so many unsuccessful attempts at getting pregnant. Maybe looking into some other options, such as adoption, might be a next step.

1. *A 37-year-old White male, talking to a hotline worker about his marriage.*

    "I think my wife is having an affair. She hasn't said it in so many words, but I can just tell. She's not home much and when she is, she seems miles away. She is beautiful and any guy would love to have her on his arm. I don't know how to ask her or even if I want to know. We've been married for seven years--some times have been better than others. This is the first time I've felt so scared."

a)   Generalize the problem:

b)   Most important pieces of information:

i.
ii.
iii.

c)   Your information-giving response:

2. *A 40-year-old White female, talking about her alcohol usage to an intake caseworker.*

    "I drink a lot. I don't deny that, but an alcoholic, that's a joke. Alcoholics are bums on the street, drinking a bottle of whisky out of a brown paper bag. My father, now he was an alcoholic. He'd leave for days at a time, and he never held down a job. He was a loser who never amounted to anything. I have a good job. I make decent money. There has never been a time that I haven't been able to control my drinking. Do I fit the alcohol profile?"

a)   Generalize the problem:

b)   Most important pieces of information:

i.
ii.

iii.

c)   Your information-giving response:

3.   *A 12-year-old girl, talking to the community outreach worker about her mother.*

"My mother was diagnosed as having schizophrenia when I was little. I don't know what that means, exactly, but she does weird things. She believes that people are following us, and sometimes she hears voices. My Dad doesn't want to talk to me about why my Mom acts so strange. He says I'm too young to understand. Is this schizophrenia thing hereditary? Will I end up like her?"

a)   Generalize the problem:

b)   Most important pieces of information:

i.
ii.
iii.

c)   Your information-giving response:

4.   *A 22-year-old Italian American female, talking with another social work student about her guilt surrounding a cousin's sexual victimization.*

"I knew my cousin was being molested by her father. She kind of hinted about it when we were younger, maybe 10 or so. Now I am in social work classes, and we are learning about sexual abuse. I should have done something then. Now I feel so guilty for doing nothing."

a)   Generalize the problem:

b)   Most important pieces of information:

i.
ii.
iii.

c)   Your information-giving response:

5.   *A 21-year-old male, talking with a crisis counselor on the hotline.*

"I'll never feel okay again. Losing my Dad, having him die so unexpectedly, left me with no chance to say goodbye. He wouldn't want me to drop out of school, but I don't have the strength to keep up with my work or the motivation to study. I always counted on him, and now he's gone. I'm at such a loss. How do people get through this?"

a)   Generalize the problem:

b)   Most important pieces of information:

i.
ii.
iii.

c)   Your information-giving response:

6.   *A 25-year-old female, talking to the domestic violence shelter intake worker.*

"Last night, I was beaten up by my boyfriend. This is probably the fourth or fifth time. He treated me nicely when we first met, but now he gets so jealous. He refuses to let me see my friends or my Mom, and I'm sure he followed me home from work last night. He's starting to really scare me. That's why I came to the shelter."

a)   Generalize the problem:

b)   Most important pieces of information:

i.
ii.
iii.

c)   Your information-giving response:

7.   *A 17-year-old female, talking with a Child Protection Service social worker.*

"I told that other social worker, the one at school that I don't use drugs that often and frankly this is my body and my baby. I appreciate your concern, but it's none of your business. I'm 17, and old enough to make my own decisions. It pisses me off that now Child Protection Services is involved. It's my life, my child, my choice."

a)   Generalize the problem:

b)   Most important pieces of information:

i.
ii.
iii.

c)   Your information-giving response:

8.   *A 70-year-old man, talking to the hospital social worker about his finances and future.*

"My wife and I need help. Everyone says, "Go talk to the social worker." We're just about broke, and with my wife here in the hospital, we can't pay for all her medical bills or get help once she gets home. She had a stroke, so she'll need a lot of care, but...I don't want her going into a nursing home, no matter what. She wouldn't want that either."

a)   Generalize the problem:

b)   Most important pieces of information:

i.
ii.
iii.

c)   Your information-giving response:

9.   *A 10-year-old girl, talking with the school social worker.*

"Last week my parents told us they're getting a divorce. It's been coming for a long time, but I really want them to stay together. My sister says there is no chance of them staying married, but I don't believe that. Please give me some ideas about how I can prevent this from happening."

a)   Generalize the problem:

b)   Most important pieces of information:

i.
ii.

iii.

c)   Your information-giving response:

10.   *A mother talking to the school social worker about her 6-year-old daughter.*

   "My daughter is having such a hard time making friends. She's so demanding and bossy to everyone. She's always been like this, but since her brother was born, it's gotten much worse. At school Susie spends most of her time alone now—the other kids want nothing to do with her. I've tried every thing I can think of, but she's driving me crazy. Her teacher suggested that I talk to you."

a)   Generalize the problem:

b)   Most important pieces of information:

i.
ii.
iii.

c)   Your information-giving response:

PART II

Social Worker: Role play the information given in case # 10, a parent talking about her 6-year-old child. Use the pitfalls advice giving and overwhelming the client with too much information (and irrelevant information) in the interview.

Client: Respond genuinely to the social worker (and try not to laugh). Continue for 5 minutes. Now, role play the scenario again. This time, offer information appropriately. Be sure to prioritize it and generalize it appropriately. Discuss the differences between the two role plays.

CONFRONTATION

Read the following items and identify:

a) Issues you would address related to the problem (at least two); and
b) Your confrontational response. <u>Be sure to include a paraphrase or reflection of feeling response either before or after delivering your confrontation.</u>

Example:

A 26-year-old Vietnamese female has expressed an interest in working on improving her relationships with people in her life. The client has informed the social worker that she can only meet at 1:00 p.m. on Wednesday. For the past two weeks she has come at 1:15 p.m. and today she did not attend at all.

a)   What issue(s) would you address?

<u>**Her lateness**</u>
<u>**Does she really want to be in counseling?**</u>
<u>**What seems to be getting in the way of her attending the counseling sessions?**</u>

b)   Confrontational response:

<u>**I'm concerned that you have either been late for our sessions or not coming at all. You asked to meet on Wednesdays and you are not following through. I wonder if you are truly committed to this process.**</u>

---

1. *A 38-year-old male is fighting for greater visitation rights with his two children. He has shared with the social worker that he is having a sexual relationship with a coworker. The divorce decree states that he is not to have any overnight guests while the children are with him. He also reports that his ex-wife plans to take him back to court. She wants the judge to order only "supervised day time only visits" until the children are older (they are 6 and 10).*

a)   What issue(s) would you address?

i.
ii.
iii.

b)   Your confrontational response:

2. *A 17-year-old female who is 4 months pregnant comes to your agency, stating that she wants to keep the baby. She is excited about becoming a parent. During her session, she casually mentions that she is drinking alcohol and smoking marijuana. She reports that she feels good most of the time, but has recently been experiencing low energy and a loss of appetite.*

a)   What issue(s) would you address?

i.

ii.

iii.

b) Your confrontational response:

3. *A 14-year-old male was caught breaking and entering into a local business. This is his second offense. He is on probation and there is a good possibility of serving time in a juvenile facility. He appears to be fairly confident that nothing is going to happen.*

a)   What issue(s) would you address?

i.

ii.

iii.

b)   Your confrontational response:

4. *A 48-year-old male who has experienced multiple sexual relationships. He states that he is careful in selecting partners, and always asks if they have been exposed to AIDS or any other sexually transmitted infections. He uses protection periodically. He enjoys his freedom and sees nothing problematic about his behavior.*

a)   What issue(s) would you address?

i.
ii.
iii.

b)   Your confrontational response:

5. *A 30-year-old female has been married for five years to a controlling man. She recently lost 20 pounds because her husband told her she was too fat. Although she wants a child, she agreed not to get pregnant because she would no longer be physically attractive to him. She states that she loves her husband and can't imagine her life without him.*

a)   What issue(s) would you address?

i.
ii.
iii.

b)   Your confrontational response:

6. *A 45-year-old male who is schizophrenic refuses to take his anti-psychotic medication because the side effects include headaches and nausea. He states that in the past he has experienced long periods of feeling fine and has no need to take the medication. The staff at his current day treatment program has informed you that he must continue taking his medication or he will be terminated from the program.*

a)   What issue(s) would you address?

i.
ii.
iii.

b)   Your confrontational response:

7. *A 35-year-old woman admits to physically abusing her children, ages 8 and 12. She reports that she has taken parenting classes and has learned "time-out" procedures. During a family session, you observe the client raising her voice and threatening to hurt her eldest daughter.*

a)   What issue(s) would you address?

i.

ii.

iii.

b)   Your confrontational response:

8. *An 18-year-old college student, who has a four-year scholarship, is currently failing all of his classes. He reports that his instructors are hard on him and expect too much from freshmen. He did exceptionally well academically in high school and was the star of his football team. Recently he stopped going to all of his classes, stating that "It's a lost cause." He reports that next year he will attend the community college at home and live with his parents. As he continues talking, tears are running down his face.*

a)   What issue(s) would you address?

i.

ii.

iii.

b)   Your confrontational response:

9. *A 20-year-old female college student admits to having "weird eating habits." She eats one piece of toast for breakfast and a cup of soup for dinner. She is proud of her ability to limit her food intake and has lost 10 pounds in the last two weeks.*

a)   What issue(s) would you address?

i.
ii.
iii.

b)   Your confrontational response:

10. *A 13-year-old girl is currently living in a foster home. During a weekend visit with her mother, she ran away. Two days later, she was picked up by the police. She reports that she ran away from home because she didn't want to go back to the foster family. Her plan is to keep running until she can live permanently with her mom.*

a)   What issue(s) would you address?

i.
ii.
iii.

b)   Your confrontational response:

PART II

> With your practice partner (s), discuss issues related to using the pitfall of premature confrontation What are some issues regarding cultural differences and how confrontations might be interpreted?
>
> Identify when confrontations are appropriate.
>
> Social Worker: Using the confrontation in case # 5, what issues are important to address? Given the nature of the client's relationship with her husband, what interviewing approach should you take? Continue this role play for 10 minutes. Discuss the client's strengths.

INTERPRETATION

Read the following items and identify:

a) At least two underlying issues that need to be addressed; and
b) Your interpretive response. <u>Be sure to use a paraphrase or reflection of feeling response after offering your interpretation.</u>

Example:

A 28-year-old woman is currently in a violent relationship. She informs you that she doesn't mind a few punches now and then. "It's better than being alone. Look, I grew up in violent home, I am used to it." She's been in two other relationships, both of which were violent.

a)   What underlying issues should be addressed? (at least two)

i.   <u>pattern of abuse</u>
ii.   <u>self-esteem</u>
iii.   <u>fear of being alone</u>

b)   Interpretative response.

<u>I get the sense that somehow that you feel you deserve to be abused, that you're not worth being treated with respect.</u>

1 *A 45-year-old man who is currently unemployed reports that he is looking for work, but no one is hiring a "middle-aged has-been." He also reports that there have been other times in his life when he has been unemployed for over six months. He was a midlevel manager at a welding company prior to his layoff. He is the sole financial support for his family.*

a)   What underlying issues could you address?

i.
ii.
iii.

b)   Your interpretative response.

2   *A 56-year-old woman is currently the caretaker of her elderly parents. Her mother, age 80, is able to manage fairly well. Her father, age 85, has been diagnosed with Alzheimer's Disease and is no longer able to recognize his family or do any self-care tasks. Your client refuses to place him in a nursing home, stating "He'd never forgive me. Finally, after all these years, I'm able to repay him for all the trouble I caused. I never was the daughter he was proud of. My sister, the perfect one, is now nowhere to be found. I guess she's too busy." [stated softly]*

a)   What underlying issues could you address?

i.
ii.
iii.

b)   Your interpretative response.

3   *A 14-year-old girl who has always excelled in her academic classes recently has refused to answer questions during class and no longer completes homework assignments. She appears uninterested in any school activities and states "I'm tired of sticking out. I hate people thinking that I'm the school brain."*

a)   What underlying issues could you address?

i.
ii.
iii.

b)   Your interpretative response.

4   *A 35-year-old woman, who is a single parent, reports that her 8-year-old daughter, Karen, has refused to go to school for the past 4 weeks. Recently the mother has decided "not to force the issue" because it's been nice having her company at home. She's now thinking about home schooling.*

a)   What underlying issues could you address?

i.

ii.
iii.

b)   Your interpretative response.

5   *A 25-year-old man is considering leaving his job as a social worker and joining the priesthood. He has always felt a "calling" to help others and believes that he can best fulfill that need through his religion. Recently he ended a five-year relationship with his college sweetheart who is "pressuring me into getting married."*

a)   What underlying issues would you address?

i.
ii.
iii.

b)   Your interpretative response.

6   *A 62-year-old divorced man has made the decision to retire after a successful career as an architect. He reports that he wants to sell his company, but has yet to find the "right buyer." He acknowledges that he has always focused on his career and doesn't have many outside interests or hobbies. His daughter, recently widowed with two children, would like him to move to Chicago and "help her get back on her feet." His relationship with her has been strained since he divorced her mother 15 years ago.*

a)   What underlying issues would you address?

i.
ii.
iii.

b)   Your interpretative response.

7 *A 30-year-old single woman reports that she loves children, wants to get married, and "have it all." She has been in several relationships during the past 10 years and has turned down two marriage proposals. The product of divorced parents, she feels it is essential to be "absolutely sure." She is waiting until the "perfect person" comes into her life. She also states that her younger brother is gay. She's sure it's because of all the conflicts between her parents while they were growing up that he is now a homosexual.*

a)　　　What underlying issues would you address?

i.

ii.

iii.

b)　　　Your interpretative response.

8 *A 48-year-old man is currently attending an outpatient alcohol and drug treatment program. He reports having trouble staying sober. Recently his wife was promoted and she is now an executive at a major corporation. He is very proud of her accomplishments, but in a passing comment he states "I wish it was me. I've worked hard all my life, but she gets the glory."*

a)　　　What underlying issues would you address?

i.

ii.

iii.

b)　　　Your interpretative response.

9 *A 30-year-old woman reports that her best friend has no time for her anymore, now that she has a boyfriend. Although she would like to be in a relationship, she doesn't want to get hurt. Her pattern of behavior includes excessive jealousy; saying one thing yet doing something else; and "testing" the other person. She states that it is hard for her to trust people, especially men. She's afraid they'll leave her too, "just like my Dad did."*

a)   What underlying issues would you address?

i.

ii.

iii.

b)   Your interpretative response.

10 *A 37-year-old man who was recently diagnosed with cancer. He has started chemotherapy and is experiencing debilitating side effects. His physician reports that the prognosis for this client is very promising, but he must continue with the treatment. The client is unsure about whether he can handle all the struggles associated with his treatment. He states that he never imagined being so scared and wonders whether he'll ever feel like himself again. His wife is very supportive, but tends not to assert herself in their relationship. He has always been the decision-maker.*

a)   What underlying issues would you address?

i.

ii.

iii.

c)   Your interpretative response.

PART II

With your practice partner(s), talk about a time that you experienced some new insight into your behaviors, patterns, thought processes etc.
What was it like to have the "light bulb go on for you?
What led up to this acquisition of new insight?
How can you use this personal experience to relate to clients, especially those who may not trust you or feel very threatened by a new way of looking at their situation?

If you choose to self-disclose to the client about a shared insight or experience, what might you say??

PITFALLS

In this section, you are presented with 14 scenarios. All of them have at least two problematic social worker responses. In completing these exercises, you may want to refer to this list of pitfalls covered in the CD-ROM and textbook:

- advice giving;
- inappropriate use of humor;
- interrupting the client/abrupt transitions;
- judgmental response;
- offering false assurance/minimizing the problem and insincerity;
- premature confrontation
- inappropriate social worker self-disclosure;
- inappropriate /irrelevant questions
- premature problem solving;
- overwhelming the client with too much or incorrect (inappropriate) information

---

Read each case and complete the following:

a) In your own words, identify the mistakes that are made;
b) Explain why those problematic responses could lead to barriers in furthering the relationship; and
c) Provide a correct social worker response.

I. Example:

The client is a 38-year-old female who has just miscarried for the third time.

Client: This is awful. Three miscarriages, and my husband and I really want a baby. And I just feel, I don't know, if I'm paying for something that I have done before. But this is terrible.

Social Worker: So, this is your third miscarriage. I know this great doctor who deals with problem pregnancies.

Client: Oh, yeah, tell me about him.

Social Worker: He's wonderful. He helped my sister with her pregnancy. You should go see him as soon as possible.

Client: What's his phone number?

---

continued

> **Social Worker** Oh, I'll just set up your appointment right now because it's too stressful :for you to worry about. You go home and rest.
>
> **a)** **What mistakes were made?**
>
> **i.** premature problem-solving
> **ii.** inappropriate self-disclosure
> **iii.** minimizing the problem
>
> **b)** **How might that response lead to barriers in furthering the relationship?**
>
> **Client feels discounted, didn't explore feelings, doing "for" versus "with" the client.**
>
> **c)** **Corrected response:** You've suffered a great loss.

Case 1:

11-year-old female who is sharing for the first time that she has been sexually abused by her stepfather.

CL: My stepfather. He touched me in places I know he is not supposed to touch. He told me that it was okay, but it doesn't feel okay.

SW: I have to contact Child Protection Services right away.

CL: No, please don't! He told me that he loves me. And we have done a couple of things that were a lot of fun together. He took me to a baseball game, and bought me ice cream. And took me to movies. He told me not to tell Mommy about it.

SW: Sharon, I'm really glad that you told me this secret. Lots of children are sexually abused. Sexual abuse is something that makes kids feel bad, like they've done something to deserve this. Now that I know, I have to contact the agency responsible for investigating sexual abuse.

CL: You know, maybe I do things to make him touch me in that way.

SW: You are not responsible for an adult's behavior. It's his problem. He needs help. No matter what, you are not to blame. Abusers try to put the responsibility on the child. It's wrong for him to do that. Wait here while I make the call.

a)   What mistakes were made?

i.

ii.

iii.

b)   How might that response lead to barriers in furthering the relationship?

c)   Your corrected response:

Case 2:

A 54-year-old male whose job performance is slipping; he has some concerns about his future with the company.

CL: I've been this company's CEO for the past 25 years. I've been on top of the ladder for a long time, but I've seen a lot of things in the past year slipping. Dividends haven't been where they should be and, I don't know. People are starting to question me; I've started to question myself.

SW: Are you saying that you are slacking off on the job??

CL: Well, I wouldn't call it slacking off. I just don't have the drive for success that I use to have.

SW: It seems to me that maybe you don't care about your job. Maybe it's time for a change.

CL: I wouldn't say I don't care, but...

SW: You just said you are not doing the same quality on the job, no wonder you're in a rut. What do you plan to do to change your situation?

a)   What mistakes were made?

i.

ii.

iii.

b)   How might that response lead to barriers in furthering the relationship?

c)   Your corrected response:

Case 3:

A 22-year-old man who is in counseling at the insistence of his girlfriend and parents.

CL: It's my fourth year in college and my grades are not where they are supposed to be. My parents said they were going to cut me off financially if I didn't get my grades up. My girlfriend has been really getting on me, too, to do well in classes. Another thing, they think I have a drinking problem. I don't know if they are right or not.

SW: You know it is really important for you to do well in your classes if you want to get a job someday.

CL: Yeah I know.

SW: And you know it is wrong to drink because it causes problems with your girlfriend and with school, not to mention, multiple health problems down the road.

CL: Well, I guess that's true.

SW: How much do you drink each day?

CL: Maybe five or six beers a night, no more than my friends drink.

SW: Wow! Sounds like you're on your way to becoming an alcoholic.

a)   What mistakes were made?

i.
ii.
iii.

b) How might that response lead to barriers in furthering the relationship?

c) Your corrected response:

Case 4:

A 30-year-old African-American male who was severely injured in a recent accident.

CL: Yeah. I had this accident two weeks ago, driving my truck. I went right through the window. I'm probably going to lose my right leg.

SW: I'm sorry to hear that.

CL: Yeah. I'm sorry, too. Don't know if I can drive a truck without the use of both legs. The doctors say that with a prosthetic and rehabilitation I'll be able to walk. I don't know how kindly I'll take to a fake leg.

SW: When will you know about the surgery?

CL: I'll know in a couple of days.

SW: If your leg is amputated, hopefully after a while, you'll get used to the idea. It takes time. Rehab can work wonders.

CL: If I lose my leg, I don't know if the firm will want me to keep driving. Maybe they have an office job for me, but I've never been real good at shuffling papers. Truck driving is basically all I've ever known.

SW: It's too early to worry about the worst, especially when no decision has been made yet. Have you always been so quick to jump to a bad conclusion?

CL: No, but there are bills to pay, you know. There's a whole family to support. This one truck accident and everything falls apart.

SW: But right now you don't know for sure how things will end up. Looking at all your strengths, I know you'll get through this. Plus, you'll be eligible for Workmen's Compensation, since this is a job-related injury.

CL: Yeah, but these are pretty rough times and there are hard days ahead of me. Truck driving is all I've really ever known.

SW: Let's get more information from the doctors, then we can move on to plan B.

a) What mistakes were made?

i.
ii.
iii.

b) How might that response lead to barriers in furthering the relationship?

c) Your corrected response:

Case 5:

A 14-year-old female was caught shoplifting.

CL: I got caught shoplifting yesterday. I went into the dressing room and put a shirt underneath my own shirt and the security guard caught me. Now they say they're going to press charges. It's a new department store policy. I'm 14, so they can't try me as an adult, which is a good thing. But obviously my mother is very angry at me.

SW: I know your mom is mad now, but I'm sure with time she'll get over it.

CL: Yeah, I guess so.

SW: Is this your first offense?

CL: Yeah.

SW: Then don't worry. They never prosecute first offenders harshly.

CL: Really?

SW: Sure, this whole thing will be over soon.

CL: Yeah, but my teachers know about it. They've been talking to me about it a lot. They make it seem like a bad situation.

SW: It sounds like the teachers are trying to scare you. I'm not saying it's okay to shoplift, but it's your first offense.

a)   What mistakes were made?

i.
ii.
iii.

b)   How might that response lead to barriers in furthering the relationship?

c)   Your corrected response:

Case 6:

A 35-year-old woman who is frustrated with her neighbor.

CL: You know my next-door neighbor, Betty? We've been friends for a long time. But she is starting to test my patience, really.

SW: Go on.

CL: I'm home. I've got these three kids and I'm home all day. And, Betty, she just says to her daughter, "Why don't you go next door and play with Sue," my daughter. And her daughter comes over, which is fine. And the next thing I hear from Betty is that she's going out. She's gone, and I don't know where to find her. And her daughter is here with me for hours and hours at a time.

SW: Well, does her daughter cause problems with your three kids?

CL: No, my children like having her over.

SW: Does she break things or roughhouse? Does she cry or complain about being at your place?

CL: No, she's really a good kid.

SW: Then it seems to me that you don't have a problem. Be glad that your kids have a good friend.

CL: But, I want Betty to at least ask me rather than just sending Sue over.

SW: Your other alternative is to say something, but that may cause your friendship with Betty to end.

a) What mistakes were made?

i.
ii.
iii.

b) How might that response lead to barriers in furthering the relationship?

c) Your corrected response:

Case 7:

A 15-year-old girl who hates school. She recently hit her teacher.

CL: I hate these teachers. They're just pissing me off! Yesterday my English teacher wanted to keep me after school because I didn't do my homework. Screw her, you know? I got so mad I slapped her.

SW: So, you think your teacher is a punching bag?

CL: Yep! I know she is.

SW: Well, when I was in school, we had this teacher we called Miss Latrine because she smelled really bad.

CL: That's hilarious. We call my English teacher Big Nose for obvious reasons.

SW: Really, what other nicknames do you have?

a) What mistakes were made?

i.
ii.
iii.

b) How might that response lead to barriers in furthering the relationship?

c) Your corrected response:

Case 8:

A 36-year-old male who is frustrated with his parents' over-involvement in his life.

CL: It's my mother and father. They make me angry. They don't treat me like I'm 32; they treat me like I'm two. They want to know who my girlfriends are. They want to dictate where I work and where I live. They still want me to live at home, and I don't want to live at home. I want to live my own life.

SW: So here you are, an adult, and your parents treat you as though you can't make any decisions for yourself? Or if you do, they're wrong?

CL: That's right. And sometimes I screw up just to spite them, just to get them angry. I think I got fired from my last job just so I could see the look on their faces after I told them I got fired from this really good job. I don't know what they expect from me. It's like I'm not their little baby boy anymore. I'm a man, I'm an adult. I need to make mistakes and I need to do things on my own.

SW: So, what was the job you got fired from?

CL: Oh, I worked at an insurance company as a consultant.

SW: Did you find that to be a fulfilling job?

CL: Yeah, I guess. But weren't we talking about my relationship with my parents though?

SW: Yes we were, but I need to know a little more about you. Do you currently have a girlfriend?

CL: No, not now.

a) What mistakes were made?

i.
ii.
iii.

b) How might that response lead to barriers in furthering the relationship?

c) Your corrected response:

Case 9:

A 17- year-old African-American female who is experiencing trouble at home, particularly with her father.

SW: Juanita, you were talking about the difficulties you were having at home. The problems with your father and those things were getting so bad that you decided to leave. Tell me what's been going on since the last time we met.

CL: I'm back at home, but my dad won't talk to me anymore. He's really upset that I ran away from home. My mother, I guess, didn't really deal with it well and was very upset. She cried all the time and couldn't eat. And he blames me for all that.

He hates me more than he did before and won't even speak to me. So walking around our house is like, is like walking on eggshells. I hate being there. None of this is my fault.

SW: Well, let's set some goals that you can work on in dealing with your father.

CL: Okay, what kind of goals?

SW: Well, maybe you could try to start one conversation with him each day.

CL: I'm not sure I'm ready to do that.

SW: If you want things to improve, this is what I'd suggest.

CL: Well, I don't know.

SW: How about trying to say one nice thing to him between now and our next session? That will help open up communication.

a)   What mistakes were made?

i.
ii.
iii.

b)   How might that response lead to barriers in furthering the relationship?

c)   Your corrected response:

Case 10:

A 20-year-old White female who was recently released from jail.

SW: Hi, Andrea, how have you been recently?

CL: Well, I've been okay since...

SW: So, that's nice. What is going on in your life now?

CL: I got out of jail about…

SW: You were in jail?

CL: Yeah, I was in jail for hitting my supervisor

SW: That's terrible. Why did you hit your supervisor? You knew you'd get in trouble.

CL: She set me off. It's just so hard to be a black wo…

SW: Keep going.

CL: To be a black woman in an all white office.

SW: But that's always a reality in your life—you can't just punch someone out because you don't like her attitude. Did you get fired?

CL: No, but I've been reassigned to another unit.

SW: Good. It's best to keep your opinions and hands to yourself so this doesn't happen again. Next time you could loose your job for good.

a)   What mistakes were made?

i.
ii.
iii.

b)   How might that response lead to barriers in furthering the relationship?

c)   Your corrected response:

Case 11:

A 40-year-old female whose boyfriend recently broke up with her.

SW: Hi, Tiffany. How are you today?

CL: Fine. How are you?

SW: (silence)

CL: So, how are you?

SW: I'm okay. What brought you in today?

CL: Well, my boyfriend just broke up with me. It's been really hard to figure out if I want to date anyone else or just be single for a while. I'm getting older and starting to worry about my marriage prospects.

SW: (silence)

CL: And I don't know what to do.

SW: (silence)

CL: And I was wondering if you could help me.

SW: Oh...?

CL: See, I hate to be alone. I can't stand not having someone in my life.

SW: OK. What other problems do you have?

a) What mistakes were made?

i.
ii.
iii.

b) How might that response lead to barriers in furthering the relationship?

c)   Your corrected response:

Case 12:

A 16-year-old female who is pregnant and searching for guidance.

SW: So how have you been doing, Jennifer?

CL: Well, okay, okay I guess. Actually, I'm not okay.

SW: What's been going on?

CL: I just found out yesterday that I'm pregnant, and I don't know what to do.

SW: Are you positive that you are pregnant?

CL: Yes, I am.

SW: Have you discussed it with your parents yet?

CL: No, I haven't. And I don't know if I should.

SW: Why not? It's really important that your parents know.

CL: I know it is, but it's just too hard.

SW: I realize that, but your parents can help you make decisions for you and the baby.

CL: I guess.

SW: So, you could tell them right now and ask them to come over and meet with us.

CL: Well, if you think that's best, I will.

SW: It is.

CL: What if they freak out?

SW: I'm sure they'll be upset, but honesty is always the best policy. How long do you think you can hide the pregnancy from them?

a)   What mistakes were made?

i.
ii.
iii.

b)   How might that response lead to barriers in furthering the relationship?

c)   Your corrected response:

Case 13:

23-year-old Hispanic male who is trying to get through college.

SW: The last time we met, you were talking about your birthday coming up
       and turning 24.

CL: Yeah. Well, I'm going to be 24 in December and all my friends have graduated.
       And I'm not quite there yet. Everybody looks at me and they're saying, "Oh, he's
       still in college. He's never going to get out. He's wasting his life."

SW: How do you see it?

CL: I feel badly about the whole thing. I transferred a lot, trying to find a decent
       major. And basically, I'm happy with social work. I'd like to get out sooner and
       start working so I can pay off all the loans that I have after the last six years of
       school.

SW: I'm sure that even if you have to stay in school longer, you will get your loans
       paid off.

CL: I don't know. I owe a lot of money.

SW: Most graduates owe a lot of money, but they make it.

CL: I guess most do, but I'm still worried about it.

SW: It's scary to owe a lot of money. I know. I had college loans too. It took me 10 years to pay them off, but I did and now things are fine. I'm proud of myself, I accomplished a lot.

a)   What mistakes were made?

i.
ii.
iii.

b)   How might that response lead to barriers in furthering the relationship?

c)   Your corrected response:

Case 14:

A 28-year-old female who is frustrated with the school's treatment of her daughter.

CL: You know this is the fifth time this week that the teacher has called about my daughter, and I'm fed up. I don't see what the big deal is. So what if my daughter is spreading paint all over the walls? It seems to me that this is a creative expression. She's having fun.

SW: I wonder whether Van Gogh's first-grade teacher complained to his mother.

CL: That's how I feel. That's exactly how I feel about it. This could be creativity in the making. This kid, she just loves having fun at school. She's not a troublemaker. The teachers don't call to say she's hitting other kids or fighting or anything like that. It's always about expressing herself through art. I have this child, this prodigy, and the teacher is squashing her creativity.

SW: So, today it's Walt Whitman Elementary School, tomorrow it's the Sistine Chapel.

CL: Well...I wouldn't say that.

SW: I'd call the teacher, set up an appointment to meet, and tell her exactly how you feel.

CL: I don't want her to get mad at me.

SW: Hey—this is your daughter here. You have to stand up for her.

a) What mistakes were made?

i.
ii.
iii.

b) How might that response lead to barriers in furthering the relationship?

c) Your corrected response:

Putting it all Together

Case 1:

A 35-year-old Chinese-American male. He is seeking help regarding suspected health problem. He believes the illness may be serious.

CL: I've been fainting at different times. It's scaring me. I don't know what I have. I don't know what's wrong. I don't know if it's something physical or if it's psychological.

SW: Right now you are extremely unsure about what might be going on with you physically and emotionally.

CL: Yes, plus I'm afraid of what to tell my family. It might be something serious. I don't know if it is something, like, genetic. This could be a very bad thing and I don't know how my family would react.

SW: Part of your concern is not just for your own health, but you are scared to tell you parents, you are afraid of their reaction.

CL: And, I guess I'm also afraid of my reaction. I suppose I should go to the doctor. It sounds serious, these fainting spells. I've looked in medical books, but I can't figure out what it is. And I'm afraid that if I go to a doctor she'll tell me it's serious. I don't know if I can take it.

SW: As you're trying to figure this out, you become more and more uncertain. "What is wrong with me? Is this something that is treatable?"

CL: I feel awful. I feel scared. And I just feel in my gut that this is a terrible situation.

SW: Summarization:

Your response:

Case 2:

A 40-year-old female. She has just had a third miscarriage. She is seeking help in coping with her loss.

CL: This is just awful. Three miscarriages, and my husband and I really want a baby. And I just feel, I don't know, as if I'm paying for something that I've done before.

SW: These miscarriages have left you feeling so out of control.

CL: And I thought that after the first one that…the doctor told me that it would be all right for the next time. And then it happened again. And now it happened again…this is just screwy. I'm really depressed about it.

SW: It's a tremendous loss.

CL: I know. And after the second one, I thought that it was just not worth going through this again. I feel like this cloud is over me. I don't know what to do now. I feel hurt, and alone, and scared.

SW: Kelly, your feelings are very understandable. You suffered repeated trauma. You wanted a baby, and now it feels as though it may never happen.

CL: Why? I mean, I ask why? Nobody deserves to suffer. I'm a healthy person. I just don't understand why God is punishing me like this.

SW: You wonder, "I take good care of myself. I'm aware of my own body and the things I need to do to ensure healthy pregnancy. Now the bottom has fallen out, for the third time."

CL: I want a baby so badly; I just want to be a mom. I want to raise a child. And when I found out I was pregnant, it's like a roller coaster. Things were going so well and we, we were going to build a nursery, and then this happened.

SW: Reflection of Feeling and clarification:

Your response:

Case 3:

A 30-year-old Hispanic male. He is considering going back to school to become a physician. His family obligations and self-doubt contribute to his dilemma.

CL: Thirty years old. The big 3 – 0. When I was in my early twenties I wanted to go to college, but I couldn't. I didn't have the money. My father was sick and I had to work to pay the bills. Now I can afford to go to college, but I'm not 20 anymore. I want to be a doctor, but medical school at 30?

SW: When you think about it, it's really exciting: the possibility of a new career, going back to school. But it's challenging. There's a lot of work involved. It is a huge decision.

CL: The thought of hitting those books, long hours studying—I don't know. It's tailor-made for the young. I know I want it. I always wanted to be a doctor. It's just now that I have the chance.

SW: Now, the opportunity is there, but so is your sense of doubt.

CL: Right. Medical school is difficult. It is an uphill battle: lab work, classroom time, a lot of memorization. You know, now I'm married, I want time with my wife. I don't know what to do.

SW: Part of what I'm hearing is that you really want to do this. But to take this on at 30 with a family, with other responsibilities, poses a real challenge.

CL: Yeah. Being a doctor has always been my life's ambition. But there's a lot of sacrifice, a lot of commitment to achieve this goal.

What issues would you want to discuss the next time you meet? (List 3)
i.
ii.
iii.

Your response:

Case 4:

A 30-year-old female who is fed up with her ex-husband. He continues to break his promises.

CL: You know, we've talked about my ex. He's an absolute jerk. We have three kids. John said he wanted kids, marriage, the whole thing. Now he's dumped me, he's out of the picture. We never see him anymore and I'm broke. He said he'd be involved in their lives and now he's gone. And it really makes me mad that he made this promise to me about our kids. I don't even care about me. It's our kids. And I can hardly afford to pay the rent and now he's gone.

SW: John has left you with all the responsibility and you're furious with him.

CL: Yes. If he cared about our kids, like he said he did, he would come up with the child support. But you know what? I haven't heard from him in four months, not a dime. I just can't believe he's doing this to us.

SW: Reflection of feeling and open ended question:

Your response:

Case 5:

A 45-year old female. She is currently in an emotionally and physically abusive relationship.

CL: You know, I really love my partner, I love Elaine a lot. But this crazy stuff has to stop.

SW: Last week, we were discussing the violence that has been going on between you two.

CL: Yeah. She got so mad at me. And, no matter how much I try to make her understand, she just doesn't listen. And you know I tried talking to her, like you suggested, and you know what? It got me into bigger trouble.

SW: What do you mean by bigger trouble?

CL: She told me that the social worker is feeding me garbage. She thinks that I should do what she says. She thinks that no matter what I want to do it doesn't count. And you've been telling me that it's important to know how I feel and know what I want. And when I tell her what I want, she hits me. This counseling thing is making matters worse between us.

SW: <u>Confrontation and reflection of feeling:</u>

Your response:

Case 6:

A 35-year-old male. He is afraid of making a permanent commitment to his girlfriend. He wants things to remain "open," but is afraid of losing her.

SW: Antonio, the last time we met, you were talking about your girlfriend. You really love her but recently you have been feeling pressure from her to get married.

CL: Right. We have been together for seven years now, which is a long time. The relationship has gotten very comfortable, it's almost like putting socks on, very natural. We both understand each other. We're very open with each and know each other, pretty much inside and out. I guess the next step is to get married, and that is what she really wants. Her family is very traditional. And you know we live together and have been for four years now. I'm fine with just living with each other. I don't need a piece of paper. She wants it to be official.

SW: You want to keep things as they are.

CL: Yes! Things are fine, you know? If it's not broken, don't fix it. I always thought that things were going fine. She is even thinking of having a child, which is okay with me. But she wants to go through the formalities. My parents are divorced and everyone who's married seems to be very unhappy. And I don't know if I want that.

SW: <u>Interpretation and paraphrase:</u>

Your response:

Case 7:

A 28-year-old Native American who is unemployed. He wants to remain on the reservation, but has been unable to find a job.

CL: The water company turned off the water. I think this is final, it's the last straw. I've been unemployed for three months and delinquent on all my bills. I don't know what to do about this.

SW: That's a lot to handle right now. Did this just happen?

CL: Yeah. I've been out of a job for three months, laid off, you know. Working in an auto shop--I've been working there for 15 years, you know, living from paycheck to paycheck, but still making it. What they give you on unemployment can't even pay for necessities like electricity. So they turned it off.

SW: Now you're unsure where to turn, what to do.

CL: Yeah. Jobs sure aren't falling like leaves. I mean they're hard to find. I was born on the reservation; I grew up on the reservation. I don't want to leave. But it's looking like I'm going to have to leave. There's just no work. Plus, my wife is mad. We were married five years ago. We didn't expect this situation. I guess nobody does. Her family lives on the reservation, too. She doesn't want to leave, but we're going to have to leave. Got to find work in the city.

SW: <u>Reflection of feeling and open- ended question</u>

Your response:

Case 8:

A 35-year-old female who is waiting for her mammogram results. She is certain that cancer was found.

CL: They got the results of my tests. I went in for a mammogram. I knew it wasn't good news when the doctor called me and told me that he wanted to see me. Usually they just send a piece of paper saying your test results came back and everything's fine. This time I got a call, and I have to go in. It sounds like they found a lump on my breast.

SW: How are you feeling about this?

CL: Really scared. I've always kind of known that I was at high risk for breast cancer. My mom had breast cancer; her sister had breast cancer. Here I am, the third in the line. I'm sure it's cancer.

SW: You are anticipating the worst.

CL: Yep. I hate having mammograms, which is why I have avoided them. I figure if I don't know, at least then I don't have to deal with it. I knew I had to go in for this mammogram. It's been about two years since I've been in and that also scares me because if the cancer has been there for that long, who knows.

SW: Reflection of feeling and information giving:

Your response:

Case 9:

A 15-year-old girl who is discussing her unexpected pregnancy.

SW: The last time we met you were trying to decide what to do about your pregnancy.

CL: Things are no better. My parents want me to have an abortion. I just don't feel I can do that. My boyfriend's parents want that, too. And Gary wants that. Everybody wants me to have an abortion and I'm feeling a lot of pressure.

SW: You keep hearing, "Have an abortion, get on with your life".

CL: Yeah, they just think that having a baby is going to ruin my life. And I realize that it's going to be difficult and it's going to be hard. But I just don't know if I can live with the fact that I killed my own baby.

SW: Paraphrase and Closed-ended question

Your response:

Case 10:

A 50-year-old African-American male struggling with job related issues.

CL: You know my job is really getting me down. I used to like going to work. I had lots of friends there, but now..........I don't know.

SW: When you say "I don't know," what does that mean?

CL: I was promoted last year because I did a good job on a project. I got lots of praise. After the job change I never quite got used to all the things I need to do. Mostly, it's supervising people. I used to be their friends, now I'm kind of the boss.

SW: Now you wonder if all this was worth the promotion.

CL: Definitely! I wish I could go back to being "one of the guys." I just don't like any part of what I'm doing now.

SW: Paraphrase and open-ended question:

Your response:

Case 11:

A 32 year old male, dying of brain cancer.

CL: It is all so crazy.......I want to find my brother, but I have no idea where to look. He literally disappeared 5 years ago. And not a word since. Now, I am dying of cancer and I want to see him. I have always missed him, but now these feelings are even stronger.

SW: For you, time is of the essence.

CL: Exactly. The last time I heard from him he had just gotten out of jail. He actually sounded pretty good. It is weird though, he kinda said good-bye...

SW: What did he say?

CL: He told me that he was fine now and not to worry about him. That is a joke of course...I have worried about him since the day he was born. He never was quite right. Diagnosed with some kind of weird mental problem.....No one really talked about it though. He wanted to be like everyone else, but kids always made fun of him. I don't blame him for going off, leaving all of us behind. By now I gotta know what happened to him. Is he dead or alive? I think he wants to stay hidden, but now I am dying.....I want to know.

SW: Have you actually done any kind of search?

CL: No, I have no idea where to start and it is expensive to hire a private detective. I seem to be the only person in my family even interested in this. Everyone else wants to pretend he never existed. I don't get it.
But now I feel driven to find him. Is that crazy???

SW: No, not at all. You want some kind of closure. He is your brother....you just can't cut that off.

CL: That is what I keep telling my family. They don't want me spending my last few months focused on him.

SW: Summarization:

Your response:

Case 12:

A 25-year-old female, struggling with issues related to her ex-boyfriend. He recently got married, which has left her hurt and confused.

CL: I just found out that Andy, the guy I dated for four years, got married.

SW: That's a shock.

CL: It really was.

SW: Did you have any idea?

CL: I knew that they had been together. But I didn't think they would get married.

SW: How are you feeling about it all?

CL: I can't sleep. I can't eat …And to top it off, he's having a reception in my hometown and inviting all my friends.

SW: It's like he's rubbing this in your face?

CL: Exactly. That's his main goal; get married and hurt me.

SW: You really sound shaken by all of this. What led up to the break up?

CL: I can't even explain what happened. We had broken up a hundred times before. He was evil; he was seriously an evil person. I just gave so much to him; and finally I felt like I couldn't give anymore. But I expected him to come back to me.

SW: You gave this relationship your all. You put up with a lot from him and then he leaves and married someone else.

CL: Yeah, after knowing her for only six months.

SW: Was your hope that eventually you two would get married?

CL: Honestly no. It was that he would want me back, and I'd be able to say "no." I've always been so weak with him, unbelievably weak. He would cheat on me and come back to me, and I'd take him back. This time, I wanted to hear, "Cheryl take me back," and I'd be able to say, "No way."

SW: You wanted the satisfaction of saying to him, "I'm strong enough now. You're out of my life." And he didn't give you that opportunity?

CL: He had the nerve to bring her over to my house so we could meet. What kind of person is he? What kind of person am I to have put up with all of this crap?

SW: <u>Interpretation and reflection of feeling:</u>

Your response:

Case 12, Continued:

SW: How were you able to end the relationship with him?

CL: It was kind of a fluke. It was New Year's Eve. We had been partying together. We met some people downtown. Next thing I know, Andy's with this girl. Later he came to my house. He wanted the money I owed him. I gave it to him and slammed the door. That was it.

SW: That was the last straw. You said that you were really weak in the relationship that you put up with years of abuse. Tell me more about that.

CL: Well, when I was in college, I was in counseling trying to figure out my relationship with him. To do things that made me stronger. But every week I would go in there, and my social worker wanted to strangle me. I'd come in there, "Oh we got back together" or "Oh we broke up." She never said I was stupid, but I was. I stopped counseling because I wasn't ready to end my relationship with Andy. And now I can't understand why he is so happy and I'm not. I'm sick of it. How dare he be happy?

SW: <u>Summarization</u>

Your response:

Case 12, Continued:

SW: You're questioning, "What is it about me that I stayed in the relationship for so long?"

CL: "What's wrong with the way I look?" "Or am I not fun?" I gave him everything. I know I have low self-esteem—I can admit that. The four years that I was with him, I did nothing but be there for him. I took all kinds of abuse. There is nothing positive about me.

SW: It's hard for you to see your strengths?

CL: Yep! It's always been that way.

SW: Reflection of feeling and open-ended question:

Your response:

Case 12, Continued:

SW: Cheryl, you have said that your family has always been a source of strength for you, that they rallied behind you after you told them about Andy's marriage. They knew you'd be devastated.

CL: My family is great. I mean, they definitely didn't like him. And they're glad it's not me he married. They stuck by me and helped me. Deep down I'm sure they are disappointed in me. That I stayed with him for so long.

SW: Clarification

Your response:

Case 12, Continued

SW: You said that you see yourself as a very caring and giving person. In some ways, that also may have caused the trouble with Andy. You're always giving and wanting to take care of him.

CL: Oh yeah, definitely.

SW: Because he expected it, too?

CL: I'm just like my mom.

SW: You think you're just like your mom. What's she like?

CL: She's very caring. She would do anything for anybody, especially her children. She's a wonderful person. She and my dad have a great marriage. That's probably why they were so upset with me. They make it look so easy. Why can't it be that way for me too?

SW: <u>Information giving and interpretation:</u>

Your response:

SW: <u>Closing summarization:</u>

Your response:

NOTES

NOTES

NOTES

NOTES